Library of Congress Cataloging-in-Publication Data

Bienstock, Richard.
Aerosmith : the ultimate illustrated history of the Boston bad boys / Richard Bienstock.
      p. cm.
Includes index.
ISBN 978-0-7603-4106-3 (plc)
1. Aerosmith (Musical group) 2. Rock musicians—United States—Biography. I. Title.
ML421.A32B54 2011
782.42166092'2—dc22
[B]

2011004333

Publisher: Michael Dregni
Acquisition and Project Editor: Dennis Pernu
Photo Researcher: Dennis Pernu
Design Manager: LeAnn Kuhlmann
Design and Layout: Sandra Salamony
Hand-drawn Title Typography: Reesa Del Duca—Ballyhoo Society Graphic Design

Printed in China

Front Cover: *Rockin' the Joint* tour, Staples Center, Los Angeles, February 22, 2006. KEVIN MAZUR/WIREIMAGE FOR HK MANAGEMENT/GETTY IMAGES

Page 1: *Rocks* tour, RFK Stadium, Washington, D.C., May 30, 1976. FIN COSTELLO/REDFERNS/GETTY IMAGES

Page 2: Cocked, Locked, Ready to Rock tour, BankAtlantic Center, August 10, 2010, in Sunrise, Florida. LARRY MARANO/GETTY IMAGES

Page 5: Opening night on the *Rockin' the Joint* tour, Nassau Coliseum, Uniondale, New York, November 8, 2005. KEVIN MAZUR/WIREIMAGE/GETTY IMAGES

Page 6: Route of All Evil tour, Hollywood Bowl, Hollywood, California, November 7, 2006. ALL © KEVIN ESTRADA/KEVINESTRADA.COM

Endpapers: World Series of Rock, Municipal Stadium, Cleveland, Ohio, July 28, 1979. © ROBERT ALFORD

Back Cover: Photo montage. AP PHOTO/PRNEWSFOTO

contents

chapter 1

Movin' Out

August 12, 2010. Jones Beach Theater, Long Island, New York. Another year, another tour, another full house. Nine p.m., the shed goes dark to match the sky above. Cue drum count-off; cue Joe Perry "Toys in the Attic" intro lick; cue curtain drop. In a flash, night becomes day, and it's *Lights!/Voices scream/nothin's seen/real's the dream. . .*

Onstage, the cast remains the same: Joey Kramer and Tom Hamilton clustered in back; Brad Whitford, shades on and ball cap pulled low, riffing stage right; Joe Perry, head down, leg cocked, black hair in face, planted stage left. Perched on a catwalk dead center, like ripe fruit dangling off the end of a branch, all mouth, hair, and multicolored scarves, Steven Tyler— the last (or is it the eternal?) child.

Leavin' the things that are real behind . . .

"Toys" wraps with Tyler and Perry, forever the dual eye of this enduring hurricane, at close range around one microphone, voices and, practically, bodies entwined. Then it's on to and through a set list that doubles as a primer on several decades' worth of classic American rock 'n' roll. Cue smoke; cue Perry guitar smash, cue crowd cheers—*Good night!*

"They hated us at the clubs. Because we did our own songs and the owners would go, 'Ooh, but the kids can't dance to it, they don't know those things.' The problem was they would just stand there in awe!"

—Steven Tyler, quoted by Sylvie Simmons in *Sounds*, July 1979

Facing page: Aerosmith's first publicity photo, 1972.
GEMS/REDFERNS/GETTY IMAGES

Some forty years into their career, and firmly ensconced as rock elder statesmen, Aerosmith remain as thrilling and combustible as ever—onstage and off. Just months prior to embarking on this recent round of live dates, the five men otherwise known as the Bad Boys of Boston—and, hyperbole be damned, America's Greatest Rock 'n' Roll Band—stood on the precipice, hardly for the first time in their long history, of ripping apart at the seams. Before 2010 came to a close they threatened the very same once more.

But Aerosmith has weathered this particular storm, and dozens others, time and again. Credit to anyone, in fact, who can identify another band that ascended to such dizzying heights and then plummeted to equally profound depths, only to rise anew, transcending time, trend, and age for a second (is it now a third? fourth?) act filled with still vaster, if not wholly unimagined, raves and rewards. *America's Greatest Rock 'n' Roll Band*? Quite likely (know one that's done it better, and for longer?). *The Bad Boys of Boston*? Absolutely, though Aerosmith's story begins in earnest in the sleepy resort region of Lake Sunapee, New Hampshire, and, years earlier, New York City.

Harlem, to be exact. . .

Steven Victor Tallarico was born March 26, 1948, with music in his blood. Giovanni, his paternal grandfather and an accomplished cellist, emigrated from southern Italy to the United States in the late 1800s. He and his three brothers formed a classical quartet that worked in ballrooms and hotels across the country. Father Victor was a Julliard-trained pianist who also played professionally, later finding employ as a music teacher in the New York City public school system. He and wife Susan were residing in Harlem, not far from the Apollo Theater, when Steven arrived. The family, including

Steven Tyler, 1973. © RON POWNALL/ROCKROLLPHOTO.COM

Chain Reaction, New York City, circa 1967.

older sister Lynda, eventually settled in Yonkers, just north of New York City. Speaking to *Musician* magazine in 1990, Steven summarized his formative years by saying that he "grew up under [his] father's piano. . . . My father talked to me playing Debussy and Beethoven. That's where my emotion comes from."

Preternaturally hyperactive and a self-described problem child, music was just one of many life-shaping forces in young Steven's life. Summers were spent at Trow-Rico Lodge, a 250-acre family-owned musical retreat on Lake Sunapee, in New Hampshire. Ensconced

in the creative environs of Trow-Rico, Steven got an early taste of the performer's life—he performed skits at Friday-night parties and, when the adults turned their backs, got drunk on homemade hard cider. Back in Yonkers, he began getting into trouble at school, fought with older kids who called him "nigger lips" for his prodigious mouth ("My mom said, 'All the better to kiss the girls with,'" Tyler told MTV), and, along with his friend Ray Tabano, joined a street gang called the Green Mountain Boys. Tyler also tried his hand at piano, but when his father's instruction didn't hold, he switched

to drums. At fifteen, he joined Victor's big band, Vic Tallarico's Orchestra, playing for the society set around Sunapee. "Like Johnny Carson's theme song, 'Begin the Beguine,' that type of shit," Tyler told *Rock Scene* in 1986.

But with his teenage years came drugs, liquor, girls, and rock 'n' roll. When the British Invasion hit U.S. shores, Tyler was a goner. "I remember the first Stones album, the Who, the Rats from England, the Pretty Things," he told *Spin* magazine in 1988. "Mick Jagger, the baddest boy on the block, my idol. I said, 'Fuck, I can do that too.'" He was well on his way. At eighteen, Tyler was making regular pilgrimages to Greenwich Village, where he and his friends spent long nights hopped up on booze, acid, and amyl nitrates, engaging in myriad carnal delights and taking in lots of rock shows—everyone from the Lovin' Spoonful and the Fugs to the Animals and the Rolling Stones.

By this time Tyler was fronting his own band—though from behind the drum kit. The Strangers (later altered to the Strangeurs to avoid conflict with an older New York act of the same name) worked rooms from Long Island to Lake Sunapee, playing four sets a night and brandishing business cards that read "English Sounds, American R&B." The band, with Tabano on bass, was raw but driven, and no one more so than Tyler, whose leadership qualities and perfectionist tendencies were already coming to the fore. In time,

the Strangeurs landed a manager and secured opening slots for everyone from the Kingsmen to the Byrds. (A March 1966 review in the *Yonkers Herald Statesman* said of the latter show "Lead singer Steven Tallarico came on like Mick Jagger of the Stones: bottom lip hanging, tambourine slapping against thigh.") A gig at Iona College in New Rochelle supporting the Beach Boys in July of that year led to an audition with Date Records, a subsidiary of CBS, who signed the Strangeurs and quickly rechristened them Chain Reaction. The band's debut single, "The Sun" b/w "When I Needed You," was a slice of Brit-influenced, mildly psychedelic pop. It received some airplay in the greater New York area throughout the fall, and Chain Reaction gigged hard across the region, including an opening slot for Tyler's idols, the Yardbirds (with Jimmy Page on guitar), at Staples High in Westport, Connecticut, on October 22, 1966.

If Chain Reaction weren't exactly full-blown rock stars, they certainly looked and acted the part, wearing their hair long and dressing in the Carnaby Street style of the Stones and other British acts. Meanwhile, the increasingly extroverted Tyler was becoming something of a regional hero around Yonkers and Lake Sunapee. Chain Reaction packed in the kids at local Sunapee hangouts like the Barn, and raised a mild ruckus at joints like the Anchorage, a Sunapee

Harbor ice cream parlor. They'd stroll in, order French fries, and leave a rock-star-sized mess for the shaggy-haired, bespectacled dishwasher to clean up. In a 2002 interview with *Blender* magazine, Tyler revealed the identity of the poor, disgruntled employee: "That was Joe [Perry]," he said. "It turned out he was mad because we always threw food, and he had to clean up after us."

But things soon began sputtering out for Chain Reaction. A second single issued on Verve, "You Should Have Been Here Yesterday" b/w "Ever Lovin' Man," stiffed, and in June of 1967 the band ground to a halt. Tyler started a few short-lived projects and, for a moment, sang backup for the Left Banke (of "Walk Away Renee" fame). In August 1969 he left Yonkers for upstate New York, where he and Tabano snuck into the Woodstock festival, took in electrifying sets by the Band and the Who, got blitzed on pills, and ran into an old Yonkers drummer acquaintance, Joey Kramer. Afterward, Tyler retreated to Lake Sunapee and headed out one night to meet up with a drug-dealer friend at the Barn. Onstage was a raw and ragtag power trio called the Jam Band with Tom Hamilton on bass and a dark, intense nineteen-year-old Joe Perry on guitar.

"When I first saw these guys they were terrible," Tyler said of the Jam Band in a 1999 issue of *Mojo*. "They weren't in tune and they weren't in time, but they did [Peter Green's] 'Rattlesnake Shake' and there was a fuckin' energy that all the bands I'd been in before couldn't do ever."

Tyler was smitten and saw his future before his eyes. "What was shining through," he said, "was the core of Aerosmith."

 It could be said that Anthony Joseph Perry seemed destined for a life of quiet desperation. That things turned out quite differently can be credited to hardheaded

determination and sheer force of will. Joe was born on September 20, 1950, in Lawrence, Massachusetts. Soon after, dad Anthony moved the family (mom Mary, Joe, and younger sister Anne-Marie) to nearby Hopedale, a small suburban enclave home to Anthony's employer, the Draper Corporation, a manufacturer of looms for the textile industry.

School didn't figure prominently in young Joe's interests, which ran

Joe Perry, 1974. © RON POWNALL/ROCKROLLPHOTO.COM

more toward guns and, from very early on, the guitar. He recalled on a 2005 episode of A&E's *Breakfast with the Arts*: "I've always been fascinated with the guitar. My Portuguese uncle played something that kind of looked like a ukulele, this Portuguese instrument. I remember at family dinners he would take this little homemade instrument out from behind the couch and sing Portuguese folksongs. So I always just loved the idea of that kind of instrument, the neck and the strings and all that. Even though my parents exposed me to piano and clarinet . . . all I wanted to do was play guitar."

By the age of nine Joe had pestered his parents into buying him his first guitar, a right-handed Sears, Roebuck Silvertone. A natural southpaw, Joe simply adapted and began playing the instrument as a righty. Lessons followed, but not for long. "I took one lesson from a guy," Perry told *Guitar Player*'s Steven Rosen in 1979, "and then a week later I saw a hearse in front of his house. He had died. I just took it as an omen." Instruction went out the window, but Perry's musical desires only heightened in intensity. "It was the only thing I could do really good," he told *RIP* magazine. "It wasn't anything my parents condoned—not that that mattered."

He got his hands on a Guild Starfire 5 and absorbed the sounds of everyone from Roy Orbison, Ike & Tina Turner, and the Shadows to the Beatles, the Rolling Stones, and the Yardbirds, teaching himself to play along the way. The next step was finding a group. "I just played around and eventually got into

a band," he told Rosen. "I don't remember the name of that first band, but I do remember I didn't play guitar, because I wasn't good enough. I sang. But after a while, I threw everybody out of the band and picked up the guitar and said, 'I'm starting a band—does anybody want to play in it?' And that was it."

His music education was in high gear, but his grades continued to suffer. In danger of flunking out of high school, fifteen-year-old Joe was shipped off to Vermont Academy, a prep school, to redo tenth grade. There, he didn't fare much better. "I really started to hate the system at [Vermont Academy]," he said in *Circus Raves* in 1975. "Every time I picked up the guitar, people would yell at me. They wanted me to cut my hair, but I kept it as long as it could

be. I quit prep school with only a month to go to graduation. At my parents' insistence, I re-registered in my hometown high school, but the principal insisted that I cut my hair, and I never graduated."

Instead, Perry took on a minimum-wage job at the local foundry. "I had to deal with all the redneck greasers who worked there," he told *Circus Raves*. He toiled five days a week pouring molten steel, heading up to Boston on weekends to catch the major bands that came through venues like the Boston Tea Party. He recalled that time in *Vintage Guitar* magazine in 1997: "That's when I really heard loud guitar and it wasn't just some distant thing coming in on the radio. These guys were doing it live and doing stuff that was incredible. Peter Green, I must

have seen Fleetwood Mac about seven or eight times [there]." Following a Jeff Beck Group gig at the Tea Party on October 22, 1968, Perry picked up a Gibson Les Paul similar to the one Beck played onstage. "I actually sat in front of his amps when they were doing 'Plynth' and 'Shapes of Things' and I had to have a Les Paul after that," he said. "[I]t was really those same guys who influenced me to play—Beck, Hendrix, Clapton, Page, and Peter Green—that influenced the gear."

By the summer of 1969, Perry had worked his way through several Hopedale-area bands with minimal success. But he also had an ongoing gig up in New Hampshire, where, like the Tallaricos, his parents owned a (considerably more modest) vacation home on Lake Sunapee. Perry passed summers working odd jobs, including washing dishes at the Anchorage. But most of his free time was spent jamming with Tom Hamilton, a lanky blond kid from nearby New London, New Hampshire, who played bass.

Tom Hamilton, 1973. © RON POWNALL/ROCKROLLPHOTO.COM

Like Perry, Hamilton was a self-taught and instinctual player with a particular fondness for loud British blues rock. The two quickly bonded, and in the summer of 1967 formed their first band, Pipe Dream, soon to be followed by Plastic Glass. By 1969, the project had morphed into the harder-edged Jam Band. "We played our guitars out of tune and it didn't matter," Perry told *Rock Scene* in 1985. "The energy mattered."

Born on New Year's Eve, 1951, Tom Hamilton spent his early childhood in Colorado Springs, Colorado, relocating with his family to Virginia after his father, an air force man, found work at the Pentagon. In typical military-family fashion, the Hamiltons (father George, mother Betty, older brother Scott, older sister Perry, and younger sister Cecily) moved often, jumping around western Massachusetts before finally settling in New London when Tom was a teenager.

By then Hamilton had received full indoctrination into rock 'n' roll courtesy of Scott, who spun Ventures records for his younger brother and taught him a few chords on his Fender Stratocaster. Tom was taken with the sounds of the British Invasion bands. "The Beatles were the biggest for me," Hamilton told *Vintage Guitar*'s Lisa Sharken. "Then the Stones and the Yardbirds came along." As a teenager, he began growing his hair out, experimenting with pot and psychedelics, and heading down to Boston to take in rock shows. "Every weekend I could I went to concerts in Boston," he told *Sounds* in 1979. "The equipment trucks outside—even that would give me a big rush. . . . The whole electricity of the situation got me off."

He began teaching himself to play guitar in earnest, eventually picking up a Fender Precision bass when a local group, Sam Citrus and the Merciless Tangerine, had an opening. Describing his style in the 1997 Aerosmith autobiography

Walk This Way, he recalled "I'd make up my own bass parts that sounded like I knew what I was doing, but in retrospect I was probably playing a lot of fucked-up notes and sounding out of key. But the bands I was in always went for feel rather than precision." Which made him the perfect foil for Joe Perry when the two met a few years later in Sunapee through a mutual friend, drummer David "Pudge" Scott. Together they formed Pipe Dream, and eventually the Jam Band. "As far as harmonic theory, and whether the notes were right, we weren't that worried about it," Hamilton said. "We were just worried about playing loud and fast."

Tyler noted as much when he caught the Jam Band at the Barn that August night in 1969, as they barreled their way through covers of everything from "Rattlesnake Shake" to Ten Years After's "I'm Going Home" to Kokomo Arnold's "Milk Cow Blues." "They had a lot of raunch," he noted in *Rolling Stone* in 1975. "And I figured I could take a step back and gradually build with them." For their part, Perry and Hamilton recognized Tyler's more advanced status. "Steven was kind of the local hero because he had the song on the jukebox at the hamburger place where I worked," Perry told MTV. In the same interview, Hamilton said, "He was in bands that were just unbelievable. We used to sneak in to see them play at places that would just be so sold out, there wasn't a chance of getting a ticket. So here was this guy that everyone assumed was just going to be a monster someday."

The following day, still on a high from what he had witnessed at the Barn, Tyler ran into Perry near Trow-Rico, where he remembers blurting out to the guitarist, "Maybe someday we'll have a band!" But it would be another year before the two would come together. In the meantime, Tyler returned to Yonkers, where he formed the Chain, again with Ray Tabano, and then William Proud, with ex–Chain Reaction keyboardist Don Solomon. In the summer of 1970, William Proud landed a gig as the house band at a club in Southampton, Long Island, slogging through four sets a night. But the years of grinding away on the club circuit had begun to take their toll on Tyler. As he said to *Rock Scene* in 1986, "I was burned up. I remember being at the end of my rope." One night onstage with William Proud, he hit the wall. "I was drumming, and I jumped over the drum set and really got into a fistfight with the guitar player. Things just weren't happening. I split, packed my suitcase, and headed up to New Hampshire, where Joe was playing in his band."

Once back in Sunapee, Tyler quickly sought out Perry. But their first meeting didn't exactly find the two on equal footing. Tyler, who'd caught wind of an opportunity to audition for the vocalist slot in the Jeff Beck Group following Rod Stewart's departure, summoned the Jam Band to the Barn to back him on his demo tape. The Beck gig turned out to be a bust, but after the demo sessions Tyler and Perry got to talking. "At the time he was playing drums and singing, and he wasn't

satisfied with that," Perry told *Rock Scene*. "Steven felt like getting up there and shaking his ass, singing." The two began jamming, and sparks flew. "I always liked to create mayhem and have unlimited energy and smash guitars and go crazy and play fast loud rock and roll," Perry explained to *Sounds*. "That was the thing Steven liked about me when he first saw me. And Steven was into arrangements and getting things just *right*. I was like the unholy terror and he was the restraint."

But Perry was already moving on, informing Tyler that he and Hamilton planned to split New Hampshire at the end of the summer and try their luck in Boston. Tyler said he was in. "Steven was very taken with Joe's fire. It was a case of two very kindred spirits getting together, and all you could do was stand there and watch in awe," Hamilton recalled in *Walk This Way*.

Perry and Hamilton left for Boston in September 1970, with the plan for Tyler to join them shortly. They moved into a two-bedroom rental apartment at 1325 Commonwealth Avenue, near Boston University, and soon hooked up with Tyler's childhood friend and former bandmate Ray Tabano, now running a leather shop on Newbury Street. Tyler insisted on bringing Tabano on board as a second guitarist in the new project, to which Perry, accustomed to playing in the power trio format of the Jam Band, begrudgingly agreed. (The compromise? Hamilton, whose skills as a musician hardly impressed Tyler, stayed put on bass at Perry's behest.) But Tabano's inclusion proved fateful when, a

Joey Kramer, 1973. © RON POWNALL/ROCKROLLPHOTO.COM

few weeks after joining up with Perry and Hamilton, an old Yonkers acquaintance walked into his leather shop looking for a gig. His name was Joey Kramer.

For Joseph Michael Kramer, playing drums was much more than a hobby—it was a way out, a coping mechanism for a childhood scarred by mental anguish and physical abuse. Born in the Bronx on June 21, 1950, his parents, Mickey and Doris, were first-generation Americans of Eastern European Jewish descent. Mickey, an army infantryman in World War II, had been injured

storming the beaches at Normandy; with the help of a GI loan, he and Doris moved the family—Joey and three younger sisters—to Yonkers, where Mickey started his own business and worked as a salesman.

Mickey was a strict disciplinarian with a nasty temper that often turned physically violent. "I never told anyone while the abuse was in progress, because I wasn't really conscious that it was abuse," Kramer told the *Hartford Courant* in 2009. "I just thought that was the way it was between my father and me." But when young Joey discovered the drums in the basement of a junior-high friend, he found an outlet for the torment at home. In *Walk This Way* he said, "You

couldn't hit your dad, but you sure could hit the drums. I sure as hell needed something."

At thirteen Kramer bought his first drum kit, purchased with money he earned selling a beloved minibike. He studied drummers like Ringo Starr, the Young Rascals' Dino Danelli, and Dave Clark of the Dave Clark Five; around this time, he also joined his first band, the Dynamics, followed soon after by the King Bees. The King Bees had it together enough to land a slot in a battle of the bands competition at Kramer's junior high school—but come the day of the show, Kramer was without a kit, Mickey having confiscated it as punishment for a bad report card. In a serendipitous turn, an older brother of the King Bees' bass player had a band whose drummer agreed to let Kramer borrow his kit. That drummer was Steven Tallarico. On the day of the show, as Kramer recalled in his 2009 autobiography *Hit Hard*, "[Steven] showed up wearing plaid pants, zipper boots, and a fur vest, with this gorgeous girl on his arm. He was already a local legend, the best singer of anybody we'd ever been around."

The two eventually crossed paths again at Woodstock, but in the intervening years Kramer proceeded to work his way through various bands—and schools. After almost flunking out of tenth grade (mostly for not bothering to show up), he was shipped off to New Rochelle Academy, a private school in Westchester County, New York. After that was nearby Thornton-Donovan, where he finally earned his diploma, and also started getting high (back home, his dealer was a kid a few years his senior named Ray Tabano).

After graduation Kramer enrolled at Boston's Chamberlain Junior College and landed a drumming gig in the backing band for the Unique Four, an all-black soul group who drilled him in the sounds of Kool & the Gang, James Brown, and Earth, Wind & Fire. (In the mid-1970s, the Unique Four would find success as the funk and disco act Tavares.) "I used to go with these guys to see artists like the Temptations and the O'Jays," Kramer told *M Music and Musicians* magazine in 2010. "They would sit me down and say, 'Watch the drummer, because he's accentuating the dance steps.'" They

also contributed to his chemical education. "Another thing I loved about the Unique Four," Kramer commented in *Hit Hard*, "[was] the drugs—serious dope."

But the hard living eventually caught up with him, and Kramer found himself laid out with a severe case of hepatitis. He left college and the Unique Four, and spent the summer of 1970 recuperating at home. He returned to Boston in the fall, enrolling at Berklee College of Music. Soon after he got wind that Tabano was in town, and one day Kramer stopped in at his leather shop to ask about bands looking for a drummer. Tabano hooked him up with Perry and Hamilton, who set up an audition at Kramer's apartment. As he recounted in *Hit Hard*: "I remember when they walked into the living room—Joe with his horn-rimmed glasses, bell bottoms that only reached down to his ankles, cowboy boots, and a long shag haircut with a blond streak in it, and I was thinking, *Who the fuck is this guy*? But once I started playing, I could see him and Tom smiling ear to ear. All of a sudden they were saying, 'When can we rehearse?'"

When Perry subsequently mentioned that a singer, Steven Tallarico, was coming up from New York to join their band, Kramer grew more eager. Tyler was similarly pleased by this coincidental turn of events, as it signaled the end of his days singing from behind a drum kit.

In the fall of 1970, Kramer and Tyler joined Perry and Hamilton at 1325 Commonwealth. Perry recalled those days to MTV: "Every room in the house was a bedroom, except the

kitchen. So every room also doubled as something else. Tom's room had the piano in it. We weren't unlike so many other kids coming into Boston for school with so much idealism and being away from home for the first time. The only thing was, we didn't go to school. We partied. It was around the clock, pretty much."

It was also at Commonwealth where they began writing their first original song—a bluesy and hypnotic Tyler/Perry composition titled "Movin' Out"—and brainstormed names for their new band. After rolling through a spate of clunkers, Kramer piped in with a neologism he had coined as a teenager and used to scribble on his class notebooks. It had a familiar ring, reminiscent of a book the other members remembered from their school days. But whereas they believed Kramer to be saying the word *Arrowsmith*, much like the title of the 1920s Sinclair Lewis novel, he clarified that the spelling was in fact *Aerosmith*. "A 'smith' is a master craftsman," Kramer explained in *Hit Hard*. "Aerosmith would be masters at getting you off the ground, getting you up, getting you high." The rest of the members dug it—or at least found it more appealing than their other frontrunner, Spike Jones and the Hookers.

With a band name under their belts, the newly minted Aerosmith settled into the daily grind of trying to make it in Boston. Tyler took on work at a bagel factory, while Perry spent his days sweeping floors in a synagogue. The band subsisted on whatever food they could scrounge together, not to mention all the booze

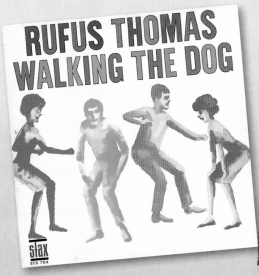

The early Aerosmith repertoire included covers of Rufus Thomas' Stax chestnut "Walking the Dog," Peter Green's "Rattlesnake Shake" (from Fleetwood Mac's *Then Play On*), and the Yardbirds' take on "Train Kept a Rollin'" (from their *Having a Rave Up* LP). The last has appeared on Aerosmith set lists for decades.

and dope they could get their hands on. "We started shooting cocaine as early as 1970," Perry told Matt Smith of *Melody Maker* in 1989. "We didn't have enough money to do it that much, but once a week we'd split a half a gram or something."

But these were hardly carefree days. Tyler admitted, in an uncredited interview in Martin Huxley's *Aerosmith: The Fall and the Rise of Rock's Greatest Band*, that "times were pretty tough. We ate a lot of brown rice back then. We managed to get a free practice room at a Boston University dorm by promising to play some dances for them. . . . They'd even sneak us free meals at the cafeteria when we were hard up."

In the basement of BU, Tyler quickly emerged as Aerosmith's leader and musical director, putting his less-seasoned bandmates through their paces. "It was like we were the students and he was the teacher," Perry told biographer Davis. "He taught us order and discipline and we taught him energy

and raw power." But according to Hamilton, Tyler's criticism could be "harsh." And given that he had spent much of his career as a drummer, no one bore a greater brunt of his wrath than Kramer. "Steven had a reputation for being a perfectionist," Kramer noted in *Hit Hard*, "and the drummer was going to be a lightning rod for every obsessive-compulsive bone in his body."

But if Tyler was steering the ship, Perry was powering the motor. As Tabano observed in *Walk This Way*, "It's hard to stress enough that Joe Perry . . . knew where he wanted to go and what was going to happen if he kept at it. He had such incredible drive in addition to his talent. Him and Steven dragged the rest of us up with them."

After spending much of the fall of 1970 woodshedding at BU, Aerosmith made their live debut on November 6 at Nipmuc Regional High School in Upton,

"American bands usually fall into one of two categories. They are either denim-clad cowpokes, bearded, laidback to the point of collapse . . . or they are glamorous, big city wrecks, fixin' to die in their makeup. So it comes as a pleasure to detect what appears, from a distance at any rate, to be a good healthy rock group, with a drop of technique and a bit of guts."

—Chris Welch, *Melody Maker*, June 28, 1975

IN THE SUMMER OF 1970, THE ORIGINAL AEROSMITH FORMS IN NEW HAMPSHIRE WITH TALLARICO (NOW TYLER) ON DRUMS, JOE PERRY ON GUITAR, AND TOM HAMILTON ON BASS.

TYLER LEAVES IN 1971, BUT BRAD WHITFORD AND JOEY KRAMER JOIN. TYLER SOON REJOINS AS LEAD SINGER.

JOE PERRY   STEVEN TYLER   BRAD WHITFORD   JOEY KRAMER   TOM HAMILTON

THEY PLAY AT VARIOUS CLUBS AND RESORTS FOR THIRTY DOLLARS A NIGHT.

THE BARN

AFTER A WHILE, THEY DECIDE TO RELOCATE.

FORGET THIS S**T! I'LL BET THERE'S A LOT OF ACTION IN BOSTON!

BOSTON?!!

Massachusetts, just minutes from Perry's childhood home in Hopedale. Opening with the R&B standard "Route 66," they blasted through covers of some personal favorites—the ever-present "Rattlesnake Shake," the Yardbirds' take on "Train Kept a Rollin'," Rufus Thomas' "Walking the Dog," and Led Zeppelin's "Good Times, Bad Times." They also performed two originals that night: "Movin' Out" and "Somebody," a holdover from Tyler's days in William Proud. If the set itself went off without a hitch, things were somewhat rockier backstage. "Steven and Joe had a big argument that first night about Joe playing too loud," recalled Hamilton to *Rolling Stone*'s David Wild in 1990. "And so began an Aerosmith tradition."

Significant as well was the location of the gig: a suburban high school outside the city lines. That the band's debut didn't take place at a bar or club was by design. In their earliest days, they deliberately bypassed the largely covers-dominated Boston club circuit in favor of unusual venues—schools, frat houses, ski lodges, roadhouses— where they could work in their original material. "We never got into the club circuit, 'cause they didn't want to hear original music back then," Perry told *Rock Scene*. "If you couldn't play a whole set of what was on the jukebox then they just didn't hire you. So we used to just promote our own shows. We'd hire out the town hall, and put up posters. . . . It was why a lot of Boston bands didn't really recognize us as a Boston band, 'cause we didn't play the game like everyone else. We did it our own way."

Moreover, Boston wasn't much of a rock 'n' roll town at the time. The city was still reeling from the "Bosstown Sound" fiasco of the late '60s, a record company marketing campaign that attempted to translate the success of the San Francisco psychedelic boom to the Northeast, to disastrous results. Hometown heroes like the Beacon Street Union and Orpheus, among others, were plucked from the local clubs and pumped up with media hype, only to come up lacking on the national stage. This mainstream failure dampened the city's taste for original rock 'n' roll for years to come (local stars the J. Geils Band were the exception), and by the turn of the '70s, clubs owners were more concerned with moving booze than supporting original music. "They hated us at the clubs. Because we did our own songs and the owners would go, 'Ooh, but the kids can't dance to it, they don't know those things,'" Tyler told *Sounds* in 1979. "The problem was they would just stand there in awe! They wouldn't dance so they didn't drink." Still, high schools didn't exactly pay as well as more established venues: "We used to get, like, $125," Tabano told A&E's *Biography*. "Okay, there's five of us, and we had a roadie, we had a truck, we had all this equipment. After everything was paid for we'd wind up with like about 19 cents each."

But they made their way, settling into a routine of free rehearsals at BU during the week and gigs at odd regional venues on the weekends. They were gelling as a unit, with the exception of Tabano, who, despite ties to both Tyler and Kramer that

extended back to their Yonkers roots, was, as Tyler told VH1's *Behind the Music*, "such a wiseass and a tough guy that he pissed everyone off." Hamilton further explained to journalist Joy Williams that "He wanted things to go his way, and his level of playing really didn't justify all the tantrums and fighting that went on as a result of his personality." It was clear to all involved that Tabano's days were numbered. "We said, 'We gotta get somebody else who's on the same path we [are],'" Perry told VH1.

In the summer of 1971, Aerosmith headed to Lake Sunapee for a gig; while there, Perry and Hamilton went to see Tyler's old William Proud bandmate, Twitty Farren, play in Sunapee Harbor with his new project, Justin Thyme. The band was good, but the guitarist, a nineteen-year-old hotshot named Brad Whitford, was positively smoking. The writing was on the wall.

Brad Ernest Whitford was born on February 23, 1952, to father E. Russell, a systems analyst with the industrial corporation Raytheon, and mother Joyce, in Reading, Massachusetts, a suburb just north of Boston. The second of three boys, Brad came to music at an early age and through an unlikely instrument: the trumpet. Brother Donald played in his high-school band, and Brad followed in his older sibling's footsteps, picking up the instrument in grade school. But the brass didn't take, and in junior high he got into rock 'n' roll—"the Beatles were the initial firestarters, along with a lot of

Brad Whitford, 1973. © RON POWNALL/ROCKROLLPHOTO.COM

started playing," he told Sharken, "I always thought that you could learn from anybody, whether he was a good or bad player. There's always some aspect of their playing that you could look at and pick up."

By junior high Whitford had joined his first band, Symbols of Resistance, followed by several more—Teapot Dome, Spring Rain, Earth Incorporated, and the Morlocks. By high school, he was firmly under the spell of harder-edged British and American players like Jimi Hendrix, Jeff Beck, and Humble Pie's Peter Frampton. But it was Jimmy Page who held the greatest sway—Whitford recalled seeing Led Zeppelin perform at the Carousel Theater in Framingham, Massachusetts, in August 1969 as a "life-changing" experience. "It was one of those nights that [Page] was in tune with the cosmos and it was absolutely mind-blowing," he told *Vintage Guitar*. "He was playing all those great solos note for note, like 'Communication Breakdown,' and it was just devastating. I swear I bought a Les Paul the next day."

After a short stint at Berklee the following year, Whitford grabbed his Les Paul and Marshall and left Boston, spending much of the summer of '71 playing guitar on Nantucket Island. Eventually he hooked up with Twitty Farren and Justin Thyme, and late that summer found himself playing in Sunapee Harbor for an audience that included Joe Perry and Tom Hamilton. Whitford recalled the pair in *Walk This Way*: "They looked more serious, more rock and roll than most people in bands, like they were really living

English stuff, like the Dave Clark Five and the Stones," he told *Vintage Guitar*'s Lisa Sharken—and began fiddling with his father's guitar, a "cheapo" acoustic.

Brad's parents were supportive of their son's budding musical interests and bought him his first electric guitar, a red and black Winston that, with a bit of resourcefulness, he figured out how to crank through the speaker of the family television set. He took some lessons but mostly taught himself from listening to records, the radio, and everyone around him. "From the time I first

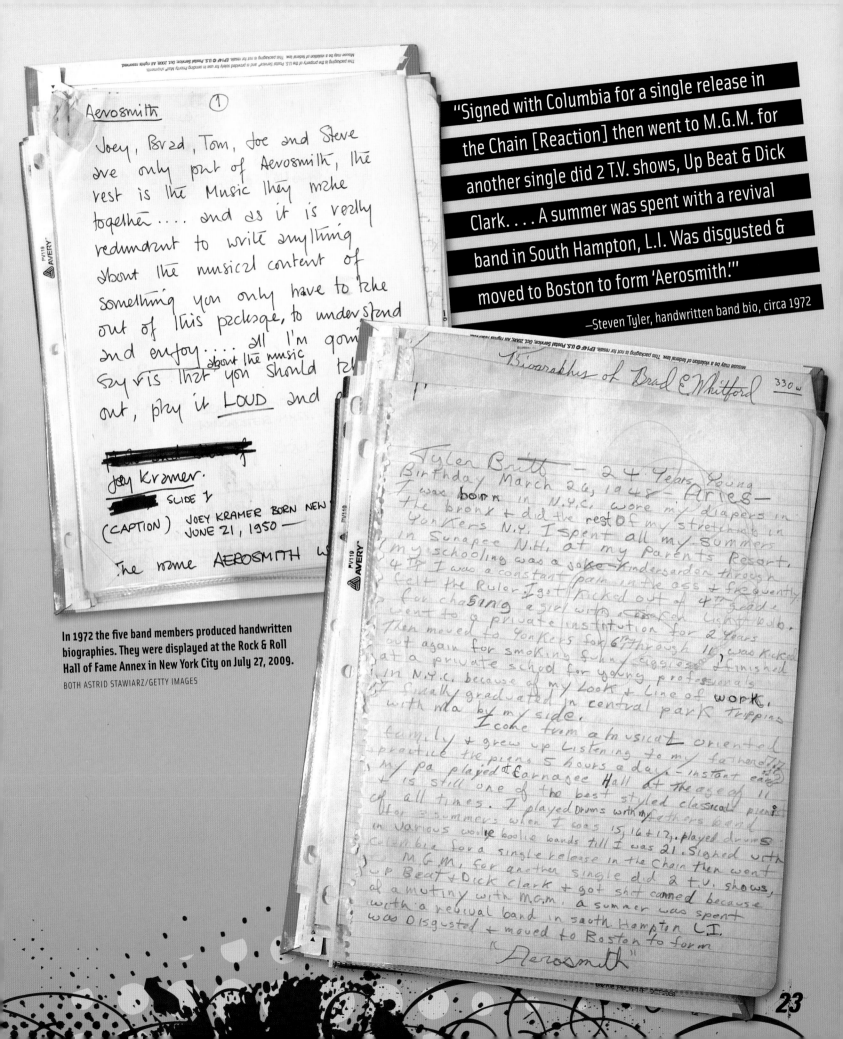

Aerosmith ①

Joey, Brad, Tom, Joe and Steve are only part of Aerosmith, the rest is the Music they make together..... and as it is really redundant to write anything about the musical content of something you only have to take out of this package, to understand and enjoy.... all I'm gonna say is that you should take it out, play it LOUD and

Joey Kramer.
SLIDE 1
(CAPTION) JOEY KRAMER BORN NEW JUNE 21, 1950 —

The name AEROSMITH w

In 1972 the five band members produced handwritten biographies. They were displayed at the Rock & Roll Hall of Fame Annex in New York City on July 27, 2009.

Biography of Brad E. Whitford   330 w

Tyler Britt — 24 Years Young
Birthday March 26, 1948 - Aries -
I was born in N.Y.C. wore my diapers in the bronx + did the rest of my stretching in Yonkers N.Y. I spent all my summers in Sunapee N.H. at my parents resort. My schooling was a joke kindergarden through 4th I was a constant pain in the ass + frequently felt the Ruler. I got kicked out of 4th grade for chasing a girl with a loaded light bulb. Went to a private institution for 2 years. Then moved to Yonkers for 6th through 11. I was kicked out again for smoking funny giggles. I finished at a private school for young professionals in N.Y.C. because of my look + line of work. I finally graduated in central park tripping with ma by my side.
        I come from a musical oriented family + grew up listening to my father practice the piano 5 hours a day - instant ear. My pa played at Carnagee Hall at the age of 11 + is still one of the best styled classical pianist of all times. I played drums with my fathers band for 3 summers when I was 15, 16 + 17. played drums in various woolie boolie bands till I was 21. Signed with Columbia for a single release in the Chain then went to M.G.M. for another single did 2 t.v. shows, up Beat + Dick Clark + got shit canned because of a mutiny with m.g.m. a summer was spent with a revival band in south Hampton L.I. was disgusted + moved to Boston to form
        "Aerosmith"

it instead of just having a fantasy about it. They had the right clothes, the right hair, the right attitude. They had the gang you wanted to be in." Characteristically, the guitarist was considerably less effusive about his own importance in that evening's events: "I guess I had the right gear and was playing the right notes that night," he said. Perry and Hamilton apparently thought so too. Within weeks, Whitford and his Les Paul moved into 1325 Commonwealth.

With Whitford on board in place of Tabano, Aerosmith was complete.

"The change in musicianship was like night and day," Kramer said in *Hit Hard*. "Brad played rhythm behind Joe's lead, but he was so skilled that now we had, essentially, two lead players, with Brad's precision playing off against Joe's raw passion." The band kicked into high gear, writing, rehearsing, and gigging to steadily growing crowds throughout the fall and into winter. A high point came on December 2, when they played the Academy of Music in New York City, third on a bill behind Humble Pie and Edgar

Winter's White Trash. But despite their musical headway, the business end of the band was sagging. They were pulling in roughly $300 per gig, a fraction of what could have been earned on the cover-band circuit. With money tight, they were slapped with an eviction notice for failure to pay rent, and also booted from their basement rehearsal space at BU.

But in the first months of 1972, a chain of events kicked into gear that would alter Aerosmith's fortunes for good. Through an acquaintance, the band hooked up with John O'Toole,

AEROSMITH SPEAKS OUT ON EARLY CRITICISM:

A COMPARISON IS RIDICULOUS! SURE, JAGGER AND I HAVE PHYSICAL RESEMBLANCES, BUT WE HAVE TWO DIFFERENT SINGING STYLES!

YEAH, THE CRITICS ARE SPENDING TOO MUCH TIME COMPARING OUR LOOKS AND NOT ENOUGH LISTENING TO OUR MUSIC!

IN 1972, THEY ARE FIRST NOTICED BY CLIVE DAVIS AT MAX'S KANSAS CITY. TYLER'S STAGE PRESENCE AND PERRY'S HEAVY BLUES RIFFS MAKE THEM HARD TO IGNORE.

THEY'VE GOT WHAT IT TAKES TO BE BIG!

who ran Boston's Fenway Theatre and offered them the stage as a daytime rehearsal space, free of charge. They'd arrive early in the morning, rehearse through the day, and then stash their gear under the stage in time for the Fenway's national acts to load in for that night's show. More significantly, O'Toole introduced them to "Father" Frank Connelly, a big-time Boston promoter who had booked the Beatles into Boston Garden years earlier and was connected around town in ways both legitimate and unspoken. Connelly attended one rehearsal at the Fenway and offered Aerosmith a management contract, which they eagerly signed on the spot. "Frank was the first guy . . . who said we were on to something," said Whitford (Huxley, uncredited). More than giving them someone in their corner, the contracts promised the members a steady income, which took care of their nagging rent problems. "Our first contract came when we were holding an eviction notice in our hands. Literally," Perry told *Rock Scene* in 1986.

Though a skilled promoter, Connelly's reach didn't extend far outside Boston. In an effort to bring bigger fish to the table, he talked the band up to the management team of Steven Leber and David Krebs, then causing a stir in the Big Apple with another group of longhaired, ragtag rock 'n' rollers led by a big-lipped,

big-personality singer: the New York Dolls. Leber and Krebs saw similar fire in Aerosmith and booked the band into hip Manhattan spot Max's Kansas City for three showcases.

For the second show, Leber and Krebs pulled out all the stops, inviting Atlantic Records' Jerry Greenberg and Ahmet Ertegun, and Columbia head Clive Davis. "There were limos all over the place, and all the different labels were there," Tyler told *Rock Scene*. The band, all long hair and tattered, gypsy-glam rags, took the tiny stage by storm, Tyler (who around this time changed his surname) strutting and swinging his silk-scarved mic stand with abandon. "We did our set," he said, "and it was just perfect." At least one other person in attendance agreed: Greenberg and Ertegun passed on the band, but Davis was captivated. After the show, Tyler remembered, "Clive Davis came over and put his arms around us and said, 'You're gonna be big stars.' It was the real thing. Just like you read about in the books."

In the summer of 1972, Davis signed Aerosmith for a recoupable

advance of $125,000, which was then divided between the band and their now two sets of managers, Frank Connelly and Leber and Krebs. After years of struggle, they had a record deal—or, more accurately, Leber and Krebs did. Aerosmith had in fact signed not to Columbia, but rather to Contemporary Communications Corporation (CCC), a Leber-Krebs company, which then entered into a production deal with Columbia to deliver Aerosmith albums to the label. Furthermore, the contracts entitled management to hefty chunks of the band's future publishing royalties. Years later, Tyler fumed to *Mojo*'s Phil Sutcliffe, "That gave the management total control to get the money first. And how about giving them 50 percent of your publishing! We did that. In that contract there's a clause including the phrase 'in perpetuity,' which means as long as you fucking live your manager gets a piece of you."

These early contracts would eventually come back to haunt the band, as well as instigate full-scale war with Leber-Krebs. But this was all much further down the road. In the present, Aerosmith was officially a Columbia Records recording group. Triumphant, they returned to Boston to record their debut album.

chapter 2

Good Evenin' People, Welcome to the Show

"We weren't too ambitious when we started out," Steven Tyler has said. "We just wanted to be the biggest thing that ever walked the planet, the greatest rock band that ever was. We just wanted everything. We just wanted it *all*." Indeed, in late 1972, with Columbia contract in hand, Tyler and Aerosmith may have felt they had taken their first decisive steps toward world domination. But in the short term at least, the world had other plans for them.

"Cream, the Yardbirds and Led Zeppelin. . . . They were all so classy and powerful sounding. We couldn't think of an American band like that. We wanted to be the first one."

—Tom Hamilton, quoted by David Wild in *Rolling Stone*, April 1990

That October, the band entered Intermedia Sound on Boston's Newbury Street to begin recording their major-label debut. At the helm was Adrian Barber, a British producer selected by Krebs for his work with artists like Cream and the Allman Brothers Band. Cut mostly live on sixteen tracks in just over two weeks, *Aerosmith* was a raw, no-frills document of the still very green band. "You can tell that it's a really basic album—there's nothing on it!" Tyler told *Rock Scene*. "It's bone dry—it has two guitars, a bass, drums, a singer and a Mellotron for the *coup de grace*."

Facing page: Masonic Hall Auditorium, Detroit, October 12, 1973. © CHARLIE AURINGER

ORPHEUM THEATRE
413 Washington St. — Boston, Mass.

Sat. Eve. at 8:00

MARCH
3
1973

W. B. C. N. presents
DAVID BROMBERG
AEROSMITH

ADMISSION $4.00
NON-REFUNDABLE

PP 113 ORCHESTRA
LEFT CNTR

GOOD ONLY
SATURDAY EVE.
MARCH
3
1973

ORPHEUM THEATRE
ORCHESTRA

LEFT
CNTR

PP 113

GLOBE TICKET CO. (S) 260

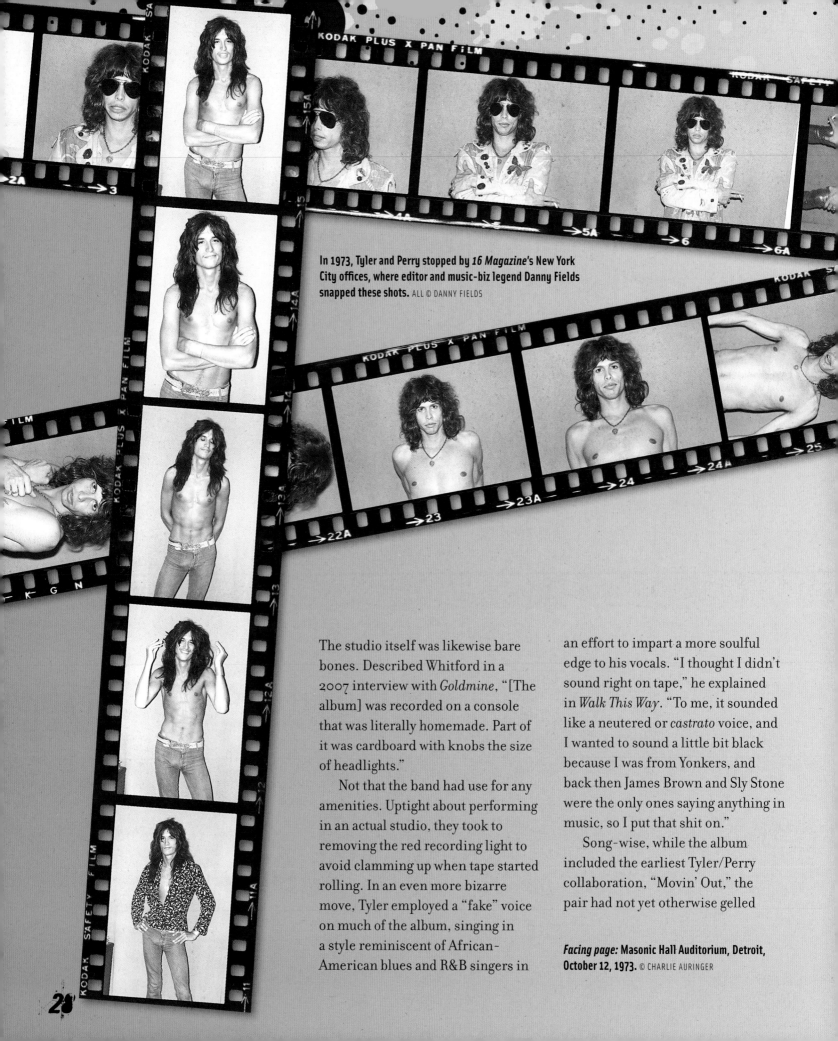

In 1973, Tyler and Perry stopped by *16 Magazine*'s New York City offices, where editor and music-biz legend Danny Fields snapped these shots. ALL © DANNY FIELDS

The studio itself was likewise bare bones. Described Whitford in a 2007 interview with *Goldmine*, "[The album] was recorded on a console that was literally homemade. Part of it was cardboard with knobs the size of headlights."

Not that the band had use for any amenities. Uptight about performing in an actual studio, they took to removing the red recording light to avoid clamming up when tape started rolling. In an even more bizarre move, Tyler employed a "fake" voice on much of the album, singing in a style reminiscent of African-American blues and R&B singers in

an effort to impart a more soulful edge to his vocals. "I thought I didn't sound right on tape," he explained in *Walk This Way*. "To me, it sounded like a neutered or *castrato* voice, and I wanted to sound a little bit black because I was from Yonkers, and back then James Brown and Sly Stone were the only ones saying anything in music, so I put that shit on."

Song-wise, while the album included the earliest Tyler/Perry collaboration, "Movin' Out," the pair had not yet otherwise gelled

Facing page: **Masonic Hall Auditorium, Detroit, October 12, 1973.** © CHARLIE AURINGER

Masonic Hall Auditorium, Detroit, October 12, 1973. © CHARLIE AURINGER

as a writing team. As a result, *Aerosmith* was for the most part a Tyler affair (plus a version of their live cover staple, "Walkin' the Dog"), with the singer contributing six original tracks: "One Way Street," "Somebody" (written years earlier with a roadie for William Proud), "Mama Kin" and "Write Me" (both featuring sax from session man David Woodford), and "Make It," whose opening line, *Good evenin' people, welcome to the show*, would kick off both the album and many Aerosmith gigs to come.

And then there was a swelling ballad titled "Dream On," which Tyler first conceived as a teenager on a Steinway piano up at Trow-Rico and continued to mold at 1325 Commonwealth. The band adapted his piano part—"Joe played the right hand; Brad played the left," he told *Guitar World*—and in the studio, Tyler added strings and flute flourishes on Mellotron. "I used to wake up hearing it," Hamilton recalled to *Guitar World* of the song's development. "The piano was in my room, and Steven would be in there. He'd come in and start playing it. I liked it from the beginning." Not all of Hamilton's bandmates felt similarly. "To me rock and roll's all about energy and putting on a show . . . but 'Dream On' was a ballad," Perry told *Classic Rock* in 2002. "I didn't appreciate the musicality of it until later." But Tyler knew the song was special. "I was so sure of [it]," he told *Blender*, adding, "It's about the hunger to be somebody. 'Dream until your dreams come true.'"

But those dreams were still a ways off. *Aerosmith* was released on

Masonic Hall Auditorium, Detroit, October 12, 1973. © CHARLIE AURINGER

January 13, 1973, to less than sterling fanfare—in fact, there was no fanfare whatsoever. "No press, no radio, no airplay, no reviews, no interviews, no party," Perry told Davis. "The album got completely ignored and there was a lot of anger and flipping out." This lack of enthusiasm extended to their record label, which around the same time issued the debut album of another new artist, Bruce Springsteen. It was clear where Columbia's priorities lay: Reportedly, for every dollar the label funneled into promotion for *Aerosmith*, $100 was put toward Springsteen's *Greetings from Asbury Park, N.J.*

Recognizing they were on their own, Leber and Krebs put the band on the road to take their music directly to the people. Their first major tour, supporting the instrumental fusion-rock act Mahavishnu Orchestra, was hardly an ideal fit. But, Kramer told *Penthouse* in 1993, "It was either go out on the road with them or not go out on the road. So we were all like, 'No! We're going!'" Predictably, Aerosmith's gritty, blue-collar blooze rock was not exactly well received by the headlining band, or its fans. "After us," Perry recalled in a 1979 interview with *Rolling Stone*, "[Mahavishnu leader and guitarist] John McLaughlin would ask for a moment of silence. I guess he figured they needed it." Things only got

progressively worse: In the spring of '73, Aerosmith went out as the opener for the Kinks and suffered abuse at the hand of Ray Davies, who denied them time for soundchecks and dismissively referred to them as "Harry Smith."

But the Kinks dates provided a boost in recognition, which served to up their asking fee from roughly $300 to $1,500 per show, and thanks to a pair of supportive DJs, *Aerosmith* started receiving spins in the prime Boston and Detroit radio markets. And while the band continued to be roundly ignored by major print outlets like *Rolling Stone*, the hipper, Detroit-based *CREEM* stepped up with the first national

Masonic Hall Auditorium, Detroit, October 12, 1973. © CHARLIE AURINGER

was issued in June 1973. Pushed by Boston radio, by the end of the summer it was a smash in the New England area. Eventually, the song became a minor hit nationally, reaching No. 59 on *Billboard* and providing Aerosmith a temporary stay of execution.

On the live front, the band continued to tour hard, gigging five nights a week on their own and embarking on a string of dates as support for Mott the Hoople. On August 10, they opened for Sha Na Na at Suffolk Downs Racetrack near Boston, and worked the hometown crowd of 35,000 into a frenzy. "Into the third song a barrage of beer cans filled the air," the *Boston Globe* reported. "[T]he show was stopped at least twice as Steve Tyler, pseudo-Mick Jagger lead singer for Aerosmith, scolded the bubbly little teens." "We played every place and every night that we could." Recalled Joe Perry on A&E's *Biography*, "And I remember many times playing two shows a day, playing like a college outdoor festival in the afternoon and then playing a club that night."

The nonstop pace paid off: by the end of the year, *Aerosmith* had squeaked into the *Billboard* album chart—just barely—at No. 166.

Facing page: Masonic Hall Auditorium, Detroit, October 12, 1973. © CHARLIE AURINGER

review of the album, declaring, rather perceptively, "*Aerosmith* is as good as coming in your pants at a drive-in at age 12 with your little sister's babysitter calling the action." Indeed, the ill-treatment and neglect Aerosmith seemingly received at the hands of the music world cognoscenti further underscored the fact that the band's real significance would be to a new and younger generation of American rock 'n' roll fans—those looking for something fresher, louder, and distinctly theirs. "I think what we wanted to do, without ever really saying it, was to be the American equivalent of all the great British bands like Cream, the Yardbirds and Led

Zeppelin," Hamilton told *Rolling Stone* in 1990. "They were all so classy and powerful sounding. We couldn't think of an American band like that. We wanted to be the first one."

Regardless, the music business is a game of numbers, and the numbers were not on Aerosmith's side. Faced with a paltry 30,000 copies in sales for their debut, Columbia informed management that the label wouldn't pick up the band's option, essentially dropping them from the roster. In an act of desperation, Krebs begged Clive Davis (soon to be ousted himself under allegations of fiscal irresponsibility) to release "Dream On" as a single. Davis relented, and the track, backed with "Somebody,"

Aerosmith

by Daniel Bukszpan

Many bands from the classic rock era needed to make a few records before they really got warmed up. Led Zeppelin's debut, which is rightly regarded as a classic by just about anybody you'd care to ask, was in reality one-half brilliant original material and one-half regurgitated blues filler that made for rousing live material and fell completely flat on vinyl. It wasn't until their fourth album that they came into their own and created forty-five perfect minutes of music.

Aerosmith needed no such limbering. Their self-titled debut showcased a group in remarkable command of their sound, with talent and attitude to burn. Listening to it, it's obvious that there was never a point in the recording where they all shrugged and said to each other "What do we do next?" It sounds like the album they had been preparing for, and rehearsing for, all their lives.

The debut kicks off with "Make It," an uptempo stomper propelled as much by Joey Kramer's clanging ride cymbal as its ascending main riff. Steven Tyler bids us good evening and welcomes us to the show, and the richness of his voice cuts a striking contrast to the raspy and reedy instrument it later became. The song is followed by "Somebody," which keeps the tempo lively and the guitars sassy. You can hear the genesis of glam metal in the major-key exuberance of its riffs, and if you close your eyes, you can see half the cast of *The Decline of Western Civilization, Part II: The Metal Years* plagiarizing the song as the basis for entire one-hit wonder careers.

"Dream On" is next. It's a piece of music that's impossible to speak about objectively. Anyone over the age of five has heard it on the radio at least 657,023 times; it's the equal of "Freebird" in that it's not really a song anymore but a cultural icon. It casts a long shadow over all rock musicians, who have aspired either to match it or to rebuff it. But despite the song's status, the band members have always seemed comfortable with the song, and unlike Robert Plant with "Stairway to Heaven," they've never tried to distance themselves from it. A good thing too, since Aerosmith will be associated with "Dream On" until the end of time, even if Joe Perry captures Osama bin Laden or Brad Whitford cures herpes.

"Dream On" b/w "Mama Kin," Japan, 1973.

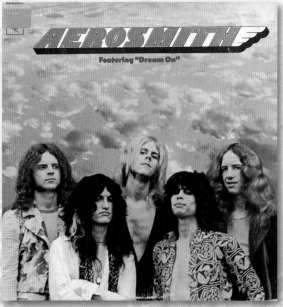

The band's self-titled debut got a boost when Columbia agreed to release the proto power ballad "Dream On" as a single in June 1973. Subsequent pressings of the LP referred to the single.

As for the song itself, it's a minor-key number containing some Bach-like flourishes, but otherwise it pretty much stays away from the classical motifs associated with the heavy metal ballad (see Rainbow or the Scorpions). It's more akin to something Paul McCartney might have toyed with around 1965. It also has something that no other power ballad has: a groove! Despite its slow tempo, the song never plods, and even at its heaviest moments it has a pulse and a swing, neither of which detract from its epic qualities.

"Dream On" ends in a tidy four and a half minutes, and it's the unenviable task of "One Way Street" to follow it. Aerosmith owe their entire careers to the Mick Taylor–era Rolling Stones, and the harmonica-heavy "One Way Street" could easily be the B-side of "Gimme Shelter." Joey Kramer and Tom Hamilton lay down a very solid groove on this one, making a strong case for themselves as the stars of the album.

Side two kicks off with "Mama Kin," another uptempo barn-burner with a distinct glam flavor. Hey, it was 1973 and the New York Dolls and KISS could be heard indulging in the same sounds. It's too bad that '80s hair metal would ruin the genre for everyone, making it impossible to hear it today without thinking of barfly skanks fellating Bret Michaels on the Rock of Love tour bus.

"Write Me a Letter" is the most underrated song on Aerosmith's debut. Another solid shuffle of the sly, head-and-shoulder bopping variety, it recalls Molly Hatchet, not least of all because Tyler sounds like the late, great Hatchet singer Danny Joe Brown on the track. "Movin' Out" follows and is perhaps the nearest thing to a misfire on the debut. Fortunately, they quickly regain their mojo on the album's closer, "Walkin' the Dog," a 1963 Rufus Thomas chestnut from the Stax catalog. The muted guitar waka-wakas after the choruses are pretty hard to beat, and without them the song might be just

another 12-bar blues, stale as chalk dust. It's here that the band draws another comparison to the Stones. "Walkin' the Dog" is an unremarkable composition in its own right, but with solid grooves and clever breakdowns, Aerosmith redeems it. None of the Stones are virtuoso players and none of their songs are particularly sophisticated, but they've always managed to be more than the sum of their parts. The members of Aerosmith are better musicians than the Stones, but their alchemical touch is the same. They're able to make something out of nothing, using solid grooves, ingenuity, and heartfelt sleaze.

Over the course of its eight songs and thirty-six minutes, Aerosmith's debut demonstrates that they knew exactly what they were doing, and it mapped out their next four decades with stunning clarity. Not bad for a band that spent most of their daylight hours getting high and watching reruns of the Three Stooges.

chapter 3

Getting Wings

The pressure was still on, and in December 1973 Aerosmith entered the Record Plant in New York City to begin work on the follow-up to their debut. The band had been working up new material throughout the summer and fall, and, as a result of their incessant gigging, the riffs and rhythms were coming tighter, harder, and more dynamic. Just as significant to their musical development was the introduction of a new face, producer Jack Douglas, who would heavily impact the band's sound going forward.

A Bronx native who cut his teeth engineering records for the Who, Alice Cooper, and John Lennon, among others, Douglas had also engineered the debut effort from the New York Dolls. He was turned on to Aerosmith by famed producer Bob Ezrin, who had earlier passed on the band. Douglas decided to check them out. "I saw them at a high school in New England and was blown away," Douglas said in a 2000 interview with KNAC.com. "They were noisy and full of energy, like the old Yardbirds."

"I would rather have a kid who went to the show write the article than a critic who has been around for so long, he saw the Stones. And he goes: 'Ah, well Joe Perry looks like Keith, and we have the Tyler-esque Jagger, or the Jagger-esque Tyler.'"

—Steven Tyler, quoted by Chris Welch in *Melody Maker*, October 1976

Facing page: *Get Your Wings* tour, Michigan Palace, Detroit, 1974. By most accounts, Aerosmith played this venue no fewer than three times in the first half of 1974.

© CHARLIE AURINGER

Facing page, inset: *Get Your Wings* tour with Blue Öyster Cult, Cape Cod Coliseum, South Yarmouth, Massachusetts.

ORCHESTRA

EE R
SEC. ROW SEAT

CAPE COD COLISEUM

SEPT
1
1974

Sun. Eve. at
DON LAW pres
AEROSMITH
ADMISSION $6.

Michigan Palace, Detroit, 1974. © ROBERT ALFORD

Though he didn't have much production experience (leading Columbia to install A&R rep Ray Colcord as a co-producer), Douglas was a skilled technician and arranger who was able to harness that noisy energy on tape. "There were many long hours of practice to get them to sound professional by my standards," he said in *Walk This Way*. "They were a young band and they were afraid of the studio."

The resulting effort, *Get Your Wings*, was, as Kramer said in *Hit Hard*, "harder, louder, more kickass." The album opened with the strutting and funky, "Same Old Song and Dance," a classic Tyler/Perry composition topped off with a glitzy four-piece horn section led by session aces the Brecker Brothers. "A great tune," Perry told this writer in 2002. "I wish we'd written more stuff like that." From there, the record was once again largely a Tyler effort, with the singer contributing the hard-hitting "S.O.S. (Too Bad)," the evocative acoustic ballad "Seasons of Wither," and the dark and seedy "Lord of the Thighs." "We started to get more into the nastiness," Douglas told VH1's *Behind the Music*. "They were singing about dope and sex and rock 'n' roll life." Kramer, meanwhile, received his first cowriting credit, alongside Tyler, on the album's closing track, "Pandora's Box."

But the centerpiece of *Get Your Wings* was a cover, a colossal take on Tiny Bradshaw's "Train Kept a Rollin'" played in the style of Aerosmith's heroes, the Yardbirds.

Get Your Wings tour, Michigan Palace, Detroit, 1974. © CHARLIE AURINGER

"Proto-metal for sure," Perry told *Guitar World* in 1997. The band initially had hoped to tack a live reading of the song to the album. When this proved impractical, Douglas merely grabbed the studio take, blasted it through the Record Plant's stairwell, which he lined with microphones to capture the resultant echoes and delays, and then overdubbed audience applause taken from tracks left over from his work on George Harrison's *Concert for Bangladesh* film mix.

This version of the song is also notable for another, less acknowledged sleight of hand: Legend has it that neither Perry

Get Your Wings tour. Like a number of bands that later went on to huge things, Aerosmith played a number of dates in support of Mott the Hoople.

★★★ SECOND SHOW ADDED ★★★

MOTT THE HOOPLE
AEROSMITH
FRIDAY, APRIL 12 1974
2 SHOWS 7:30 & 11:30 PM
SANTA MONICA CIVIC AUDITORIUM
RESERVED SEATS $6.50, $5.50, $4.50 AVAILABLE
AT ALL WALLACH'S STORES, LIBERTY & MUTUAL
AGENCIES, TICKETRON AND SANTA MONICA
CIVIC AUDITORIUM BOX OFFICE.

Get Your Wings tour, Michigan Palace, Detroit, 1974. ALL © ROBERT ALFORD

nor Whitford performed the guitar solos on "Train." Rather, Douglas brought in guitarists Dick Wagner and Steve Hunter, go-to studio men for executive producer Ezrin, who had used them as ringers on Alice Cooper's *School's Out* and *Billion Dollar Babies*, respectively, and who came to the general public's attention as the crack guitar team on Lou Reed's *Rock 'n' Roll Animal*. In a 2010 interview with Rick Allen of *Vintage Guitar*, Hunter confirmed their involvement in "Train Kept a Rollin'": "The straight solo is me, and then there's a version that sounds like a live version [in the second half of the song]. That's Dick Wagner. I think Joe and Brad are playing the rhythm guitars."

Douglas revealed the same to KNAC.com: "Brad wanted to make the guitar parts really technical and neither he nor Joe were up to that skill level yet, so I brought in Hunter and Wagner," the producer confirmed for KNAC.com. "Those flashy, brilliant solos in 'Train Kept a Rollin'' and 'Same Old Song and Dance' are Hunter/Wagner [Note: the duo has since clarified the latter song features only Wagner]. Later, they sat Joe and Brad down and taught them everything they'd done. By the next disc, we didn't need them. Strangely enough, the band wasn't against using the session guys, especially Steven Tyler. They wanted a hit—they got one."

But it was only through their own hard work that the album became a success. *Get Your Wings*, with a cover photo that debuted the band's winged logo (reportedly designed

by former guitarist Ray Tabano, who had returned to the fold as a paid employee), was released on March 1, 1974. "Same Old Song and Dance" was issued as the first single, but failed to chart. Ditto the second ("Train Kept a Rollin'") and third ("S.O.S.") singles, but Aerosmith knew the routine: "We toured all of 1974 and nearly killed ourselves," Kramer wrote in *Hit Hard*. They went out with everyone from Black Sabbath to Blue Öyster Cult, Lynyrd Skynyrd to KISS. They played Ohio "a thousand times," said Perry, and headlined their first shows at the Orpheum Theater in Boston. In June they flew to L.A. to tape a performance of "Train" for *The Midnight Special*. That July, they supported Leber-Krebs stablemates and media darlings the New York Dolls, and watched them implode in a blizzard of drugs and booze. "Despite all this, they had a press book you would kill for,"

Hamilton and Tyler channel their New York Dolls counterparts and tour mates, Arthur "Killer" Kane and David Johansen, somewhere in the Northeast.
RICHARD MCCAFFREY/MICHAEL OCHS ARCHIVES/ GETTY IMAGES

Get Your Wings tour, Roberts Municipal Stadium, Evansville, Indiana, September 14, 1974.
BOTH DANIEL R. PATMORE/FRANK WHITE PHOTO AGENCY

Perry said in *Walk This Way*. "We kept saying, what about us?'"

In fact, the band finally was getting noticed in the press, even if it was often only to compare them, both in sound and look, to the Rolling Stones. Tyler griped to *Melody Maker*'s Chris Welch that "I would rather have a kid who went to the show write the article than a critic who has been around for so long, he saw the Stones. And he goes, 'Ah, well Joe Perry looks like Keith [Richards], and we have the Tyler-esque Jagger, or the Jagger-esque Tyler.'" But it wasn't all digs. In the magazine's first review of the band, *Rolling Stone*'s Charley Walters

wrote of *Get Your Wings*, "Aerosmith's second album surges with pent-up fury yet avoids the excesses to which many of their peers succumb."

Though Walters may have deemed their music free of excess, life on the road was a different story. "Wherever we went we brought the party with us," Tyler said in *Walk This Way*. "Those were the days when I had to do as much as I could to keep the buzz going every waking minute." Onstage the band was on fire, and backstage things were just as volatile. Tyler and Perry were continually at one another's throats, often reprising the same argument that began at Nipmuc High ("I tell Joe Perry he

plays too loud, which he does most of the time," Tyler told Chris Welch). But a new, and potentially more destructive development had also been introduced: Tyler's growing resentment over Perry's close relationship with girlfriend Elyssa Jerret. "Here's a guy that I had been waiting all my life to have as a friend, never mind be in a band with, and he really doesn't give a fuck about me," Tyler told *Behind the Music*. "He'd rather be off with Elyssa." Said Whitford to A&E's *Biography*, "I refused to go into whatever dressing room we had when the show was over, because [Steven and Joe] would have frighteningly explosive

Backstage at the Schaefer Music Festival, Central Park, New York City, September 7, 1974. SONY BMG MUSIC ENTERTAINMENT/GETTY IMAGES

arguments." He added to VH1, "The sexual tension between Steven, Elyssa and Joe, back then I mean it was just incredible."

But the band carried on, raging from one gig to the next. "We were like a drugged-out circus act, going from town to town with two tons of gear in a forty foot tractor trailer," Kramer said in *Hit Hard*. "We toured so much that when I got home, I'd pick up the phone and try to order from room service." Even so, *Get Your Wings* peaked at No. 100, which translated to a half-million copies—a gold record.

"We were like a drugged-out circus act going from town to town. . . . We toured so much t...

—Joey Kramer, *Hit Hard*, 2009

Get Your Wings

by Jaan Uhelszki

With the release of *Get Your Wings*, Aerosmith shrugged off most—but not all—of the messy British influences of their first album, learned to write first-rate songs, and zeroed in on their signature sound. In the process, they defined American hard rock in the 1970s. It was also with *Wings* that Steven Tyler and Joe Perry cracked open the backstage door, revealing dark obsessions with sex, drugs, and haughty women in songs like the "Lord of the Thighs," "Same Old Song and Dance," and "Women of the World."

Despite accolades from such spiritual descendants as Guns N' Roses and Mötley Crüe, *Get Your Wings* didn't hurl Aerosmith into the roiling waters of the mainstream, but it did get them into fighting shape for the bumpy journey to the top of rock's slag heap, engineering their preening bluster, dangerous power, perilous indulgence, and sprawling protean talent into a well-lubricated machine (emphasis on the lubrication, as history would later prove), a rock 'n' roll Harley-Davidson.

Aerosmith's self-titled debut had introduced a band aimed in the right direction. "Mama Kin," a fire-breathing talisman of a song, would become a GN'R live staple fifteen years down the road, and the wistful "Dream On" might just be the world's first power ballad. Despite the raw, screeching talent, the debut stalled at No. 166, largely ignored by a public more interested in Helen Reddy, Elton John, and Jim Croce.

When Columbia Records head Clive Davis sent a notice to the band saying he wasn't picking up their option, the band's then-manager David Krebs begged Davis to release "Dream On" as a single to show that his band really had what it took to snag more fans. The ploy worked—the single shot up to a healthy No. 59 and Aerosmith was given a reprieve.

They became a band on a mission, jettisoning British producer Adrian Barber, who had been hired because of his

Get Your Wings didn't hurl Aerosmith into the roiling waters of the mainstream, but it did get them into fighting shape for the bumpy journey to the top of rock's slag heap.

impressive credentials as an engineer for Cream, the Velvet Underground, the Allman Brothers, and Vanilla Fudge. Barber did little more than let the Boston boys have their way on their debut, recording the whole thing live and offering little guidance. "It was so simple," explained drummer Joey Kramer. "If we were good, Adrian would yell 'Yes! It's got the bloody fire!'"

Clearly, Aerosmith needed more. They thought they'd find it in Bob Ezrin, the Canadian studio savant who had produced the first four Alice Cooper records and Lou Reed's *Berlin*. But Ezrin wasn't interested. He suggested instead that the band recruit engineer Jack Douglas.

"Bob Ezrin said to me 'they're too raw and they have terrible attitudes . . . I don't want anything to do with them,'" Douglas told *Record Review* magazine in 1981.

Undaunted, Douglas took a train to Boston to see them play. "I thought I saw the American Yardbirds," Douglas remembered. "Not a copy. Not an imitation, but the real thing. . . . They played 'Train Kept a Rollin'' and I was floored. I was thinking to myself, 'This is the great American rock band.'"

Douglas immediately told the band that he didn't think much of their debut—it didn't capture who they were. His first thought: "What can I do to make them sound like themselves?" Lofty ambitions for someone who had produced just one album, Alice Cooper's *Muscle of Love*. That record went platinum; still, the label wanted him to have a copilot, so Ray Colcord was called in to co-produce. (Ezrin took an executive producer credit on the eventual album.)

The band brought an arsenal of songs to their first preproduction meeting with Douglas. Frank Connelly, one of their managers, insisted they move back in together to write the second album, so they squeezed into an apartment on Beacon Street in Brookline, Massachusetts. For four months that summer and fall, the band rehearsed incessantly, holing up in the basement of a store called Drummer's Image on Boston's Newbury Street.

Filing into the infamous Record Plant a week before Christmas 1973, they were bedazzled by the artists who had passed through those doors before them. "All of a sudden we're in New York sitting in the same seats Mick and Keith were sitting in a few weeks before," said Perry. "We were pretty much in awe of the Record Plant that we just did what Jack told us to do."

Like Barber before him, Douglas recorded the band live, but he added his own embellishments. "I took the track we cut in the studio and some really big speakers and I blasted it into the famous stairwell at the Record Plant," he recalled. "We were on the tenth floor and I put microphones on the eighth, sixth, and second floors so we could get various delays and make it sound live . . . I had worked with George Harrison on the film mix of the *Concert for Bangladesh* and I had all this applause from Madison Square Garden. I just slowly moved this out to the stairwell and brought in the crowd. Sounds pretty live. Most people were fooled."

Whatever Aerosmith accomplished on *Get Your Wings* or in concert, they did it with a sense of humor. Unlike Led Zeppelin, or even the mighty Stones, this was a populist band—five guys caught up in their own excesses and who really seemed to like being rock stars. They might have dressed more flamboyantly, dated more fetching women, and drank more expensive wine than the rest of us, but when you really got down to it, they were not that different from their fans.

Wings put Aerosmith on the road to superstardom, but they were accidental superstars, flawed heroes in spandex who may have had high ambitions, but never perched on Mount Olympus looking down at the rest of us like some of their rock brethren. Pouty and often precious, yes, but always reliably irreverent and riff-happy, Aerosmith gave classic rock a good name.

Kutztown, Pennsylvania, circa 1974.

chapter 4

Walk This Way

By the end of 1974, Aerosmith was building a career in earnest. *Get Your Wings* had nestled its way into the lower regions of the *Billboard* album charts and proceeded to remain there for much of the year—no thanks, per the usual, to radio or the press, who in large part continued to at best ignore (the former) and at worst slag (the latter) the band.

"We really put everything we had in *Toys*. . . . We were like a well-oiled machine at that time and had lots of dynamite songs that we couldn't wait to get down on tape."

—Tom Hamilton, quoted by Peter Makowski in *Metal Hammer*, March 1988

Instead, Aerosmith worked for their dinner on the road. Still a minor act on the West Coast and virtually unknown in the South, the band crisscrossed the country as support for everyone from Lynyrd Skynyrd to Blue Öyster Cult to REO Speedwagon, with the occasional headline gig in the Northeast and Midwest, their strongest markets. "I'll tell you why," Joe Perry explained to the Detroit-based *CREEM*, one of the band's few early proponents in the media. "No press. No airplay. No single. No support from the record company. In L.A., it's

*Facing page: **Toys in the Attic** tour, Cobo Arena, Detroit, May 28–30, 1975.* © ROBERT MATHEU

just the band name on the marquee at the Whisky—below somebody else. The only reason we've gotten anywhere in Detroit is that we came here and played third on the bill a couple of times, then second. The people started calling radio stations, asking for our songs, and now we're headlining. But, we haven't gotten any press compared to Bad Company or even the [New York] Dolls."

"We literally fought our way into the business that year," Brad Whitford told biographer Stephen Davis. And if at the end of it all they weren't exactly full-blown rock stars, at the very least they still had jobs:

as Perry told this writer in 2002, at the time there had been talk at Columbia—yet again—of dropping the band entirely.

It was under these shaky conditions that Aerosmith entered the studio to begin work on their third album. The band commenced preproduction that winter with Jack Douglas at Angus Studios, a converted barn in Ashland, Massachusetts, before returning to New York City and holing up at the Record Plant for two months of recording in January and February 1975.

The album that resulted from those sessions, *Toys in the Attic*, was

a monster. "We really put everything we had in *Toys*," Tom Hamilton told *Metal Hammer* in 1988. "I guess the reason it turned out so well was because we had the perfect combination of great songs and the kind of fired-up spirit that you get after a lot of touring. We were like a well-oiled machine at that time and had lots of dynamite songs that we couldn't wait to get down on tape." They were also working with a little extra fuel in the tank. "We'd go in with an ounce of blow at three in the afternoon and leave at four o'clock the next day," Tyler told VH1 of the sessions. "And we'd have a song."

"*Toys* was the one where it really clicked," Tom Hamilton told *Guitar World* in 1997. "We were starting to have . . . a solid idea of how to make a record as a band."

Toys in the Attic **tour, Cobo Arena, Detroit, May 28–30, 1975**. BOTH © ROBERT MATHEU

Toys in the Attic kicked off in barn-burning fashion with the Tyler/Perry title track, which grafted a rollicking, "Communication Breakdown"–style riff to an insistent chanted vocal—a benchmark 'Smith tune, according to Perry. Next up was the sinewy blues "Uncle Salty," one of two Hamilton compositions, while Whitford offered up the album's heaviest cut, the psychedelic sludgefest "Round and Round." Elsewhere, the band spread its wings on a cover of Bull Moose

Jackson's version of "Big Ten Inch Record," an obscure and heavy-on-the-innuendo '50s R&B tune, here decked out with horns and boogie-woogie piano (courtesy ex–Ronnie Hawkins and the Hawks pianist Scott Cushnie, who would subsequently join the band on tour that year), and the sweeping album-closing ballad, "You See Me Crying," resurrected from Tyler's Chain Reaction days and adorned with a lavish, live-in-the-studio string arrangement.

"[*Toys*] was the one where it really clicked," Hamilton told *Guitar World* in 1997. "We were starting to have a solid relationship with Jack, and a solid idea of how to make a record as a band."

It would also prove to be the one where Steven Tyler truly found his voice as a lyricist, as easy with evocative, slice-of-life storytelling (from "No More No More": *Blood stains the iv'ries on my daddy's baby grand / Ain't seen the daylight since I*

"Sweet Emotion" b/w "Uncle Salty," Germany, 1975.

"Sweet Emotion" b/w "Uncle Salty," promo disc, Germany, 1975.

started this band) as he was with a sly turn of phrase (the *love at first bite* refrain at the core of "Adam's Apple").

But the singer's increasingly well-honed wit was at its finest and most salacious on "Walk This Way." Built on a jive Joe Perry lick—"I was into James Brown and the Meters at that point and was trying to play something funky," Perry said of the song's origins—the title was lifted from a line in the Mel Brooks film *Young Frankenstein*, which the band members, sans Tyler, took in at a late showing one night in nearby Times Square.

Back at the Record Plant, they presented the singer with the title and music, and he ran with it, jotting down lyrics in stream-of-consciousness fashion on the studio's stairwell wall as the backing track played in his headphones: "There were the old make-out parties and the girl who was just a

little bit older than you and showed you where to put your finger," Tyler told Stephen Davis. "This was called showing you how to walk. Walk this way." The protagonist in Tyler's rapid-fire narrative takes things quite a bit further, progressing from masturbation to oral sex to bedding the neighbor's daughter, a schoolgirl, and a cheerleader (not to mention her sister and her cousin) in short order, a breathlessly rendered picture of youth in horny bloom.

The *Toys* sessions wrapped in late February, but not before the band tacked one last track onto the album, this one based on an old riff Hamilton had kept in his back pocket since his high school days. Of the song that would become "Sweet Emotion," the bassist recalled, "It was at the end of the recording and Jack said, 'Tomorrow's jam day, if anybody's got a spare riff hanging

**Long Beach Arena,
Long Beach, California.**

**Roberts Municipal Stadium,
Evansville, Indiana.**

around.' I said, 'Yeah, I do.' So I spent the day showing everybody everything, and we took it from there, refining it into what it is. And then Steven had the idea of taking that intro riff, which became the chorus bass line under the 'sweet emotion' part, and transposing it from A to E, and making it a really heavy thing."

Which is not to say that Tyler wasted many minutes ruminating on the musical implications of the now famous key change. "We didn't know how to end it," he said. "We got into a big fight. Blew cocaine all over the place. Finally I said, 'Just fucking play a drum fill and we'll go into [the outro].' And we did. It was a magic moment."

Toys in the Attic was released on April 8, 1975, and Aerosmith's fortunes seemed to shift almost overnight. If the reviews weren't glowing (Robert Christgau of the *Village Voice* commented, "These boys are learning a trade in record time—even the sludgy numbers get crazy"), at least they weren't wholly derisive. More importantly, the album sold. *Toys* went gold in five months, and the first single, "Sweet Emotion," busted onto the *Billboard* charts, becoming the band's first Top 40 hit that July.

In addition, the band suddenly found itself out from under the inauspicious hand of "Father" Frank Connelly, now suffering from cancer, who sold his remaining interest in Aerosmith to Steve Leber and David Krebs. There was no love lost between Connelly and the band: legend has it that mixed in with the backward handclaps that punctuate the pre-chorus instrumental section of "Sweet Emotion" is the sound of the members sarcastically chanting, again with backward masking, "Thanks, Frank!"

With Leber-Krebs now in the driver's seat, Aerosmith took their show back on the road. The *Toys in the Attic* tour kicked off with dates in the Midwest and Northeast, including back-to-back headlining gigs, with support from Foghat, at the hometown Boston Garden on April 18 and 19. Then it was on to the West Coast to open a string of dates for ZZ Top, including a tide-turning show at the L.A. Forum, where, at the end of the year, they'd return as headliner. In Cleveland Aerosmith went before 60,000 fans as part of the World Series of Rock, and back in New York City, they played Central Park for the Schaefer Music Festival.

With an exhaustive road schedule and consistently knockout shows, Aerosmith was quickly emerging as America's hardest working—and hardest playing—rock 'n' roll act. "I've been going to a lot of concerts lately," Tyler told *Rolling Stone* that year, "watching groups who are so

fucking outrageous on record that you'd think they'd get out there onstage and shake ass. But they just stand there. The songs we write aren't the kind that you can come out and fucking genuflect. We play kick-ass music."

The fans took notice—and one strain of fan in particular. The band and the press began referring to the seas of blue-collar, denim-clad, and occasionally rowdy longhairs that populated Aerosmith shows in large numbers as the Blue Army—"our people," commented Perry. "The only problem," Joey Kramer said of the Blue Army in *Hit Hard*, "was all the crap they threw onto the stage, including cherry bombs and M-80s."

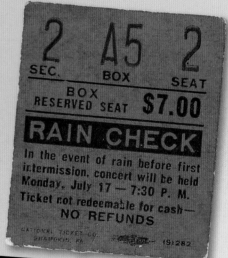

Wollman Rink, Central Park, New York City.

"Aerosmith may already be the most popular band ever to come out of Boston . . . it is their reputation for powerhouse raunch that sold out Detroit's Cobo Hall two consecutive nights: the little girls may understand, but the boys like the music because it's tough."

—Wayne Robins, *CREEM*, September 1975

Things were getting more unruly all around. Cocaine and pills were mainstays on the road—lines were cut on top of guitar amps during shows, while Tyler kept the scarves on his mic stand loaded down with Tuinals for easy access. At the L.A. Forum with ZZ Top in June, a problem with the onstage monitors led Tyler to threaten to bail on the gig; backstage, the singer was known to fly into a rage if turkey loaf, rather than the specified turkey on the bone, was found in the buffet; post-show in Nebraska, Tyler and Kramer were arrested for throwing fireworks out the window of Kramer's room at the Hilton Inn.

Meanwhile, Perry's relationship with his girlfriend Elyssa Jerret was forming a deep chasm within the band, with Tyler in particular blaming her constant presence for Perry's pulling away from the others—a sentiment touched on in the lyrics to "Sweet Emotion." This, however, didn't prevent the singer and guitarist from stealing away together during Joe and Elyssa's wedding at the Boston Ritz that summer to snort some heroin together. "Really strong heroin," Perry told Stephen Davis. "It was all I could do to keep from throwing up on the cake." (Not that the guitarist was the only one pairing off: Earlier in the year Hamilton had married longtime girlfriend Terry Cohen, and Whitford would soon follow with his girlfriend, Lori Phillips. Tyler,

Opening for ZZ Top at the Forum, Inglewood, California, June 19, 1975, on the night of the infamous faulty monitor incident.

MARK SULLIVAN/GETTY IMAGES

World Series of Rock, Municipal Stadium, Cleveland, August 23, 1975. Aerosmith played before 60,000 fans at the seventh installment of the famed 1970s concert series. The Faces, Uriah Heep, and Blue Öyster Cult were also on the bill. ALL © ROBERT ALFORD

AEROSMITH
AUGUST 29

SCHAEFFER MUSIC FESTIVAL
CENTRAL PARK, 7 PM, TICKETS: $2.50, $1.50
TOYS IN THE ATTIC
ON COLUMBIA RECORDS AND TAPES.

An exhaustive *Toys in the Attic* tour included an August 1975 gig at the Schaefer Music Festival in Central Park, New York City. It was their second appearance at the annual summer-long series. COURTESY FILMPOSTERS.COM

meanwhile, was nurturing a serious relationship with an underage girl; the two began cohabitating after the singer approached her parents to sign legal guardianship papers. Scandalous, perhaps, but as he told *Blender*'s Ben Mitchell in 2002, "She sure didn't act 16.")

But nothing could stanch the band's collective high. The remainder of the year was spent sharing stages with everyone from the Faces to Black Sabbath, and the continued success of *Toys in the Attic* pulled Aerosmith's earlier records up with it. By the end of 1975, all three efforts were on the charts, and "Dream On," which had stiffed when issued as Aerosmith's debut single two years earlier, was on its way

to becoming their first Top 10 hit. Eventually "Walk This Way" would follow. From here on out, it would be strictly headlining dates on the road.

For the first time real money was rolling in, much of it courtesy of royalty checks for *Toys in the Attic*. The band members enjoyed the financial fruits of their labors by purchasing toys of their own—Porsches, Ferraris, and Corvettes, as well as plenty of substances to keep the party going indefinitely. "With more money in the pipeline," Kramer said in *Hit Hard*, "Aerosmith became the single biggest market for drugs in New England." They also dropped a down payment on an empty warehouse in Waltham, Massachusetts, outside of Boston.

Christened "A. Wherehouse," the facility functioned as a band rehearsal space, office, and all-around clubhouse. Said Kramer, "Like most guys who get a lot of fame and a lot of money before they know what to do with it, we carried on pretty much like the thirteen-year-old boys who came to see us."

Of course, what goes up must eventually come down. "What none of us realized," the drummer noted, "was that we had just reached our early peak."

The Forum, Inglewood, California.

Toys in the Attic tour, Madison Square Garden, New York City, December 3, 1975. RICHARD E. AARON/REDFERNS/GETTY IMAGES

Toys in the Attic

by Greg Kot

Aerosmith was only three years removed from touring in front of crowds so small that the band could hear crickets between poorly received songs. In those three years they became a band to be reckoned with. By the winter of 1975, as they settled into the Record Plant in New York with producer Jack Douglas to record their third studio album, *Toys in the Attic*, they still hadn't had a hit, but they were road-tested, confident, and jacked up.

With high-grade drug abuse, there's a fine line between a heightened sense of confidence/ daring and total insanity. Aerosmith would trip over that line and crash countless times in subsequent years, but at this moment they were on the right side of the edge and flying. What's sometimes missed by readers who gobble up all those ultra-transparent interviews that Steven Tyler and Joe Perry have given about this era is that Aerosmith was as serious about their music as they were about anything in life, including sex and drugs—and given this band's outrageous appetites, that's saying something. After playing nearly every day for three years, Aerosmith came into the studio sounding like a vastly improved band from the one that debuted with *Aerosmith* in 1973, the rhythm section in particular.

Tyler and Perry were the public face of the band, and they came armed for battle; Perry's riffs are all-timers in "Walk This Way" and "Sweet Emotion," in particular, and Tyler is at his salty, cackling, swaggering best as a vocalist and even a conceptualist (don't laugh—more on this later). But the engine room was where the rumble really started to happen. The opening title track set the tone, a street fight with bassist Tom Hamilton, drummer Joey Kramer, and rhythm guitarist Brad Whitford taking the first swings. Rather than just bashing out his parts, Kramer orchestrated them, creating a range of textures, fills, and accents that gave each song a rhythmic personality.

Hamilton's the biggest revelation, though; he sounds like a different, better bassist. He took to heart a joke that Douglas had made about his performance on Aeromsith's previous album, *Get Your Wings*, and woodshedded his way into becoming a more nimble musician. In many ways, he's the secret weapon on *Toys* and a major reason why Aerosmith was able to translate its appreciation for blues and R&B into a swinging hard-rock sound all its own. While other '70s classic-rockers were all about

> With high-grade drug abuse, there's a fine line between a heightened sense of confidence and total insanity, but at this moment Aerosmith was on the right side of the edge and flying.

riffs, Aerosmith added a sense of groove, a shimmy in the hips that matched Tyler's lip-smacking lyrics.

No wonder they reached back to cover "Big Ten Inch Record," a song too risqué to invite widespread radio airplay when saxophonist Bull Moose Jackson recorded it in 1952 with his hard-charging big band. Given Tyler's love of double entendres and his penchant for pushing the imagery in his lyrics just short of out-and-out lewdness, it's little wonder he loved the song, and he gives it a bravura performance worthy of a chitlin' circuit house party. The band swings with confidence and exhibits a feel for syncopation and the space between the notes that did not come easily to other suburban-bred '70s rockers.

The groove is never better than on "Walk This Way." Perry's funky guitar springs out of a rhythm pocket so deep that it sounds like something James Brown could've invented. Perry says he conjured the riff while watching a Godzilla movie, and it's that huge and iconic, one of those instantly recognized sounds on par with the opening of the Beatles' "Hard Days Night" or the Rolling Stones' "Brown Sugar." Hamilton and Kramer give the song a strut that never falters, while Tyler unleashes a stream of sex-charged wordplay that suggests the clever acrobatics of a great rap vocal, somewhere between Cab Calloway and Slick Rick. No wonder Run-DMC jumped on this sucker a decade later for their breakthrough hit.

The album has its share of '70s clichés: the doubled guitar line in "Adam's Apple" (very Thin Lizzy, very Judas Priest); the strings-and-horns power-ballad bombast of "You See Me Crying" (a bigger, clunkier version of "Dream On"); the plodding hard rock of "Round and Round" (the most dated-sounding track on the album, like a Black Sabbath leftover). But some of those clichés sounded damn good—Perry's talk-box in "Sweet Emotion," for example. It's more a texture than a showboating centerpiece in

a brilliantly orchestrated arrangement. The talk-box distortion aligns the song with another killer Hamilton bass line and studio musician Jay Messina's marimba. Douglas uses the studio as an instrument—backward harmonies and handclaps, the sound of a shotgun—to enhance the mood as it flips between druggy reverie (not for nothing was the song used to open the quintessential '70s stoner film, *Dazed and Confused*) and biting putdowns (Tyler riffing on the rift between Perry's future wife and the rest of the group).

Aerosmith took great pleasure in evolving into "a people's band," unburdened by heavyweight intellectual pretensions. But there's more going on in *Toys* than just boys-will-be-boys kicks. The cover art depicts a collection of discarded stuffed animals coming to life; in the lower left corner a child enters this surreal scene clutching a set of keys. A quote Tyler once gave me in an interview seems to comment on that illustration: "It's OK to let the kid out, to go on stage and feel like you're 20 again even if you're 41."

Toys is about that search for wonder which the real world erodes. In many of the songs, innocence and mental stability are casualties. The title track's narrator is "leaving the things that are real behind." "Uncle Salty" depicts an abused orphan reduced to fantasizing about the "sunny day" outside her window. "Adam's Apple" cleverly flips the biblical script about who was to blame for original sin—talk about a fall from grace. And then there's "No More No More," about the drudgery of the road, with a great, ringing riff that Paul Westerberg surely had in the back of his mind when he was writing the Replacements' equally disillusioned "Unsatisfied."

So besides being a great party album, a volatile cocktail of testosterone riffs, and boogie perfect for both headbanging and dancing, *Toys in the Attic* is the sound of a band keeping it together—if only barely—before the drugs take over and the music becomes an afterthought. They're still that kid with the keys on the album cover, playing on their own island of misfit toys. ✈

"Toys in the Attic" b/w "Sweet Emotion," Japan, 1975.

"Sweet Emotion" b/w "Uncle Salty" (a.k.a. "Dulce Emocion" b/w "Tio Salty"), Spain, 1975.

chapter 5

Rocks

As 1975 turned into 1976, Aerosmith was indeed flying high. "We were America's band," Perry told *Rolling Stone*. "We were the garage band that made it really big—the ultimate party band. We were the guys who you could actually see. It wasn't like Led Zeppelin was out there on the road in America all the time. The Stones weren't always coming to your town. We were."

Coming off the road at the end of the year, and with the three-year-old "Dream On" a bona fide hit single across the country, the band set to work on their fourth album, beginning preproduction with Jack Douglas at their own Wherehouse before moving to the Record Plant in New York City.

But progress was slow: Tyler was struggling with lyrics to the

"They've retooled Led Zeppelin till the English warhorse is all glitz and flow, beating the s*** out of Boston and Ted Nugent and Blue Öyster Cult in the process."

—Robert Christgau, 1976

Facing page: **Rocks** tour, RFK Stadium, Washington, D.C., May 30, 1976. FIN COSTELLO/REDFERNS/GETTY IMAGES

Facing page, inset: June 24, 1976, Sam Houston Coliseum, Houston, Texas.

59

Descending into Detroit for the May 8, 1976, show at the nearby Silverdome. FIN COSTELLO/REDFERNS/GETTY IMAGES

new songs, and Perry, reeling from the recent death of his father from cancer, had retreated further into Elyssa and, more dangerously, heroin. Much of the time, Kramer, Hamilton, and Whitford worked up tracks with Douglas independent of the singer and guitarist. (The rhythm section by this time had taken to referring to themselves as the LI3, or Less Interesting Three, an in-joke on the manner in which they were regarded, both within the band's organization and by the press.) But despite the fractured nature of their working process, musically the band was on a creative high, resulting in some of their most diverse and exciting material to date. "We cut all the basics at the Wherehouse," Douglas said to KNAC.com of the early sessions. "A big, metal, roaring, huge room. I used stage monitors . . . to blow the sound right back at them. And that's when they started to stretch out. Joe would ask what he should be listening to and I'd hip him to John Coltrane for solo ideas—and he'd get to that! Even in preproduction, I knew it was great."

Rocks, with production credit shared, for the first time, by Douglas and Aerosmith, proved to be their strongest and most ferocious set to date, the sound reflected in the album's cover art: five sharply cut diamonds against a stark black background. The enduring Tyler/Perry cut "Back in the Saddle" kicked off the record in grand style, a swaggering statement of intent carried on Tyler's raw-throated vocals and Perry's deep-in-the-pocket riff, played on a Fender Bass VI six-string bass. "I was very high on heroin when

I wrote [it]," Perry told *Guitar World*. "That riff just floated right through me." Of its unusual instrumentation, he commented, "I got turned onto the six-string bass from watching Peter Green play one with Fleetwood Mac. I always thought that was a cool thing."

The album featured several more top-notch Tyler/Perry collaborations, including "Lick and a Promise" and "Rats in the Cellar." (The latter, commented Perry, was "our answer to 'Toys in the Attic.' We were getting lower and more down and dirty. So the cellar seemed like a good place to go.") Perry also received his first solo writing credit, for "Combination," a down-and-dirty drug tale with a hard-as-nails groove for which the guitarist assumed co-lead vocals with Tyler.

In general, the sessions were dominated by a sense of experimentation. To lend "Back

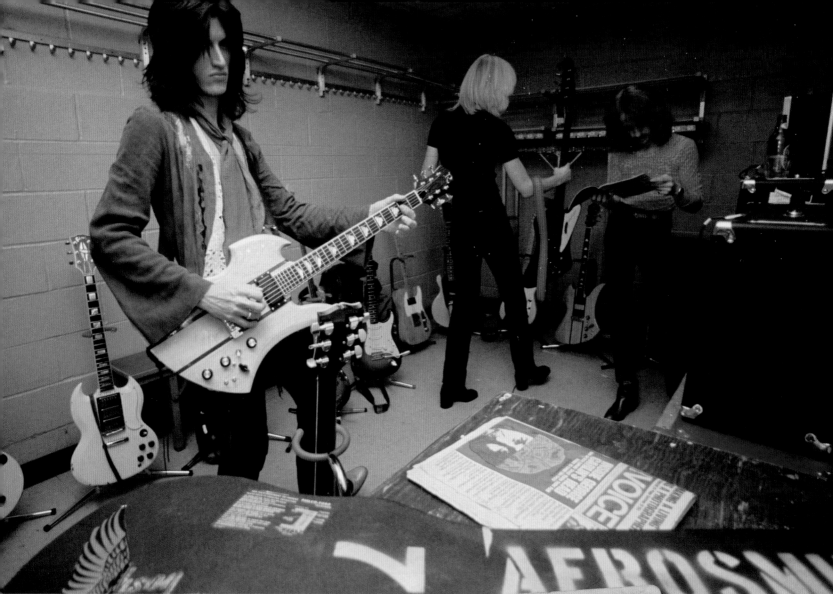

Perry (with a B.C. Rich Mockingbird guitar), Hamilton, and Kramer backstage at Madison Square Garden, New York City, May 10, 1976. FIN COSTELLO/REDFERNS/GETTY IMAGES

CELLAR DOOR CONCERTS
Presents

Aerosmith
5/17 MIA
#5

BACKSTAGE PASS

Jai Alai Fronton, Miami, Florida.

Sound Seventy Productions INC.

AEROSMITH
MAY 10 1976 H'VILLE

Date   City

Von Braun Civic Center, Huntsville, Alabama.

Stage Pass

mid SOUTH

6-19-76
Jackson, Miss.

Mississippi Coliseum, Jackson, Mississippi.

STADIUM   AEROSMITH

LIF.   9 2   IOG.A.
                     DATE/EVENT CODE
R CONCERTS   003/20
                  ENTRANCE
PRESENTS
H   雨雨雨   07/10
        OUTDOOR   EST. PRICE
ANGES   14119612RM0298
6   4:00P $10.00
                     TOTAL

Anaheim Stadium, Anaheim, California.

in the Saddle" an appropriate "cowboy" vibe, Perry and David Johansen, then laying low with the band following the implosion of the New York Dolls, gaffer-taped tambourines and bells to Tyler's boots and had him stomp a wooden board. For Whitford's supremely funky "Last Child," Douglas brought in Paul Prestopino, formerly of the folk combo the Weavers, to add some down-home banjo. Hamilton's "Sick as a Dog," meanwhile, featured some real-time mid-song instrument reshuffling: "Tom played rhythm guitar," Perry told *Guitar World*. "I played bass for the first half of the song. Then I put down the bass and played guitar in the end, and Steven picked up the bass and played it the rest of the song—all live in the studio. One take!"

Rocks was released on May 3, 1976, and promptly exploded. On May 21 it was awarded gold status; on July 9 it went platinum, one of the first records in history to do so (1976 being the year the designation was introduced). More firsts would follow. The band debuted at Madison Square Garden on May 10, opening for Black Sabbath (though Perry, following a coke-and-pills marathon with Elyssa, almost missed the gig, still fast asleep at home in Massachusetts just hours before show time). Two days earlier, they headlined their biggest show to date, at the Pontiac Silverdome in Michigan, where Kramer treated the 80,000-strong Blue Army to his first drum solo. "When the audience responded I could feel the joy in every cell

continued on page 66

Whitford's supremely funky "Last Child" b/w "Combination," Japan, 1976.

Joe Freeman Coliseum, San Antonio, Texas.

Jefferson Civic Coliseum, Birmingham, Alabama.

Balboa Stadium, San Diego, California.

Cobo Arena, Detroit.

BE-BOP PRODUCTIONS presents
AEROSMITH
★
COLISEUM
JUNE 19 1976 Jackson, Miss.
SATURDAY 8:00 P.M.
GEN. ADM.
JUNE 19, 1976
ADMIT ONE ON ABOVE DATE ONLY
003961 SEC ROW SEAT
$6.50
PRICE NO REFUND NO EXCHANGE
DAY OF SHOW
GEN. ADM.
003961 SEC ROW SEAT

BACKSTAGE PASS
COLT PARK, HARTFORD, CT.
WPLR PRESENTS
AERO-SMITH
AUGUST 9, 1976
A CONTEMPORARY CONCERT CORP.
PRESENTATION

& KMR Productions Present
AEROSMITH
and special guest Rick Derringer
AUGUST 29th
NBC ARENA HONOLULU
BACKSTAGE PASS

Belkin Productions
Presents
AEROSMITH
Detroit 10/2

Below and facing page: Rocks tour, RFK Stadium, Washington, D.C., May 30, 1976.
BOTH FIN COSTELLO/REDFERNS/GETTY IMAGES

in my body," he recalled in *Hit Hard*. "So being me, I got hooked on that high, and I did a solo every night for the next eighteen years."

The band was also joined in Michigan by a writer from *Rolling Stone*, which, after years of minimal coverage, had finally come to the table with a cover story. The piece, titled "Aerosmith's Wrench Rock" (August 26, 1976), was hardly flattering. Scribe Ed McCormack pegged Tyler as a petulant "caricature of a caricature," with a voice that "makes Alice Cooper sound like Vic Damone"; labeled Perry a "grease monkey"; and dismissed the band as "brain-damage music." Even the Blue Army took a beating: "They looked like hell," McCormack wrote. "They gobbled reds and chugalugged beer." To add insult to injury, the magazine ran a solo shot of Tyler on the issue's cover, despite Krebs and the band's insistence on a full group portrait. (When management refused the request for a solo Tyler shoot, *Rolling*

Stone photographer Annie Leibovitz merely showed up unannounced at his Beverly Hilton bungalow early one morning and got off a few somewhat unflattering clicks of the half-asleep singer. Cover done.)

But Aerosmith were unstoppable. *Rocks* peaked at No. 3 on *Billboard*, and "Last Child" made it to No. 21 on the singles chart. At one point, according to Perry, the album was moving upward of 10,000 units a day. And not every media outlet was as dismissive as *Rolling Stone*: as Robert Christgau, writing in the *Village Voice*, noted in his review, "They've retooled Led Zeppelin till the English warhorse is all glitz and flow, beating the shit out of Boston and Ted Nugent and Blue Öyster Cult in the process."

Furthermore, they were cleaning up on the road: 65,000 at Comiskey Park in Chicago on July 10, where the roof of the venue caught on fire during opener Rick Derringer's set after the Blue Army started lobbing firecrackers and M-80s; 110,000

at the Kingdome in Seattle on September 3; a week later, 56,000 at Anaheim Stadium. For Perry and Whitford, a special thrill of the summer of '76 was having Jeff Beck, enjoying newfound life as an instrumental rock/fusion artist with *Blow by Blow*, as an opener for many of these dates. "Imagine Brad and I going out there and watching this insanity go on, and then having to follow it," Perry said to *Trouser Press* of the irony of seeing his hero as the opening act. "A lot of other people wouldn't have done it."

Firmly atop the rock 'n' roll food chain in America, that October the band made their first voyage outside the States, heading to Europe for a month of shows. But the jaunt, which took them through the U.K., Germany, Sweden, Holland, Switzerland, and France, found them in defensive mode, struggling

Kingdome, Seattle, Washington.

Rocks tour, Civic Center, Providence, Rhode Island, August 7, 1976. © RON POWNALL/ROCKROLLPHOTO.COM

to prove themselves on new turf. In Germany, Tyler, with new girlfriend and former Playboy model Bebe Buell in tow, was strip-searched and arrested at customs after being found with a small amount of hash, which he then defiantly blew in the customs officer's face. In England the press was openly critical of the band. Barbara Charone of *Sounds* reviewed their October 17 gig at London's Hammersmith Odeon: "Visually, Aerosmith parody the Stones quite limply." But Tyler gave it right back: "I'll tell you man, the critics are old blokes here," he told *Melody Maker*'s Chris Welch. "They're fucking stupid, most of them."

The band soothed the rough going in Europe by returning home to close out the year with seven massive North American dates, including two nights at Boston Garden and a headlining gig at Madison Square Garden on December 16. As an added bonus, Columbia reissued "Walk This Way" as a single and, following the belated path taken by "Dream On," it became their second Top 10 hit in twelve months.

Overall 1976 had been, in the words of Perry, "a hell of a year," but the heavy touring and excessive drinking and drugging was taking its toll. The band was worn out, strung out, and very close to burned out.

SOUNDS/OCTOBER 16 1976 15p

AEROSMITH · THIN LIZZY

Sounds

The hit man

Aerosmith's Steven Tyler is out to kill; page 26

Black punks on erb

Bunny Wailer and Jamaica's new music

Tyler graces the cover of U.K. music weekly *Sounds*. In a later issue, Barbara Charone would pan the band's gig at Hammersmith Odeon.

Rocks

by Chuck Eddy

Rocks came out in May 1976, which may well make it the last hard-rock record on which a singer calls someone a "punk" before punk rock came along and changed the meaning entirely. (Competition: Brownsville Station's *School Punks* [1974], the Tubes' "White Punks on Dope" [1975], and Slick's "The Kid's a Punk" [1976]). In Aerosmith's case, the word occurs amid the heavy swinging funk of "Last Child," partly penned by rhythm guitarist Brad Whitford and screamed by Steve Tyler: *I was the laaaast child, just a punk in the streets.* The point of view seems to be that of a farm boy reminiscing about his stint in the big-city ghetto, where he misses his mule and plow and girl and mama, so he has to get back to the real nitty gritty. Where the grass is green and the girls are pretty and the howlin' owl in the woods hunts the horny-backed toad—oops, wrong bands, but same idea. Aerosmith could've named it "Home Sweet Home" since that's the song's tagline. Eventually, Mötley Crüe claimed that title.

"Last Child," which also notably takes into account South Tallahassee and sweet sassafrassies and John Paul Getty's ear, and features veteran studio folkie Paul Prestopino on banjo, is the second song on *Rocks*—Aerosmith's fourth album, probably their heaviest, and quite possibly their best; the only real challenges would be from the two LPs immediately preceding it. After this, it was a long crash and slide downhill, though of course the band's commercial, if not creative, prospects picked back up a decade down the line. Both "Last Child" and the song that precedes it on *Rocks*, future comeback-tour theme "Back in the Saddle," start out dark, gloomy, and ominous, but eventually find a pocket, the depth of which few rock bands before or since have ever equaled.

And if the lyrics of "Last Child" are country, those featured on "Back in the Saddle" are western. (Neither is Aerosmith's most C&W song, though—that'd be "Chip Away at the Stone" on *Live! Bootleg*.) "Saddle" opens the album slow

Aerosmith's fourth album was probably their heaviest. After this, it was a long slide downhill until the band's commercial prospects picked up again a decade down the line.

and slimy, revs up faster and faster, then explodes with some bucking-bronco neighs that'd maybe eventually influence 1990s frat-rappers Cypress Hill and House of Pain; Steve Tyler boasts that he's "baaaaack" and the band catapults into a groove as thumping as most any disco of the era, scoring a plot that seems to concern galloping into town by moonlight on one's trusty steed, stopping by a "crazy horse saloon," ordering a drink, and picking up a date—not that you'd ever consider such mundanities while listening to the thing. Mainly, it *roars* in an epic manner that draws a direct line from Gene Autry's 1939 cowboy classic "Back in the Saddle Again" to the Osmonds' equine 1972 metal move "Crazy Horses" to Die Kreuzen's subterranean '86 Wisconsin shriek-core *October File* to Poison's 1988 Harrisburg-to-Hollywood mascara glam, "Back to the Rocking Horse." Which is to say, if you were a budding R.O.C.K.er in the bicentennial U.S.A., you grew up on it, no matter which road you took from there. And its odd syncopated ending—all cracking whips and wah-wahs and giddy-ups—is a kissing cousin to "Life at the Outpost," Skatt Brothers' Stetson-hatted rough-trade leather-bar disco-metal masterpiece from 1979, to boot.

Simpletons pretend "Back in the Saddle" is just about being a coked-up rock star, but it's always been more empowering for regular suburban '70s school brats and their progeny than that implies. Still, it's hard to deny that, taken in noun form, *Rocks*' title might imply illegal inebriants of some sort, and there's certainly an unmistakable drug-dangers motif to the yellowing skin and eluding the NYC jailer and pushing up daisies stuff in the album's third and fastest track, "Rats in the Cellar"—bulging-bicep thrash that everybody hears as a direct sequel to "Toys in the Attic." Along with side two's high Richter-scaled natural disaster "Nobody's Fault" (as in, say, San Andreas . . . screaming, fleeing people, stilt houses toppled, debris piled to your knees!), "Rats" is probably also the most

legitimately *metal* track on *Rocks*. Or at least, if you asked somebody in an early-'80s New Wave of British Heavy Metal band, they'd say so.

You'd think *Rocks*' "Get the Lead Out" (given its classic-rock-block-radio anticipating title) would be the obvious Zeppelin rip, but nope, that one's a merely mortal mid-tempo booger-rooger with a Hank Williams "Hey Good Lookin'" quote in the middle, whereas "Nobody's Fault" has the sleek chromium density that matters. Though "Get the Lead Out" does conclude with a sort of marching band shuffle—as does the reasonably whomping "Combination," the album's lone Joe Perry–alone songwriting credit, which is basically all rhythm, no hook.

Anyway. "Combination" ends side one and then you flip the record over. (Yeah, I'm told there are now other formats besides vinyl, but they make no sense for this particular platter.) "Sick as a Dog" starts side two with some surprisingly pretty, almost Byrds-like jangle, then more sustained Steve Tyler vowels, pleading *pleeeeeease* with a paramour like he's rotting on the end of his rope, but also chiding her for being over-refined and for the cat having her tongue.

And then you actually hear some cat-scratch-fevered feline pawing and purring toward song's end, followed by an almost bubble-gummy handclap break and incidental atmospherics that could serve as a weather forecast for Guns N' Roses' "November Rain"—all sorts of subliminal doodads apparently stuck into the mix by producer Jack Douglas. (Max Bell, in his 1976 review in England's *New Musical Express*, wrote, "I still like those bits between the tracks best.")

Penultimate *Rocks* track "Lick and a Promise," sung by Tyler in the third person, seems to be named for two things a guitar hero might give a groupie on a Saturday night at the house of blue lights; the licks come from his instrument too, of course, and the promises should not be expected to be kept. It's set in a stodgy old dive, seemingly, but the na-na-na-na-nas demonstrate again that 'Smith wasn't afraid to pour some sugar on their blues. "Home Tonight" is the sweet ballad finale, Joe Perry on lap steel, your cigarette lighter in the air, "now it's time to say goodnight." Drive home safely, but be forewarned that Aerosmith's power-schlock '80s—and hair metal, too—are on the way. ◣

"Last Child" b/w "Combination," promo disc, Germany, 1976.

"Back in the Saddle" b/w "Sick as a Dog," Japan, 1976.

chapter 6

Know Where to Draw the Line

Aerosmith kicked off 1977 with their second endeavor outside the States. But in contrast to their grand European misadventure, Japan, under the guidance of legendary promoter Mr. Udo, welcomed the band with open arms—seven sold-out gigs, including two nights at Tokyo's Budokon Hall; swarms of young, screaming girls descending, Beatlemania-style, on the members (though mostly Tyler and Perry) wherever they went; and all the sake and geisha girls they could handle.

"The drugs and the debauchery—that band definitely wins the prize, hands down. They were wilder than the Stones. They were wilder than Zeppelin."

—Bebe Buell, speaking on VH1's *Behind the Music*, 2002

After a short break in Hawaii, they returned to the U.S. in late winter to begin work on their fifth album, *Draw the Line*. With live dates already penciled in for June and July, the record was scheduled to be in the bag by May. In an effort to remove any outside distractions, Krebs installed the band at the Cenacle, an isolated estate on one hundred acres in Armonk, New York, an hour north of Manhattan.

Facing page: The photo shoot that resulted in the image from which Al Hirschfield drew the famous *Draw the Line* caricature (see 8-track, facing page). The Cenacle, Armonk, New York, May 31, 1977. © RON POWNALL/ROCKROLLPHOTO.COM

AEROSMITH
DRAW THE LINE

TC8
JCA 34856

71

AEROSMITH & CBS/SONY CO-PILOT SENSATIONAL FLIGHT OVER JAPAN

The early '77 high-altitude Aerosmith tour of Japan continues to establish records. Aerosmith records selling in the stores, and Aerosmith records playing on the stations. CBS/Sony is proud to be part of the team work it takes to bring home the really successful artist tours.

CBS SONY
CBS/SONY INC.

Stateside in spring 1977, CBS made sure to point out that thousands of screaming fans had greeted the band on their first tour of Japan: seven sold-out gigs in January and February 1977.

The choice of location was thick with unintended irony: The facility had formerly housed a nunnery, and its current owner, a psychiatrist, hoped to reconstitute it as a treatment center for disturbed adolescents. Instead, he got Aerosmith—close enough. The Cenacle sessions were disjointed, to say the least. Kramer, Hamilton, and Whitford worked for days with Douglas before the others appeared on-site. When Perry did finally show—with his Porsche, Elyssa, and a new toy, a semiautomatic submachine gun, in tow, it was hardly with music on his mind. "He went up to the fourth floor, found a large living space—and didn't come down for four or five days," Douglas told VH1. "We didn't even see him." Ditto for Tyler, who, upon arrival, cased out his own secluded space and quickly vanished. "They just weren't around," Whitford said. "They were locked away in their rooms consuming whatever they were consuming" (Huxley, uncredited).

The scene was full-on decadence: "Sixty acres with a great big house, and the Record Plant installed a whole studio there for us," Perry recalled in *CREEM*. "I don't know how much it cost, but it was outrageous. They had a bar and people to serve [us], and I'd wake up at four or five in the afternoon. We had motorcycles and Porches and we'd go cruising around the countryside terrorizing everybody. We had all our

Pressing of "Walk This Way" b/w "Nobody's Fault" released in Japan in 1977 to mark the band's first tour of the country.

"Kings and Queens" b/w "Critical Mass," Japan, 1977.

The band enjoyed the financial fruits of their hit records. Perry shows off his Porsche and his not-so-cherry Corvette.
© RON POWNALL/ROCKROLLPHOTO.COM

Aerosmith belt buckle, circa 1977.

friends up there and we'd go shooting off all these guns at the shooting range, just blasting away."

Occasionally, they also attempted to work. Douglas instructed the full-service studio to be erected in the cavernous chapel, with Kramer's drum kit installed on the altar. Tyler's vocal booth was on the second floor, Whitford was ensconced in a living room, and Perry was in a big walk-in fireplace. An awkward way for a band used to playing together live in the studio to cut a record, but then again, there wasn't much recording going on. Tyler had little in the way of lyrics, and Perry would arrive at the chapel so blitzed and glassy-eyed that Douglas, disgusted, would throw him out. New material was coming so slowly that the band attempted to pad the album with covers—Otis Rush's "All Your Love," Kokomo Arnold's "Milk Cow Blues"—from their early days. But mostly, everyone just sat around and got bombed.

Tyler and Perry discuss the recording of *Draw the Line* at the Cenacle. The estate's new owner in 1977 hoped to repurpose the former nunnery as a treatment center for troubled adolescents. Instead, he got Aerosmith—close enough. © RON POWNALL/ROCKROLLPHOTO.COM

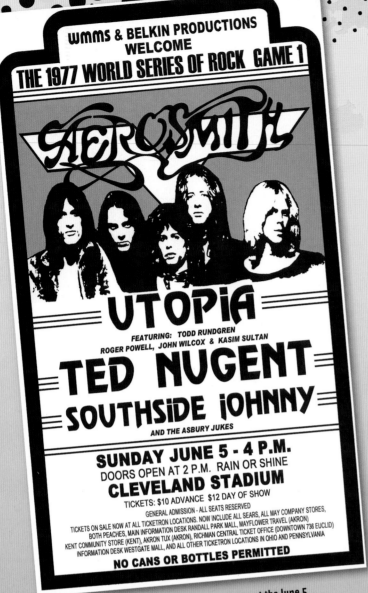

WMMS & BELKIN PRODUCTIONS
WELCOME
THE 1977 WORLD SERIES OF ROCK GAME 1

AEROSMITH

UTOPIA
FEATURING: TODD RUNDGREN
ROGER POWELL, JOHN WILCOX & KASIM SULTAN

TED NUGENT
SOUTHSIDE JOHNNY
AND THE ASBURY JUKES

SUNDAY JUNE 5 - 4 P.M.
DOORS OPEN AT 2 P.M. RAIN OR SHINE
CLEVELAND STADIUM
TICKETS: $10 ADVANCE $12 DAY OF SHOW
GENERAL ADMISSION - ALL SEATS RESERVED
TICKETS ON SALE NOW AT ALL TICKETRON LOCATIONS. NOW INCLUDE ALL SEARS, ALL MAY COMPANY STORES,
BOTH PEACHES, MAIN INFORMATION DESK RANDALL PARK MALL, MAYFLOWER TRAVEL (AKRON)
KENT COMMUNITY STORE (KENT), AKRON TUX (AKRON), RICHMAN CENTRAL TICKET OFFICE (DOWNTOWN 736 EUCLID)
INFORMATION DESK WESTGATE MALL, AND ALL OTHER TICKETRON LOCATIONS IN OHIO AND PENNSYLVANIA

NO CANS OR BOTTLES PERMITTED

Aerosmith cancelled their scheduled appearance at the June 5, 1977, installment of Cleveland's World Series of Rock.

When their time at the Cenacle was up, the new album was far from complete. But the road beckoned, and *Draw the Line* would have to be worked on in fits and starts throughout the rest of the year. The Aerosmith Express tour left the station in June of '77, and the debauchery continued. Prior to the tour kickoff, both Kramer and Perry totaled cars; once on the road, hotel rooms were chainsawed into oblivion, and television sets were fitted with extra long extension cords so that the still plugged-in boxes would explode when they hit the ground after being hurled off balconies. On July 10, at the Civic Center in Baltimore, Perry flew into a rage, pushing monitors into the audience and smashing his guitar onstage; August 20, at the Loreley Festival in Munich, Tyler collapsed three songs into their set—another night he began spitting up blood; October 10, at the Spectrum in Philadelphia, an M-80 exploded in the backstage stairwell, nearly blinding Tyler and severing an artery in Perry's hand. "It was shocking," Perry recalled to *Circus* in 1990. "I remember a flash, a real heavy impact, then my hand went numb and there was all blood spurting out."

Interband tensions, particularly between Tyler and Perry, also began spilling over onto the stage. Perry played loud as ever, and often didn't even bother to come up to the mic to provide harmony vocals. Tyler would retaliate by swinging his mic stand just inches from the guitarist's head. Recalled Kramer in *Hit Hard*, "[In] Europe, they started fighting onstage, even down to Steven pulling

A lighter moment on the Aerosmith Express tour, somewhere in Germany, early to mid-August, 1977. ELLEN POPPINGA, K & K/REDFERNS/GETTY IMAGES

Joe's amp cord out of the socket for playing too loud." It was around this time that the press took to labeling the pair the Toxic Twins, a play on the Mick-and-Keef tandem, the Glimmer Twins. While the moniker referenced their enormous chemical appetites, it could have just as handily referred to their poisoned partnership.

Tyler was also undergoing further relationship stresses: That summer, he became a father when Bebe Buell gave birth to a girl, Liv, on July 1. By this time however, Buell and Tyler had split as a result of his out-of-control behavior. "The drugs and the debauchery—that band

Admission to the 1977 Loreley Festival at which Tyler collapsed three songs into the set.

Reading Festival, Reading,
England, August 27, 1977.
© RON POWNALL/ROCKROLLPHOTO.COM

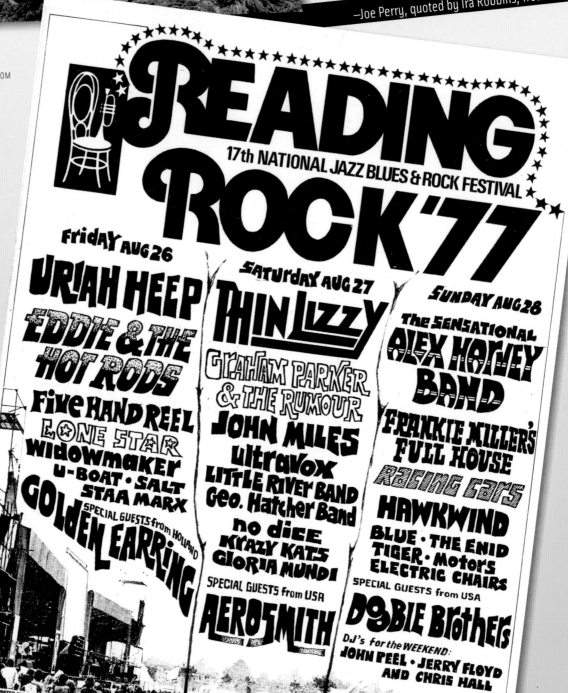

definitely wins the prize, hands down," Buell told *Behind the Music*. "They were wilder than the Stones. They were wilder than Zeppelin." Buell retreated to musician Todd Rundgren, a former boyfriend who would raise Liv as his own for years to come. Tyler was cut out of Liv's life—though, by this point, he was hardly present in his own. "I was so stoned on Tuinals," he told *Guitar World*. "You take two—whether you eat them or shove them up your ass—and you're fucking gone. You're over the line immediately. And that line is Fuck-All Land. I just didn't care anymore."

Throughout that summer and fall on the road, Aerosmith stole away at every chance to continue work

Draw the Line finally saw release on December 1, 1977, six months late and with a price tag of a half-million dollars.

Tyler on the ledge at AIR Studios, London, where the band recorded "Come Together" with George Martin in August 1977. © RON POWNALL/ROCKROLLPHOTO.COM

AEROSMITH. AMERICA'S BIGGEST DRAW.

"DRAW THE LINE!" THE NEW AEROSMITH ALBUM. ON COLUMBIA RECORDS AND TAPES.

AEROSMITH
DRAW THE LINE

PACE CONCERTS

AEROSMITH
SUMMIT
JUNE 24

The Summit, Houston, Texas.

Riverfront Coliseum, Cincinnati, Ohio.

Thurs., Sept. 29

Civic Auditorium, Omaha, Nebraska.

on the now long-overdue *Draw the Line*. Douglas traveled with the band, booking studio time in Germany, England, and the U.S. in an effort to finish the record. It finally saw release on December 1, 1977, six months late and with a price tag of half a million dollars. Though there were some strong moments—most prominently the white-hot, slide-guitar-led Tyler/Perry title track ("loud and powerful," Perry told this writer); the straight-up rocker "I Wanna Know Why"; and the punky, Perry-sung "Bright Light Fright"—the overall effort was, not surprisingly, messy and disjointed. "Get It Up" was a limp funk workout, "Critical Mass" came with lyrics reportedly penned by Douglas after Tyler came up blank, and "The Hand That Feeds" was all Whitford on guitar, as Perry couldn't even be bothered to get out of bed to play on it.

"Heroin is what did it," Douglas reasoned to KNAC.com. "They came

in with no songs, which was nothing new. They'd bring seedlings of music and we'd make that into songs. But I couldn't get them all in the same room anymore. Joe and Steven were smacked out and the 'LI3' were coke-crazy. All day they'd be doing anything but music—shooting guns, getting high, whatever. That's why *Draw the Line* is the way it is."

The press took notice: In a scathing review, *Rolling Stone* wrote "a truly horrendous record, chaotic to the point of malfunction, with an impenetrably dense sound adding to the confusion. This album shows the band in a state of shock." And yet Aerosmith was still fairly bulletproof. *Draw the Line* moved a million and a half copies in its first six weeks of release, making it the band's—and Columbia's—fastest seller to date. But due to its delayed release, the band was no longer on the road to support the album, and as a result it fizzled quickly. It was Aerosmith's first recorded misstep. "I don't think *Draw the Line* was as good as *Rocks*," Perry later admitted to Ira Robbins of *Trouser Press*. "It's not as hard-edged. It was a real self-indulgent album."

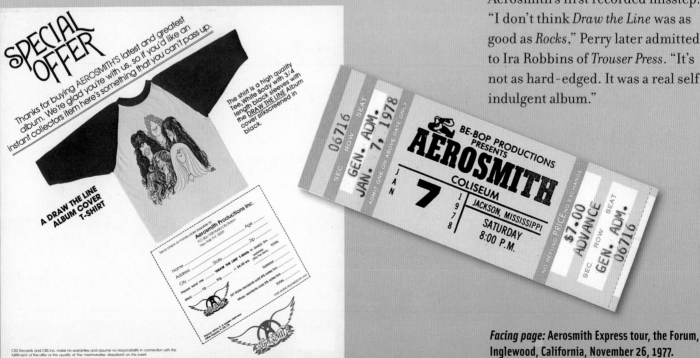

Insert included with original pressings of *Draw the Line*.

Facing page: Aerosmith Express tour, the Forum, Inglewood, California, November 26, 1977.

© KEVIN ESTRADA/KEVINESTRADA.COM

Draw the Line

by Martin Popoff

To chart the arc, *Rocks* is widely considered Aerosmith's best record, a collection of jewels demonstrating stratospheric talent applied to stellar material, touched by manic starriness on the rise. Yet *Draw the Line* is perhaps the more fascinating study of artists at their height because an almost impossible element of stress is added to the equation, Aerosmith forced to operate on fumes. But what fumes!

Drugs aplenty and recording at a haunted country locale, an abandoned convent no less, with guns, dangerous sports cars, and dramas involving barricades. Snap back to the reaction in '77: critics pondering *Draw the Line* were appropriately squeamish, vaguely dissatisfied, and often playing out some grudge because of a Tyler or Perry rock pig snub.

So were me an' my buddies, as fourteen-year-old fans, and it was roughly for the same reasons, namely that despite how much manic energy and dizziness and hype was thrown at the project—giddy exhaustion, really—there was a lack of songs that made for empty calories you could nonetheless talk about for years as the best meal you ever ate.

Ergo languishers like "Critical Mass" and flounderers like "Sight for Sore Eyes" (a sleepy "Last Child" remake with Bowery scuzz) and "Get It Up," more of this three-legged funk rock suppressed by layers of fulmination. Still, "Milk Cow Blues" was an angular, tangy way to re-treat and second-heat a blues classic. ("America's Led Zeppelin" they were called, and they lived up to it, dammit!) "Bright Light Fright" was a timely punk blast of panicked mania, double-timed for cocaine-fueled claustrophobia, sung well but short of breath by Joe Perry, and still, years later, his best contribution as a Keith (perhaps Richards' best is "Little T&A").

Elsewhere, "Kings and Queens" was always Aerosmith's "Achilles Last Stand," for which a complicated, modernized blues rock band tried to write a Purpley or Sabbatherian metal epic for God knows what reason. Still, talented rogues that they are, Aerosmith trumps Zeppelin here despite the forced nature of both tracks—Zeppelin wobbling, trashy, and contrived and Aerosmith plushly contriving. (And let's not talk about different generations here—*Presence* and *Draw the Line* are only twenty months apart.)

Draw the Line features cover art by renowned caricaturist Al Hirschfeld, best known for his work in the *New York Times*.

"I Wanna Know Why" and "The Hand That Feeds" both feed this idea, again, that we are watching a manic band of meteoric, even flame-throwing talent at near breakneck breakdown, presenting the DNA of the gosh-darn Aerosmith burning in a crucible but without any of the hard lifting having been done, nor even a nutritious breakfast. And don't think that the eerily detached cover art didn't contribute to the feeling of having died and gone to heaven, or at least having floated skyward on artificial tabs of whatever. Celebrated celebrity caricaturist Al Hirschfield was commissioned to render the boys comical yet uncommunicative, again, like (fallen) angels. His swoopy drawings are quintessentially *New York Times* but ironically a whole different New York than Aerosmith's adopted spiritual home on the dark side. Still, conceptually, shades of Rainbow's *Long Live Rock 'n' Roll* with that one, but more so, AC/DC's clinical *Flick of the Switch* puzzler.

Back to the music, you say? Gladly, for that leaves for us the magnificent flair of the immense title track. When asked—and yes, I believe it—I've called "Draw the Line" the greatest song of all time, given many blinding hammers of strength, such as that complicated (like "Celebration Day") riff, its epic structure without epic length, and finally the throat-ripping performance of Steven Tyler during the crescendo, a James Brown lung-hack that tops the similarly wince-worthy "Back in the Saddle." Nay, I'll keep talking about it. If there's magic to the Rolling Stones and that band's handicapped yet Jack-swaggered rope-a-dope lope, it's concentrated and exploded tenfold right here. And if many of the other tracks are chemicals poked about and ingested in boredom, this one has chemicals and memorably lab-blasted chemistry that closes shop through a toxic and infernal purple haze.

Alas, in some unspeakable way, you can't make rock more magical and energy-infused—and maybe even as heroic and up

on top of the wall—as what goes on when the band (through Joey Kramer like a lance) collapses into the first verse of this song and then creates giddy crescendos throughout. The result is that all the high points on the band's academically more impressive album, *Rocks*, are comparatively retired, gone home at 10:00, unsparked. Even "Sick as a Dog" and "Lick and a Promise" pale in comparison with respect to both swing and song construction.

The lesson is that if a band at the top of its druggy, delusional self-belief, if not its working best, can be left to its own devices, flame to gas tank, at least one hard rock of white light/white heat will shoot off at a violent angle from the lovable mess. That's what "Draw the Line," the long dong of a song, is—it's a confluence that lifts all boats and makes you look at them hard as sculptures that feed the concept of what just might be a concept album, the concept being, again, immense talent dramatically, catastrophically gasping on fumes, impossibly emoting and emanating beyond past glories but doing it with no safety net. Specifically only three or four songs and no

plan beyond delivering a record so they can spill back out onto the road to perdition.

And where do we sit and fit more than thirty years later? *Draw the Line* is, in fact (and surprisingly, given its release during the perfect year of 1977) one of Aerosmith's many forgotten albums—not so long gone as the band's unanimously perceived low points but strangely passed over in the minds of even medium-grade Aerosmith fans. Is this because the record feels like it sucks the soul out of you, saps the breath, exasperates? Maybe so, but try yer hand again, 'cause a revisit reveals a stark and vibrant humanity, failings and all, a feverishly beating heart that evokes the shambled charm of the Who, the emotional scarring of *Rumours*, and the squalor of *Raw Power*, rained down upon a band blessed with so much talent that blowing off large chunks of it was new and pleasurable folly in the name of the next buzz chased.

"Draw the Line" b/w "Bright Light Fright," Japan, 1977.

"Draw the Line" b/w "Bright, Light, Fright," Holland, 1977. Note the reversed photograph.

chapter 7

Critical Mass

Aerosmith may have been careening toward musical bankruptcy, but on the road the money was still pouring in. "We used to have a ritual," Perry told A&E's *Biography*. "We would get paid in the smallest bills we could and then we'd throw it all up in the air and just kind of wallow in it a little bit. And the ritual went on for quite a while until it started to be too much money to carry around. You know, we would have needed an armored truck. But as fast as it came in, it went out too."

And so Aerosmith pushed on. In March and April of 1978 they embarked on a mini-tour of small theaters and clubs, joined by keyboardist and backing vocalist Mark Radice. Though likely provoked by the beginnings of a backlash to "coliseum" rock brought on by the burgeoning punk movement, Hamilton offered a different explanation of the back-to-basics shows to Sylvie

"One hour you're onstage, you're happy . . . then as soon as you walk off you f***ing start hating it all over again."

—Joe Perry, quoted by Mark Mehler in *Circus*, December 1978

Facing page: Detroit, circa 1978. The Motor City became a frequent stop for the band, first as a support act for bands like the New York Dolls and KISS. It didn't take long for Aerosmith to become a popular headliner there. © ROBERT ALFORD

AEROSMITH 1308

THIS VOUCHER WHEN PRESENTED TO SANTA MONICA CIVIC AUDITORIUM BOX OFFICE ALLOWS THE BEARER TO PURCHASE TWO (2) TICKETS FOR PERFORMANCE FRIDAY, APRIL 7, 1978. TICKETS MUST BE PICKED UP BY 7:00 P.M. NIGHT OF PERFORMANCE.

BOX OFFICE HOURS
10 a.m. - 6 p.m. MON. thru FRI. — 10 a.m. - 5:30 p.m. SAT.
CLOSED SUNDAY — OPEN E

DILLINGHAM TICKET CO., L.A.

ENTAM PRESENTS
AEROSMITH
GREENSBORO COLISEUM COMPLEX
MAY. 5 1978
GREENSBORO, N.C.
FRIDAY 8:00 P.M.
PLUS $.25 OUTLET SERVICE CHARGE

ENTRY G SEC CTR ROW Z SEAT 14 MAY 5, 1978 ADMIT ONE THIS DATE ONLY NO RE

Simmons of *Sounds*: "What we were looking for was to go back and remember some of the excitement of the smaller gigs, not that there's any lack of it at the big ones we do."

Indeed, this touring cycle would be dominated by two massive stadium shows—with similarly sizable paydays—in the first half of the year. California Jam II, held on March 18, 1978, at Ontario Motor Speedway, an hour east of Los Angeles, saw the band headline a bill featuring Heart, Foreigner, Santana, and Leber-Krebs stablemate Ted Nugent, among others, before a crowd of more than 250,000, reportedly the largest rock concert of the late '70s. An even more sizeable audience than that which had greeted them at the speedway would watch from home when highlights from the

Ontario Motor Speedway hosted California Jam II on March 18, 1978. Aerosmith headlined a bill featuring Heart, Foreigner, Santana, and Ted Nugent, among others, before a crowd of more than 250,000, reportedly the largest rock concert of the late '70s.

The van used to transport the band in the backstage area at Cal Jam II. © ROBERT ALFORD

CALIFORNIA
O
ONTARIO MOTOR SPEEDWAY

Backstage at Cal Jam II. BOTH © ROBERT ALFORD

PETER FRAMPTON · THE BEE GEES

AEROSMITH · ALICE COOPER · EARTH WIND & FIRE · STEVE MARTIN · PAUL NICHOLAS · BILLY PRESTON

THE ORIGINAL MOTION PICTURE SOUND TRACK

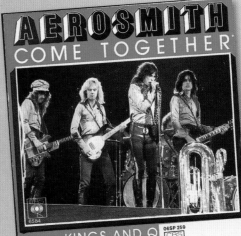

KINGS AND Q

The band at least got a single out of the *Sgt. Pepper's* move. "Come Together" b/w "Kings and Queens," Holland and Japan, both 1978.

Reportedly, Aerosmith's role as the Future Villain Band in *Sgt. Pepper's Lonely Hearts Club Band* was originally offered to the Rolling Stones—who wisely passed. One wag at the *New York Times* commented, "This isn't a movie, it's a business deal set to music."

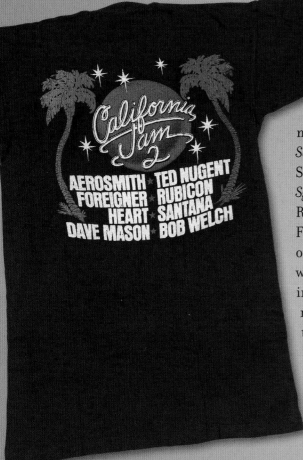

show were later aired on network television as an ABC special.

That spring, the band spent time in Los Angeles making their big-screen debut in *Saturday Night Fever* producer Robert Stigwood's movie adaptation of *Sgt. Pepper's Lonely Hearts Club Band*. Reportedly Aerosmith's role as the Future Villain Band was originally offered to the Rolling Stones, who wisely passed; Perry later joked that, in playing the villains, his band was rightly cast. They certainly acted the part, arriving sufficiently bombed for their three days of work that director Michael Schultz was led to ask, "Who are these drunks on my fucking set?"

A further point of contention between band and director came with their big scene, in which Aerosmith battled costars the Bee Gees (Sgt. Pepper's band) and Peter Frampton (as Billy Shears), the script calling for Tyler to be killed off by pop pinup boy Frampton. "We're sittin' there saying, 'There's no way that Steven's gonna get directly offed by Frampton. No way,'" said Perry (Huxley, uncredited). As Tyler explained to Sylvie Simmons, "No one beats Aerosmith."

Needless to say, the film, to no one's surprise, was a disaster (the *New York Times*: "This isn't a movie, it's a business deal set to music"; *Newsweek*: "a film with a dangerous resemblance to wallpaper"), and the accompanying soundtrack was jokingly rumored to have been the first album to ship platinum—and return double platinum. But Aerosmith emerged from the fiasco with one unequivocal positive: a

"Chip Away the Stone," promo disc, U.S., 1978.

recording session with legendary Beatles producer George Martin, with whom they cut a version of "Come Together" for the movie's soundtrack. "Kind of intimidating," Perry admitted, "but we weren't easily intimidated in those days"

(Huxley, uncredited). In June, they hit the studio once again, this time at Long View Farm in Massachusetts, to record a new song, "Chip Away the Stone." Penned by Richie Supa, a musician friend of the band's who was also managed by Leber-Krebs,

the track would see minor success as a single in the early part of the following year.

That summer the band headed back out for the final leg of the Aerosmith Express. On July 1, Aerosmith headlined the Texas World Music Festival (a.k.a. Texxas Jam) at the Cotton Bowl in Dallas to 100,000 more fans, once again with Nugent and Heart, as well as a hot, wildly energetic young act that had come up through the L.A. clubs playing Aerosmith covers: Van Halen. In comparison, Aerosmith's energy reserves ran somewhat lower in those days—come showtime, Tyler had to be carried onstage on the back of a roadie. Nevertheless, the band unleashed a rollicking set, the Toxic Twins lean and mean, Perry wielding a brand-new, fire-red B.C. Rich Bich, the spoils of a recent endorsement deal with the guitar maker. For the encore, Nugent joined the band onstage for a spirited run-through of "Milk Cow Blues," the entire performance capped off with a massive fireworks display.

The tour wrapped with a gig on August 6 at Giants Stadium in New Jersey, supported by Ted Nugent, Journey, and Mahogany Rush—only the second rock show ever staged at the massive venue. In October, Columbia issued the band's first concert document, the double album set *Live! Bootleg*, compiled largely from performances recorded by Douglas on the road over the previous year and a half, and rounded out with an alternate take of "Come Together" and two covers— Calvin Carter's "I Ain't Got You" and James Brown's "Mother Popcorn"—

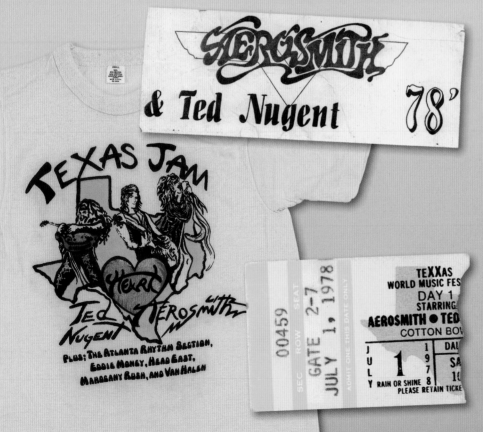

that dated from a 1973 gig at Paul's Mall in Boston. A gritty, warts-and-all effort of sometimes dubious sound quality, the record stood in stark contrast to the spit-shined live documents that populated racks at the time. A defiant Perry explained to *CREEM*, "There's so many perfect live albums coming out, all doctored and fixed—big deal. I felt like we had to top that, do a real live album, like *Live at Leeds, Get Yer Ya-Ya's Out* . . . I've let stuff go by on this album, like guitar mistakes, and I just don't want to change it. I don't want anybody fixin' it. That was *that* night."

Without missing a beat, they were back out on the road promoting the live record, this time with support from AC/DC. But disconnect and exhaustion were setting in. For much of the jaunt the band would

Aerosmith Express tour, Giants Stadium, East Rutherford, New Jersey, August 6, 1978. This was just the second rock show staged at the massive venue. © RON POWNALL/ROCKROLLPHOTO.COM

Live! Bootleg tour,
Civic Center,
St. Paul, Minnesota,
October 14, 1978.
BOTH © RON POWNALL/
ROCKROLLPHOTO.COM

Live! Bootleg tour, Cobo Arena, Detroit, September 29, 1978. BOTH © ROBERT ALFORD

alternately be based in Chicago and Boston, traveling by Learjet to each date on the tour, then leaving town immediately following the gig. Onstage the band was on autopilot, cranking out the hits while ducking M-80s and beer bottles; a 1979 issue of *Rolling Stone* captured Perry, after enduring another round of flying debris, commenting in disgust to a roadie, "Maybe if I worked harder on my guitar playing we'd attract a better class of people." Furthermore, the members were barely communicating with one another, retreating to wives and girlfriends post-gig—and sometimes before. "When we'd start 'Dream On,' Joe's over in his corner with Elyssa at the side of his amps and he'd look at her and they'd laugh. At me," Tyler said in *Walk This Way*. "It hurt really bad. The band I had with this guy was . . . gone." For his part, Perry remarked to *Circus* that year, "One hour you're onstage, you're happy . . . then as soon as you walk off you fucking start hating it all over again."

But there were some bright spots. Aerosmith finished 1978 with a platinum album for *Live! Bootleg*, as well as a hit single in "Come Together," from the *Sgt. Pepper's* soundtrack, which made it to No. 23 on the *Billboard* charts. And on December 22, Tyler became a father for the second time

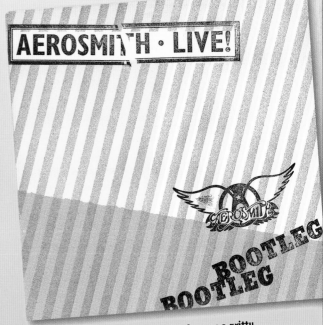

Released in October 1978, *Live! Bootleg* was a gritty, warts-and-all effort of sometimes-dubious sound quality that stood in stark contrast to the spit-shined live documents that populated racks at the time.

in as many years, when new wife Cyrinda Foxe gave birth to a baby girl, Mia Abagale. Tyler had fallen hard for Foxe, a model, actress, and New York City scenemaker who was recently separated from David Johansen. The two wed that fall in an informal ceremony in Sunapee. Speaking to VH1, the singer provided a lighthearted motivation for their union that also hinted at a deeper truth: "Elyssa hated Cyrinda," Tyler said. "So I married her."

The following year began with something rare for Aerosmith: a break. The band stayed off the road for the first four months of 1979 before eventually gathering at the Wherehouse to begin work on the follow-up to *Draw the Line*, tentatively titled *Off Your Rocker*. When they moved to Mediasound Studios in New York City to begin recording, it was without longtime producer Jack Douglas. With both band and label jittery as a result of the relatively disappointing reception to *Draw the Line*, a change was in order, and Douglas played the role of sacrificial lamb. In his place came Gary Lyons, a Brit best known for his work with Humble Pie and Foreigner.

But swapping producers was hardly the answer to their growing problems. The songs, once again, were coming slow, and Tyler's lyrics even slower. Furthermore, Tyler and Perry's relationship had deteriorated to the point where the two couldn't stand to be in the studio at the same time. With the album in limbo and studio bills piling up, Leber-Krebs sent the band back on the road to cash in with a series of massive festival dates.

Monsters of Rock, Day on the Green, Oakland, California, July 21, 1979.
COURTESY WYCO VINTAGE

Aerosmith wouldn't return in one piece. By this point Perry, fed up with the state of affairs, had it in mind to embark on a one-off solo project, a sentiment only hardened when, at a pre-tour meeting, Krebs presented him with an $80,000 bill for unpaid hotel expenses. "Now, I used to have a lot of room service," Perry commented to *Guitar World* in 1990, "but certainly not *that* much." Management's suggestion as to how he could pay it off? Record a solo album, and use the advance to cover his debts.

And so the fuse was lit. On April 8, the band headlined the California World Music Festival at the L.A. Memorial Coliseum, backed by Van Halen and Toto. Six days

later they were at the Florida World Music Festival at the Tangerine Bowl in Orlando. On July 21, the band topped the bill for Monsters of Rock at the Day on the Green in Oakland, California, supported by Nugent, AC/DC, and Frank Marino and Mahogany Rush. From there, they headed to Cleveland for the World Series of Rock on July 28, where they played to 80,000 fans alongside Nugent, AC/DC, Journey, and Thin Lizzy.

Backstage in the band's trailer, tensions were at a high. Prior to

Facing page: Aerosmith appeared at their second World Series of Rock at Cleveland Municipal Stadium on July 28, 1979. Also on the bill were Ted Nugent, Journey, Thin Lizzy, AC/DC, and the Scorpions. BOTH © ROBERT ALFORD

Above and facing page: **World Series of Rock, Municipal Stadium, Cleveland, July 28, 1979.** ALL © ROBERT ALFORD

showtime at Cleveland Stadium, sparks were igniting between the band members to such an extent that even the wives joined in, with Elyssa Perry going so far as to hurl a glass of milk at Terry Hamilton—"ironic," noted Perry to VH1, "that it was something as cliché as spilled milk."

Following what was a reportedly strong set, the band picked up fighting right where they had left off. "We came offstage and went right into the trailer, and we freaked out at Joe and started yelling at him," Hamilton recalled in *Walk This Way*. "And then Joe's answer finally was, 'Well, maybe I should leave the band then.' And Steven said, 'Yeah, maybe you fuckin' should.' And the rest of us stood there, basically agreeing with Steven. And then Joe stormed out."

It would be almost five years before Joe Perry stepped onstage with Aerosmith again.

chapter 8

We Is Goin' on Trial

Reflecting on Aerosmith's condition in the late 1970s, Steven Tyler told VH1's *Behind the Music*, "It was the end of a grand era. Everybody was tripping, everybody had blow in the room. Everybody was gakked to the nines, as stoned as you could be. It was truly days full of night. It was just a matter of time before we all killed ourselves."

Miraculously, the band members got out of the decade with their lives intact. But Aerosmith as an entity didn't fare as well. Throughout the summer and fall of 1979, rumors were rampant in the press of an impending breakup, which Perry and the rest of the band denied at every turn. In the August 23 issue of *Rolling Stone*, the guitarist characterized his upcoming solo album as merely an "extra-curricular activity." But on October 10, Leber-Krebs issued a press release stating what was

"I'm a great believer in pre-destiny. So for me to say 'No, it's not time,' I'd have been a fool."

—Joe Perry, quoted by Dave Zimmer in *CREEM*, August 1980

"He wants to do the Joe Perry Project? Then let him go ahead and do it! . . . I'm gonna miss Joe."

—Steven Tyler, quoted by Bill Flanagan in *Trouser Press*, 1979

Facing page: Club Boston, December 3, 1980.
© RON POWNALL/ROCKROLLPHOTO.COM

Tyler alone at New York Music Week press conference, Plaza Hotel, New York City, September 14, 1979.
© BOB LEAFE

as an ace session man for high-profile artists like Meat Loaf and Stevie Nicks. More recently, he had recorded two unsuccessful albums with the RCA act Flame, a female-fronted hard-rock act managed and produced by Jimmy Iovine. He came to Aerosmith through an association with Supa, signing on in October of 1979. "I only joined Aerosmith the night before the mixing of *Night in the Ruts* after Joe Perry left," Crespo recalled in an interview posted on his official website. "They got me to come in and fire off a solo to 'Three Mile Smile,' and that was pretty much it." Still, Perry received full credit in the album's liner notes and also appeared in the cover photo, an outtake from a shoot the previous year in L.A. that presented the band dressed as coal miners, originally commissioned for use for the "Chip Away the Stone" single.

But the guitarist was there in spirit only. Fed up with Aerosmith's dysfunction and pissed off at Leber-Krebs—"I started counting the money we made in past years on my fingers and said 'Something's wrong here,'" he told *Guitar World*—he began putting plans together for a solo album. Backstage at an Aerosmith gig that spring, he had run into Ralph Morman, an old Boston acquaintance whose former band, Daddy Warbux (later BUX), had been managed by Frank Connelly. Now working construction, Morman inquired as to whether Perry knew of anyone looking for a singer, to which he replied, "Yeah, me." In short order, Perry picked up bassist David Hull, of Connecticut rockers Dirty Angels, and local Boston drummer Ronnie

already patently obvious to those with any interest in the matter. It began: "Joe Perry and Aerosmith announced today in New York Perry's plans to depart the group to pursue a solo career. Perry's departure will commence upon completion of the new Aerosmith album, *Night in the Ruts*."

In truth, the guitarist left considerably before sessions wrapped. He recalled his last studio date with the band as May 30; appropriately, on that that day they cut a throwaway instrumental titled "Shit House Shuffle" (which later surfaced on the 1991 box set *Pandora's Box*). "I washed my hands of it," Perry told *CREEM* in 1980. "After a certain

point I said, 'No, I'm not going back to New York and just sit around and not do anything. It's your album, do what you want with it. You've got my work, you can use it or erase it. I'm working on something else.'"

In the end, Perry contributed to a little more than half of *Ruts*, his parts completed by Richie Supa, guitar tech Neil Thompson, and his eventual replacement Jimmy Crespo (other potential nominees for the slot included Rick Derringer guitarist Danny Johnson and ex-Scorpions and U.F.O. shredder Michael Schenker). Though a relative unknown, the twenty-five-year-old, Brooklyn-born Crespo had made a name for himself within the industry

Stewart, and set to work. "I knew it was shining down on me to do this solo thing," he told *CREEM* in 1980. "I'm a great believer in pre-destiny. So for me to say 'No, it's not time,' I'd have been a fool." Tyler took a more corporeal view about this turn of events in *Trouser Press*: "He wants to do the Joe Perry Project?" he asked rhetorically. "Then let him go ahead and do it!"

Despite Aerosmith being in shambles, *Night in the Ruts*, released on November 1, 1979, proved a surprisingly strong effort. Even in the face of the complete disintegration of Tyler and Perry's relationship, the pair managed to jointly sign their names to five of the album's nine songs—"No Surprize," "Chiquita," "Bone to Bone (Coney Island White Fish Boy)," "Cheese Cake," and "Three Mile Smile"—all of them flat-out rockers. "No Surprize" in particular proved a first-rate

Tyler/Perry composition, marrying a tough-as-nails guitar riff to a lyric that laid out, in rich and redolent detail, the history of the now shattered band, with references to the Fenway Theatre's John O'Toole, Max's Kansas City, and ol' Clive Davis, who *said he's surely gonna make us a star*. But even while looking back through slightly rose-tinted glasses, Tyler sang of the damage to come: *But with all our style / I could see in his eyes / That we is goin' on trial / An' it was no surprise*.

Elsewhere the album sagged, padded with several covers—the Yardbirds' "Think About It," the Shangri-Las' "Remember (Walking in the Sand)" (with original member Mary Weiss on backup vocals), and

the '40s-era blues cut "Reefer Head Woman"—and rounded out by an unspectacular ballad penned by Tyler to his new daughter, titled "Mia." Reviewing *Ruts* in *Rolling Stone*, David Fricke opined, "With Joe Perry now forming his own band, this isn't the time for Aerosmith to be lying down on the job."

Perry, for his part, certainly wasn't. As his former bandmates slogged through the final months of the *Night in the Ruts* sessions—which ultimately came with a price tag of a million dollars—the guitarist holed up at home and at the Wherehouse, woodshedding with his new group. On November 17, 1979, less than three weeks after *Ruts* saw release, the Joe Perry Project made its public

On January 14, 1980, Tyler and Hamilton, along with former Beatles producer George Martin, guested on *The Robert Klein Radio Show* at RCA Studios in New York City. BOTH © BOB LEAFE

Issued in March 1980, *Let the Music Do the Talking* was a fiery statement of purpose from Joe Perry.

debut at the Rathskeller, a glorified cafeteria on the Boston College campus. Both Whitford and Tyler came down to support their former bandmate, though Tyler left before the show began. A wise move—reportedly Perry played like a man reborn, sharing lead vocals with Morman and running his lean-and-mean combo through a hot set of freshly penned originals, covers of Jimi Hendrix's "Red House" and Elvis Presley's "Heartbreak Hotel," and a few choice Aerosmith cuts, including "Same Old Song and Dance," "Bright Light Fright," and "Walk This Way." "The place was packed with kids hanging from the rafters and standing on tables," Perry recalled in *Walk This Way*. "We walked off and they started chanting 'We want Joe!' and 'Two more!' We didn't know two more songs. The encore was 'Life at a Glance,' which I'd literally written the night before the gig. And that was it. The Joe Perry Project was off and running."

Soon after, the band inked a deal with Columbia, though Perry acknowledged that, given his recent track record, this took some finessing. "Aerosmith had been bringing in their albums late, going

On June 11, 1980, the Joe Perry Project's first lineup appeared in the CBS Studios in New York City prior to a concert broadcast on WNEW-FM. Shown here with Perry (from left) are vocalist Ralph Morman, an unidentified radio staffer, and drummer Ronnie Stewart. © BOB LEAFE

way over budget, and they thought they'd get more of the same from me. But I convinced them I was a walking, talking viability and not a fuckin' burned-out prima donna" (Huxley, uncredited). Indeed, his newfound enthusiasm spilled over into the recording studio. Reunited with Jack Douglas, the Project entered the Hit Factory in New York City that December, finishing the album in six weeks and, even more surprisingly, coming in under budget.

Issued in March 1980, *Let the Music Do the Talking* was a fiery statement of purpose from the guitarist. "This album was definitely a spurt of energy that was let loose after being fenced up in Aerosmith," Perry told *CREEM*. "We went into the studio and played the songs live. There was no bullshit, no magic." Far from a self-indulgent, all-guitar-all-the-time type of effort, its nine songs were tight, concise, and aggressive, a mix of straight-ahead hard rockers ("Let the Music Do the Talking," "Life at a Glance," "Shooting Star") and funky, R&B-tinged workouts ("Rockin' Train" and "Discount Dogs"). There was also one all-guns-blazing instrumental, "Break Song," which Perry described to *Guitar World*'s John Stix as "one minute and fifty seconds of screaming guitar. It's just an out-and-out sonic guitar piece."

Perry, who assumed lead vocals for roughly half the songs, was also spilling out his emotions in lyrics for the first time. The title track, penned while still a member of Aerosmith but held back from the band, was a clear indicator of his artistic intentions. "Conflict of Interest,"

The Joe Perry Project supported Journey on a number of dates, less than two years after the latter had supported Aerosmith at Giants Stadium.

meanwhile, found him venting his disgust toward Leber-Krebs and the business side of the music industry in general, a sentiment also reflected in the album's cover photo—nine suited men positioned around a glass boardroom table, their eyes fixed on Perry, standing and clutching his band's master tapes. Incidentally, one of the guitarist's first moves post-Aerosmith was to fire Leber-Krebs as his management.

The critics were largely receptive to *Let the Music Do the Talking*—with caveats. *Rolling Stone* offered the somewhat backhanded compliment "The Joe Perry Project delivers all of the rock and roll moxie that Aerosmith couldn't deliver on the prophetically titled *Night in the Ruts*.... Any singer might feel intimidated by the locomotive pace and guitar-army sound of this album. Any singer except maybe one. If Steven Tyler were here, *Let the Music Do the Talking* would probably be the finest record Aerosmith never made."

Regardless, Perry was ready to roll. That fall, he boarded a tour bus with the Project (not to mention six grand worth of heroin and another thousand in prescription drugs), playing six nights a week in largely sold-out clubs. Beginning in November, the Project spent another month and a half in larger venues as the support act for Heart. To the press Perry appeared content, telling *Hit Parader*, "I don't miss those huge arenas because the vibes in those places are cold." But times were tough. He was burning through money, Elyssa was pregnant with their first child, and the band was already falling apart (halfway through the tour Perry fired Morman, who would often show up for gigs drunk—if he showed up at all—replacing him with a New York singer named Joey Mala). Furthermore, it became clear to Perry that all the positive critical and fan reception in the world couldn't save *Let the Music Do the Talking*. Reportedly Krebs, in an effort to get Perry back in

Aerosmith, saw to it that Columbia buried the record, with little money or manpower put into radio or other promotion. The album stalled at No. 47 on *Billboard*, ultimately selling fewer than a quarter-million copies.

On another front, while relishing his new role as a solo artist, Perry admitted to *Sounds'* Sylvie Simmons in 1980 that he missed the camaraderie of playing alongside longtime co-guitarist Whitford. "It was the best rock and roll guitar combination I could ever have imagined," he lamented. "We talked about [Whitford joining the Project] but he didn't want to leave Aerosmith."

Whitford did in fact opt to continue slogging it out with Aerosmith—for the time being,

at least. The *Night in the Ruts* tour officially launched on December 5, 1979, at the Broome County Arena in Binghamton, New York. The guitarist recalled, in an interview for A&E's *Biography*, "I didn't know that we could do it without Joe. It certainly didn't feel like we could do it without Joe." And yet, Crespo worked to maintain a certain status quo: Much like Perry, he played Les Pauls and Strats, and kept his head down and dark hair in his face (one difference: his extended, unaccompanied solo during "Train Kept a Rollin'" that betrayed his skills as a speedy, more technique-oriented player). But the

chemistry—or lack thereof—between Crespo and his bandmates couldn't be so easily faked; furthermore, Tyler was hopelessly gone, routinely forgetting the words to his songs and often falling over onstage. At the Cumberland County Civic Center in Portland, Maine, only the second show of the tour, the singer collapsed midway through "Reefer Head Woman" and had to be carried offstage by two roadies. "He fell down in front of me," Whitford

Tyler collapses onstage at Cumberland County Civic Center, Portland, Maine, December 6, 1979. ALL © RON POWNALL/ROCKROLLPHOTO.COM

recalled to A&E, "and I wasn't even sure if he was alive." Show over, a week of dates canceled.

Tyler was in rapid decline and began taking his frustrations public. He grumbled to *Trouser Press*' Bill Flanagan, "There are a lot of things [Perry's] been saying in the press that just aren't true. If he keeps it up, I'm gonna have to wind up telling the truth about the whole thing and

it's not gonna be healthy." He added, unselfconsciously, "He's a very bitter man."

Perry eventually countered, telling Sylvie Simmons, "In one paragraph in an interview Steven puts me down, saying, 'you've got to be out of your mind for going from the big halls to the small halls,' and then he says, yes, he did the small halls [with Aerosmith in early 1978] because he wanted to get back to the kids. And where is he right now? From what I've heard he's either sick or spaced

out, canceling tours left, right and center, and unable to work."

Indeed, the *Night in the Ruts* tour came to an abrupt end in the fall of 1980, when, riding his motorcycle in Sunapee after picking up daughter Mia's nanny, a cocaine-and-booze-addled Tyler lost control of the bike, skidded out, and hit the dirt hard. Badly injured, with his foot nearly severed at the heel, Tyler spent the next two months laid up in the hospital. More months passed as he convalesced at home. When the cast finally came off, he recalled in *Walk This Way*, "I had this jagged Frankenstein scar on my heel and the doctors said to forget about touring, which was the kiss of death for *Night in the Ruts*."

Night in the Ruts

by Daniel Bukszpan

Aerosmith's sixth studio album was released in November 1979 as the "Me Decade" was drawing to a close, and it reflects its times accurately. A lot of people who lived through it describe the end of the '70s not as a hedonistic paradise of plentiful, consequence-free sex and endless rails of coke, but as the period when that all came crashing down to earth. The champagne stopped flowing, the hot tubs became cold, and the bill arrived in the mail, with three unpaid cycles on it and stamped "Past Due" to boot. *Night in the Ruts* is the sound of a bleary hangover and the embodiment of the morning after that defined the decade's end.

The record was made under less-than-ideal circumstances. To generate income for the debt-plagued band, the group's management sent them out on tour halfway into the recording process, and it was a disaster. Joe Perry quit the group halfway through, in effect leaving the album sessions halfway through as well. Brad Whitford pulled double duty to finish Perry's guitar parts while session musicians supplemented the rest. Somehow, the resulting album is not the total disaster that its fractured history should have guaranteed. But despite some good riffs and some other notable moments, on the whole the album is best described as one somewhat decent album side accompanied by another side composed almost entirely of profoundly dull filler.

Side one—the good side—kicks off with "No Surprize," which recounts the 1971 Max's Kansas City gig where the band was discovered. A typical Aerosmith opening cut, uptempo and swaggering, it's followed by "Chiquita," a solidly raunchy mid-tempo stomper. The song is adorned by horns that manage to make it sound heavier and more grinding than it might otherwise be without them. This is no small feat: horns have ruined many an otherwise great rock song and often herald a misguided attempt to harness bluesy "authenticity." This is a fool's errand. In this case, however, the horns give the song momentum, the feeling that the album is really going to kick into high gear now. Well played, boys.

The sound of a bleary hangover and the embodiment of the morning after that defined the end of the 1970s.

So much for momentum. "Remember (Walking in the Sand)" follows, and this arrangement of the Shangri-Las' George Morton–penned debut is a bizarre concoction. Structured like the Beatles' "I Want You (She's So Heavy)," it starts in what seems like the middle of a doo-wop song before giving way to a straighter groove, augmented by finger snaps. The confused muddle that follows somehow made it onto Billboard's Hot 100, which is probably a testament to the loyalty of the Blue Army more than anything. It's followed by the slow and greasy slide guitar workout "Cheese Cake," one of the few moments on the album when you can hear the inspired Aerosmith of old assert itself. It's no stretch to say that the song probably inspired a little sumpthin' sumpthin' atop the shag carpet of more than one van.

From here on out, the album starts to sound like one very long and repetitive extension of the song ending side one. On their own, each of the four songs is mediocre to OK, but their cumulative effect hampers the pacing of the LP. Maybe the band was going for coherence, but unfortunately

they crossed a very fine line into everything sounding the same. The songs don't bear clone-like similarity to one another—tempos jump around, dynamics change, tight little technical turnarounds happen at unexpected times—but none of it keeps the proceedings interesting.

The worst offender of the lot is the band's cover of an old, relatively obscure blues number, "Reefer Head Woman." The individual performances are all solid and Perry generates volcanic heat with a tasty wah-pedal solo. But it comes off as an unconvincing blues exercise and screams "we're out of material." Things pick up briefly with "Bone to Bone (Coney Island White Fish Boy)," whose tight funk groove sounds foretell *Permanent Vacation*-era Aerosmith. But ultimately the song makes no impression. And despite a very promising Alice Cooper–like intro with harmonized lead guitars, the bands' workout of the Yardbirds' B-side "Think About It" jumps right back into the repetitive morass, officially leaving us in how-much-longer-is-this-record?-land.

Just when all seems lost, the album makes a last attempt to engage the

listener, succeeding with "Mia." The piano ballad closes out the album on an epic and mournful note that recalls Queen or Angel, while providing a refreshing break from the preceding fifteen minutes. Had the song been sequenced in the middle of the album rather than the end, it might have made for a more satisfying LP. After an ascending bridge that again recalls the pomp of Mr. Mercury and company, the song fades out and the album ends with the sound of a single low piano note, repeating over and over. It could have been the bell tolling the death of a great American band.

That Aerosmith recovered from these doldrums and went on to experience success beyond anything that they had experienced in their classic period is astounding. But before that happened, the band had to hit bottom (as anyone who's ever staged an intervention knows). *Night in the Ruts* was that bottom. ▬

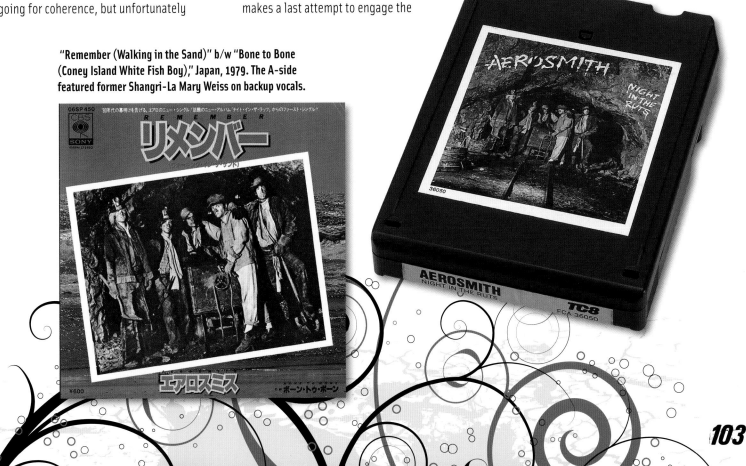

"Remember (Walking in the Sand)" b/w "Bone to Bone (Coney Island White Fish Boy)," Japan, 1979. The A-side featured former Shangri-La Mary Weiss on backup vocals.

chapter 9

Push Comes to Shove

By this time, Perry was faring only marginally better. He was stretched to the limit financially, thanks to a confluence of heavy drug debt, a row with the IRS over unpaid back taxes, and a standoff with Krebs, who, according to the guitarist, was holding back monies owed to him. Perry was having difficulty keeping the Project solvent, and was so strung out he wasn't aware that Columbia had released a best-of compilation, *Aerosmith's Greatest Hits*, in October 1980, until a fan approached him in a supermarket asking him to sign a copy.

In an effort to put his finances in order, Perry took on new management in the form of veteran Boston promoter Don Law, and in the spring of 1981, the Project, with new singer Charlie Farren (formerly of local Boston band Balloon), regrouped at the Wherehouse to begin preproduction on their sophomore effort, tentatively titled *Soldier of Fortune*. In an interview with *Guitar World*'s John Stix prior to the album's release, Perry revealed where his musical sensibilities lay, giving a nod to the sounds of the day. "I'm going to play a little more rhythm in an R&B

"I realized I didn't hate Steven or Brad or Joey. It was all the other s*** which separated us. Like being led around by our management, and chasing off after our dealers."

—Joe Perry, quoted by Robert Sandall in *Q*, November 1989

Facing page: *Rock in a Hard Place* tour, Civic Center, Providence, Rhode Island, February 17, 1984. © RON POWNALL/ROCKROLLPHOTO.COM

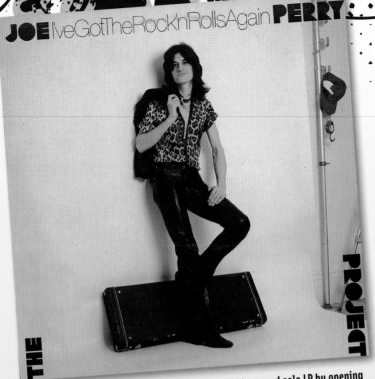

With little promo from Columbia, Perry supported his second solo LP by opening dates for Heart, ZZ Top, and Aerosmith's old Boston peers, the J. Geils Band

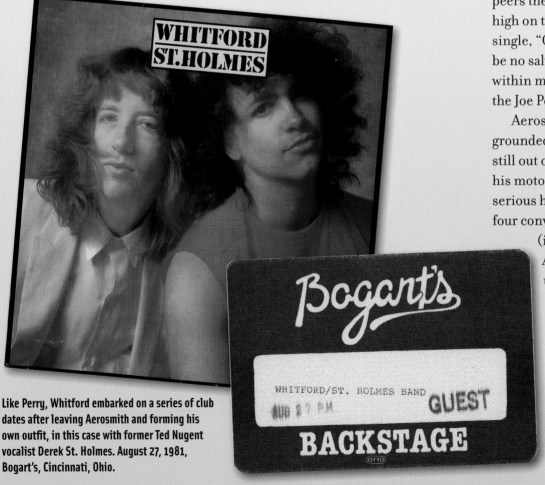

Like Perry, Whitford embarked on a series of club dates after leaving Aerosmith and forming his own outfit, in this case with former Ted Nugent vocalist Derek St. Holmes. August 27, 1981, Bogart's, Cincinnati, Ohio.

style and a little less lead," he said. "The feeling I get when I'm playing now is the same feeling I got when I first heard the Sex Pistols . . . not saying that we sound like the Sex Pistols, but I get the vibe of that kind of energy."

Sessions got underway at the Boston Opera House with Doors producer Bruce Botnick at the helm, the band tracking to the Record Plant's mobile recording truck. But despite several strong cuts, notably Farren's "East Coast, West Coast" and Perry's "South Station Blues," the album, released that June as *I've Got the Rock 'n' Rolls Again*, bombed, Columbia once again burying promotion. The Project took to the road, opening dates for Heart, ZZ Top, and Aerosmith's old Boston peers the J. Geils Band, now riding high on the charts with a smash single, "Centerfold." But there would be no salvaging the record, and within months Columbia dropped the Joe Perry Project from its roster.

Aerosmith was likewise grounded. Early in 1981, with Tyler still out of commission nursing his motorcycle injuries and also a serious heroin habit, the remaining four convened at the Wherehouse (interestingly, both Aerosmith and the Project utilized the space) to work on new material. Soon Whitford started drifting and began writing songs with Derek St. Holmes, singer and rhythm guitarist in Ted Nugent's band. Krebs landed them a deal with Columbia, and the two made quick work of an

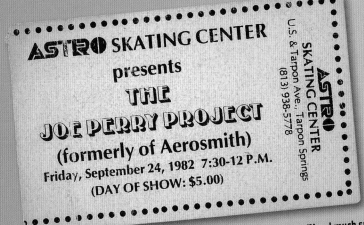

The Joe Perry Project headlined much smaller venues than the guitarist had grown accustomed to with Aerosmith. Astro Skating Center can still be found in Tarpon Springs, Florida, today.

album, gathering a rhythm section and cutting the songs in two weeks' time at Atlanta's Axis Studios. In August 1981, the label issued their effort under the moniker *Whitford/ St. Holmes*. While the record was hardly a success, it did make a lasting impression on the Aerosmith guitarist. As Whitford recalled in a 1986 interview with *Guitar for the Practicing Musician*, the experience helped him to understand "I wasn't the cog in the wheel that wasn't working. It was frustrating at that point, because nothing was getting done in Aerosmith. It was a high for my ego and my sanity to see, 'This is how you make an album.'"

Nevertheless, that September, Whitford returned to Aerosmith, and the band commenced work at New York City's Power Station with producer Tony Bongiovi for what would become *Rock in a Hard Place*. By this time, Tyler was back in the mix—but just barely. The singer, now separated from Cyrinda, had been reduced to holing up at the seedy Gorham Hotel on West 55th Street, surviving on a $20 daily stipend from Krebs, which he

would take directly to the heroin dealers on nearby Eighth Avenue. Needless to say, not much work was getting done. Whitford finally had enough. He contacted Leber-Krebs and officially tendered his resignation from Aerosmith.

Kramer, Hamilton, and Crespo came close to following him out the door. Tired of waiting around for Tyler to get his act together, the three enlisted former Peter Frampton keyboardist Bobby Mayo and singer Marge Raymond, Crespo's former bandmate in Flame, and cut seven basic tracks at Manhattan's SIR studios for a proposed project, to

be named Renegade. But Tyler soon came around, and Renegade was put on ice as Aerosmith forged ahead. "I think Steven caught wind of what we were doing and realized he had to get things moving again," Crespo later recalled. "Otherwise the band was history."

In early 1982, Aerosmith swapped Bongiovi for Jack Douglas and moved the *Rock in a Hard Place* sessions from New York to Miami's Criteria Studios. To replace Whitford, Douglas brought in a new guitarist, Rick Dufay, who contributed briefly in the final stages of the recording. The twenty-nine-year-old Dufay, who had previously released one solo album, the Douglas-produced *Tender Loving Abuse* (1980), was an outrageous personality, even for Aerosmith. According to Tyler, the guitarist claimed he had once escaped from a mental institution by jumping out a third-floor window.

Richfield Coliseum, Richfield, Ohio.

Maple Leaf Gardens, Toronto.

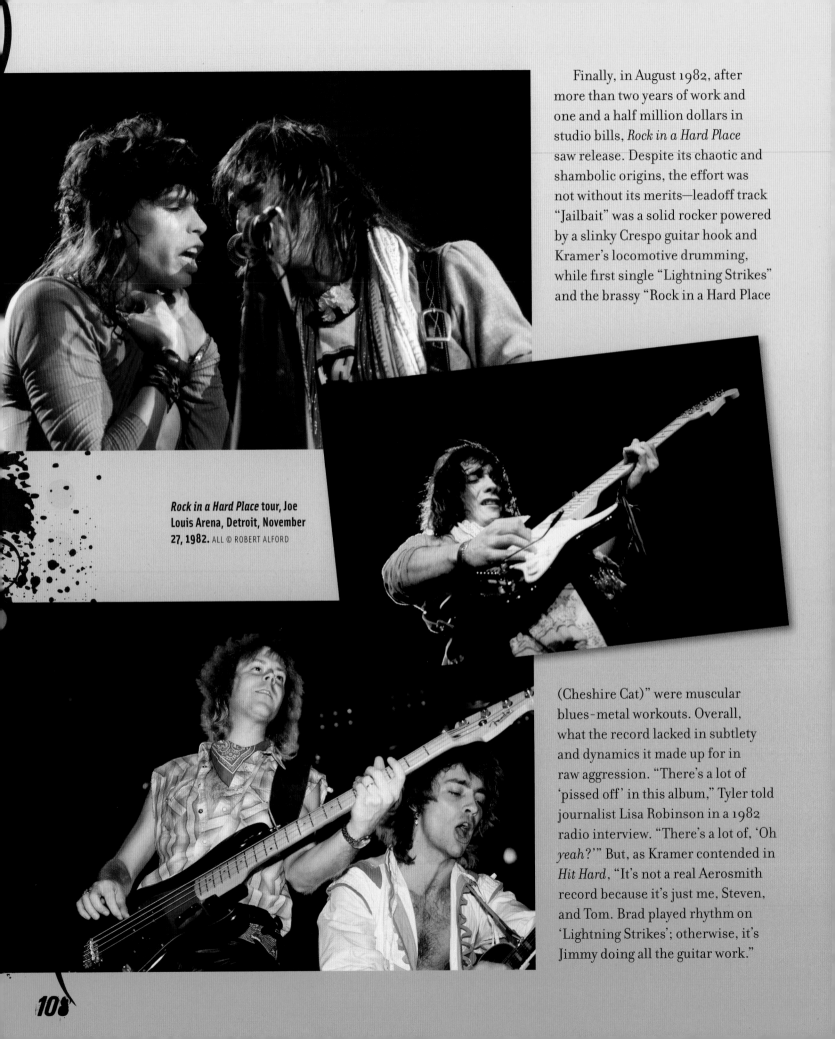

Finally, in August 1982, after more than two years of work and one and a half million dollars in studio bills, *Rock in a Hard Place* saw release. Despite its chaotic and shambolic origins, the effort was not without its merits—leadoff track "Jailbait" was a solid rocker powered by a slinky Crespo guitar hook and Kramer's locomotive drumming, while first single "Lightning Strikes" and the brassy "Rock in a Hard Place

Rock in a Hard Place tour, Joe Louis Arena, Detroit, November 27, 1982. ALL © ROBERT ALFORD

(Cheshire Cat)" were muscular blues-metal workouts. Overall, what the record lacked in subtlety and dynamics it made up for in raw aggression. "There's a lot of 'pissed off' in this album," Tyler told journalist Lisa Robinson in a 1982 radio interview. "There's a lot of, 'Oh *yeah*?'" But, as Kramer contended in *Hit Hard*, "It's not a real Aerosmith record because it's just me, Steven, and Tom. Brad played rhythm on 'Lightning Strikes'; otherwise, it's Jimmy doing all the guitar work."

Crespo, in fact, acquitted himself quite well, stepping up to fill the fairly massive songwriting void and also pushing Tyler to complete lyrics and ideas. "The good thing about Jimmy was that he was very prolific," Hamilton told *Guitar for the Practicing Musician*. "I have a lot of respect for Jimmy as a studio guy." Indeed, *Rock in a Hard Place* is as much Crespo's album as it is Tyler and Aerosmith's. But his efforts were in vain. *Rock in a Hard Place* sold poorly—their second album in a row to not reach platinum status—and made only a brief appearance on the *Billboard* charts, where it peaked at a mild No. 32. Furthermore, in a bid to make it onto the fledgling MTV, an ill-conceived video was fashioned for "Lightning Strikes" in which the band were made up to resemble a '50s greaser gang, complete with slicked-back hairdos. The clip never entered regular rotation on the network. (As a final kick two years later, the mockumentary *This Is Spinal Tap* used the image of Stonehenge—the very monument that appeared on the cover of *Rock in a Hard Place*—to make an incisive comment on the bombast and, some would say, idiocy, of hard rock and heavy metal.)

Just weeks after the album's release, Tyler sat for a lengthy, sprawling interview with journalist Lisa Robinson, during which he came off alternately defensive, agitated, vulnerable, and even delusional. Robinson questioned whether the singer had any concerns that Aerosmith's bluesy hard-rock style would be seen as out of touch next to the punk and New Wave sounds that were then in favor with

***Rock in a Hard Place* tour, Joe Louis Arena, Detroit, November 27, 1982.** © ROBERT ALFORD

youthful listeners. "Aerosmith is its own gang, its own little club," he replied. "I don't see any reason to cut my hair." He went on to state that he considered Aerosmith to be the biggest band in the country, which prompted Robinson to ask, somewhat incredulously, "You feel you're *the* biggest band in the United States?" "Sure," Tyler replied, then added, "Or we're gonna be again." He paused. "Weren't we before?"

That November, Aerosmith hit the road for their first live dates in close to two years. The shows were the debut of the Crespo/ Dufay lineup, and also included an additional musician, Bobby Mayo, on keyboards. But these weren't the only changes—there were no more limos, no more Learjets. The biggest band in the United States, at least in Tyler's eyes, was now struggling to fill clubs and small arenas. And at the occasional large-venue show, such as an April 23 date at the Tangerine

Bowl in Florida for the World Series of Rock, Aerosmith was demoted from headliner status, playing second on a bill topped by Journey. Recalled Hamilton to VH1's *Behind the Music*, "I remember playing Hartford at like this thousand-seat club that we always had packed, ever since the early days. And there was maybe 100, 200 people there, and somebody literally yelled, 'Where's Joe?' right in between a couple songs. So that's when the denial balloon started to pop."

Reportedly, the band's performances on the *Rock in a Hard Place* tour varied from moments of brilliance to sheer ineptitude, with Tyler sometimes collapsing onstage and unable to complete a show. For years, Kramer commented in *Hit Hard*, they had convinced themselves "that [we] could perform fucked up and get away with it. And it was okay . . . until it wasn't. Now it was totally out of control, and the

results were fucking humiliating." A particular low point came at the new 14,000-seat Centrum in Worchester, Massachusetts, in December 1983, one of the biggest dates of the tour. By this time, Tyler and Perry had begun making tentative inroads toward rekindling a relationship (in September of the previous year, Tyler had stopped by a Project gig at the Bottom Line in New York City), and on this night the guitarist was invited to observe his former band in action. For better or worse, when Perry arrived backstage at the Centrum it was the good old days all over again. Tyler grabbed his Toxic Twin, locked the dressing room door behind them, and dug into his stash of premium heroin. When Aerosmith hit the stage, Tyler hit the ground. "The show was meant to be a big local homecoming for the band," Kramer recalled. "But Steven passed out and once again we had to cancel. He made a fucking fool of himself."

The Centrum fiasco only amplified the fact that neither Tyler nor Perry was ready—or able—to move forward with a reunion. But it was becoming clear that, for all their bluster to the contrary, they needed one another. "Steven missed Joe like you miss a long-lost lover," Douglas told *Behind the Music*. Perry, for his part, saw his life and career evaporating without Aerosmith. A brief ray of light shone through when Whitford joined his old bandmate for a string of dates with the Project in early 1982. But Perry was sinking. He was broke, virtually homeless, and separated from Elyssa, who had reportedly taken to selling his guitars and attempting to have

The 1983 edition of the Joe Perry Project, including vocalist "Cowboy" Mach Bell, at L'amour, Brooklyn, New York, September 30, 1983. BOTH © FRANK WHITE

him jailed for nonpayment of child support. Halfhearted stabs at drying out, including a stay in a psychiatric hospital, were in vain, and on the road with a reconstituted Project—headed by singer "Cowboy" Mach Bell, previously of the Massachusetts band Thundertrain—he began suffering drug- and anxiety-induced seizures. "Joe was in pretty scary shape when I met him," Mach Bell recalled in an interview posted to the fan-generated Crossfire website, dedicated to the Joe Perry Project. "His skin had a gray/green tinge, and every time he took his hands off the Strat they trembled badly."

But Perry soldiered on. By this time he was being managed by Tim Collins, a young Boston-area booking agent who, like Don Law before him, was saddled with the Herculean task of righting the Project's course. Collins, along with his partner Steve Barrasso, landed the band a new deal with MCA, and in the spring of 1983 they hit the studio to record their third album, *Once a Rocker, Always a Rocker*. But Perry wouldn't find any more support at MCA than he had at Columbia; reportedly Irving Azoff, then president of the label, was so unimpressed with the Project that he tried to drop them before the record was even delivered. Not surprisingly, *Once a Rocker* tanked upon release in September 1983. The band continued to toil away on the road, but the Joe Perry Project was, for all intents, done.

The only course of action left for all parties was to foster reconciliation between Tyler and Perry. Collins took up the mantle. In late 1983, the Project played a show in Boston, and, he recalled in

Perry found no more support at MCA than he had at Columbia; reportedly, Irving Azoff, then president of the label, tried to drop the Project before *Once a Rocker* was even delivered.

an interview with A&E's *Biography*, "After the gig Joe had a friend, a local disc jockey [named] Mark Parenteau, and he invited us back

111

The replacements. Rick Dufay and Jimmy Crespo on the *Rock in a Hard Place* tour's stop at Brendan Byrne Arena, the Meadowlands, East Rutherford, New Jersey, December 13, 1983. BOTH © BOB LEAFE

Rock in a Hard Place tour, 1982–1984. BOTH COURTESY WYCO VINTAGE

to his house to hang out. And Joe is passed out, so Mark starts playing all the old Aerosmith records. And I got excited. I started to feel the music. And it was at that moment that I knew it was meant to be." Collins convinced Perry to contact his old singer and the two began speaking by phone. Perry recalled his feelings on the matter in a 1989 interview with *Q*'s Robert Sandall, saying he "realized I didn't hate Steven or Brad or Joey. It was all the other shit which separated us. Like being led around by our management, and chasing off after our dealers." Eventually, Collins and Perry met up with Tyler in New York. "[There] was a little bit of reminiscing and a lot of complaining," Collins recalled. "And then at one point I said, 'Guys, let's talk about the future and let go of the past. Steven looks at me and says, 'He's right. I think it's time, Joe.' And Joe says, 'I do, too.'"

But still a bit more time would be required. Through the early months of 1984 both Aerosmith and the Project continued to tour, even as Tyler and Perry worked to reconnect behind the scenes. In a fortunate twist, both were now also involved with women (Tyler with Teresa Barrick, whom he would eventually marry, and Perry with future wife Billie Montgomery, a model who had appeared in the Project's video for "Black Velvet Pants") who helped to foster, rather than rupture, their relationship—a radical shift from the days of all-out Elyssa vs. Cyrinda warfare. Speaking of Montgomery to A&E, Perry commented, "She didn't know anything about Aerosmith. We were driving along in the car one day

Rick Dufay and Tyler peruse a copy of *Hit Parader*, Los Angeles, February 1984. Behind the scenes, Tyler and Perry were working to reconnect.
© JODI SUMMERS DORLAND/RETNA LTD.

and 'Back in the Saddle' came on. I said, 'That's my guitar right there.' And she said, 'No, you're kidding me.' So I turned the radio up and said, 'That's my band.' So it was pretty easy for her to say, 'Why don't you get back with those guys?'"

The final push came about through an unlikely turn of events. In April 1984, Perry, hurting for cash, got wind of an opportunity to work as a songwriter and sideman for Alice Cooper and headed to Arizona to meet with the shock-rock legend. "I got riled," Tyler recalled to *Q*. "I phoned him up and said, 'What the fuck is this?'"

But Perry was ready to return to the fold. "I didn't want to be a hired hand," he told *Guitar for the Practicing Musician* in 1986. "With Alice Cooper it seemed like I was a square peg in a round hole. I realized just how much I missed being in Aerosmith, where I could just let it fly." That said, Perry had one condition before the reunion could be official: Leber and Krebs were out, and Collins would manage the band going forward. Though loyal to Aerosmith's longtime managers, Tyler eventually acquiesced. With Perry on board, Whitford quickly followed, and Aerosmith was back. But there would be no cause for celebration just yet: "One of [Collins'] first jobs would have to be extricating us from Krebs, which was not exactly a slam dunk," Kramer recalled in *Hit Hard*.

The Ritz, New York City, February 9, 1984.
© FRANK WHITE

Rock in a Hard Place

by Martin Popoff

So Steven's at a druggy, broke nadir and so is Joe, only Joe's actually not even in the band anymore, but off his rocker with the Joe Perry Project, about to follow-up the garage-y, combative, and serviceable *I've Got the Rock 'n' Rolls Again* with the disastrous *Once a Rocker, Always a Rocker*, third and last from that band of bandits. Even Brad Whitford would leave Aeromsith, exiting mid-recording yet showing up as rhythm guitarist on "Lightning Strikes," making *Rock in a Hard Place* the only Aerosmith album ever without the same classic five guys. In fact, significantly, it's the two guitarists who are switched, Perry and Whitford replaced by Jimmy Crespo (two records on RCA as Flame) and Rick Dufay (a Jack Douglas recommendation), both industry fringe guys with a dangerous hoodlum vibe. Not good messaging, but yeah, they looked and felt the part, like a composite of the two no-goodniks they replaced.

Surprise though, throw a million and a half dollars at it, and as long as you've got stakes, a major deal, Jack Douglas producing, egos that want to triumph despite being scabby and tired, and, finally, a brand name like Aerosmith (and an army behind the brand), a very good album falls out the back door. Also key—and it may seem obvious—is that you've got the signature voice of the band, the singer. So really, no surprise that this hobbled collective could produce robust arch-Aerosmith songs, and that two interlopers (mostly Crespo) could write and riff and solo and vibe like Perry and Whitford.

And so, digging into this improbable seventh Aerosmith record, first we dispense with the auto-pilot stuff: "Push Comes to Shove" and "Cry Me a River" are both barroom blues, the first a Van Halen

Throw in $1.5 million, producer Jack Douglas, giant egos, and a brand name like Aerosmith, and a very good album falls out the back door—even with Perry and Whitford gone.

joke-esque original (on which Steven drums), the latter the next in a long line of obscure covers, commendable in that there's more integrity to reworking a slow blues ballad than what would come later, namely power ballads written by corporate song doctors. The trunk of the album, the choogling updates or, dare I say, improvements on Led Zeppelin (the best blues metal bands, such as Aerosmith, Status Quo, Foghat, ZZ Top, and, these days, Clutch, make the blues not boring by writing riffs and eschewing tired blueprints), would be tracks like "Bitch's Brew," "Bolivian Ragamuffin," "Rock in a Hard Place (Cheshire Cat)," and the overlooked "Jig Is Up," which really does bash like the best of Zep while also upholding that rare heroic Stones thing Aerosmith managed to locate and shake in stadiums.

Moving up the food chain, "Lightning Strikes" was floated as a single and (low-budget) video, and it's a cruising metal track with back-switches, band swaggering, and heads held high, and it held its own among all of those cheeky New Wave of British Heavy Metal upstarts about to inspire and

fire what would be a ten-year golden period for metal once the idea moved stateside. But the classics are both LP side openers. First track "Jailbait" lights the fuse on the album like no paint-stripping frightener since "Toys in the Attic." It's violent, punky, chaotic, innovative in its rhythm section, a squalid mess at unsafe speeds. O'er to side two of the original vinyl, and we get the astonishing "Joanie's Butterfly," probably the band's most completely written track that is soft or acoustic (in spirit, in parts), an ambitious epic that recalls, again, the Stones but here more in an *Exile/Beggars Banquet* zone, as well as Zeppelin at their most *III*-esque. "Joanie's Butterfly" underscores a point made earlier: that for whatever confluence of reasons, somehow Aerosmith figures out how not to screw up, constructing a varied record with elbow grease, a collection of shiny (enough) diamonds befitting the band's status as U.S. rock royalty despite the bankruptcy notices pinned to the door. There's a parallel there somewhere to Paul Chapman–era UFO and Thin Lizzy at the end of Phil Lynott's fuse as well.

Anyway, to close, in temporal context, *Rock in a Hard Place* is emphatically an Aerosmith album because it tries and succeeds with that mission in mind—this isn't about a new era, letting the personalities of the new guys shine, stretching out, saying hello to the '80s. Rather, the modus operandi seemed to be—and there's a wee feel of the contrived—to spin new gold out of the bits composing an established complex oeuvre. In fact, it feels closer to the legacy and core identity than does *Done with Mirrors.* And then with *Permanent Vacation,* the band sort of chrysalizes into something else anyway, a new bells-and-whistles journey. Maybe *Rock in a Hard Place* is a bit disjointed and ever so slightly less inspired than *Night in the Ruts* (there's a bummer factor too, in that it's the last with Columbia until *Nine Lives* in '97). Nonetheless, after all these years, the record's come to be positioned as a fist-pumped coda of four similar rockable feasts, no apologies needed, all of that "America's greatest rock 'n' roll band" stuff still hat-hangable despite the house of cards assembled to execute the preposterous plan of keeping the franchise alive.

Rock in a Hard Place tour, 1982–1984.
COURTESY WYCO VINTAGE

chapter 10
Back in the Saddle

When Aerosmith reconvened in 1984, it was hardly as returning champions. Though Tyler and Perry were without doubt in the roughest condition, the LI3 were carrying their share of financial and personal burdens. Whitford, now divorced and remarried to Karen Lesser, had been reduced to selling off much of his guitar collection at bargain prices to cover his house and alimony bills.

Kramer, who likewise had a new wife, April, as well as a son and stepdaughter, was also in dire financial straits. After unloading his longtime New Hampshire residence and moving his family into a rental in White Plains, New York, he was living day-to-day off advances from Leber-Krebs (the managers would later claim these totaled as much as $2.5 million, which Kramer would subsequently spend years repaying out of the band's future royalties). Hamilton and wife Terry, who had lived the most frugally during the low years, had gotten away with merely downsizing to a modest condo in the Boston suburbs. Most significantly, all five members were still deep in the throes of drug and alcohol addiction.

"The Quiet Riots and all those guys with the leather and studs and the stacks of Marshall amps that aren't turned on better watch out. We *are* the band your mother warned you about."

—Joe Perry, quoted by Steve Pond in *Rolling Stone*, September 1984

Facing page: Back in the Saddle tour, Greek Theater, Los Angeles, August 25–26, 1984. CHRIS WALTER/WIREIMAGE/GETTY IMAGES

Back in the Saddle tour, Greek Theater, Los Angeles, August 25–26, 1984. BOTH RICHARD E. AARON/REDFERNS/GETTY IMAGES

All around the band, rock music had moved on in the time they had been away. Sleeker, more polished acts like Van Halen and Def Leppard stepped into Aerosmith's arena-shaking boots, while the Hollywood hair bands, led by the likes of Mötley Crüe and Ratt (both of whom exhibited more than a little Aerosmith in their sound and swagger), were beginning their ascent to the top of the hard-rock heap. "We left a big, gaping hole," Kramer lamented to *Rolling Stone*'s David Wild in 1990, "and we watched all these other bands fill it." The massive success of this slicker, flashier strain of rock was helped along in large part by the full-fledged support of MTV, which had yet to show an Aerosmith video on the network. But if the band was worried, they didn't show it. "The Quiet Riots and all those guys with the leather and studs and the stacks of Marshall amps that aren't turned on better watch out," Perry told *Rolling Stone*'s Steve Pond in 1984. "We *are* the band your mother warned you about." Added Tyler in the same interview: "We paved the road, so to speak. So why not fucking get in our cars and drive down it again?"

It would be easier said than done. Aerosmith's first post-reunion rehearsals, staged at the Glen Ellen Country Club an hour south of Boston, were rough going. "I had to come back to the house and wash down about six Valiums the size of manhole covers with a six-pack of beer just to calm down," Perry told Pond. Still firmly ensconced in a drug-and-booze haze, the members had trouble recalling how to play their own songs, no one more so than Tyler. According to Collins, a get-together at WBCN Boston radio disc jockey Mark Parenteau's apartment one evening revealed just how dire the situation was. Parenteau began spinning old Aerosmith records, and, hearing the *Toys in the Attic* cut "You See Me Crying," Tyler commented, "'Hey! That's great! We should cover this. Who is it?' Joe [said], 'It's *us*, fuckhead.'" The manager was shocked. "Steven hadn't recognized it," Collins continued. "He'd never sung it in concert, so he'd forgotten it."

To make matters worse, the band was at this point receiving little support from Columbia, a situation rooted in the fact that Aerosmith signed their recording contract through Leber-Krebs' production arm, Contemporary Communications Corporation, rather than directly with the label. With the band now at war with its former managers, Columbia sided with the latter. Furthermore, just months before breaking ties with Leber-Krebs, Tyler, Hamilton, and Kramer, at the time the only remaining original members of Aerosmith, had re-inked with

Contemporary—and, by extension, Columbia—for another five albums. Anticipating the legal and financial battles to come, Collins deemed the best course of action was to forego any discussion of recording new material (not that the band was in any shape to do so), and instead go out on the road to build a war chest.

Launched in June 1984, the Back in the Saddle tour saw Aerosmith play more than seventy dates over the rest of the year. There was no new album, no radio or MTV support, and no record company involvement, but the old fans came out in droves to witness the band burn through a greatest hits–style set, including one new song, a version of Perry's "Let the Music Do the Talking," now with reworked lyrics from Tyler. The shows varied wildly in quality. A sold-out New Year's Eve gig at the Orpheum Theatre in Boston was a celebratory homecoming, the band coming out swinging with a blistering "Rats in the Cellar" and hitting the stroke of midnight with Tyler belting out an *a cappella* "Auld Lang Syne" as Perry smashed his guitar to bits. Other nights were less inspiring. At the Prairie Capital Convention Center in Springfield, Illinois, Tyler, wasted on heroin, began fiddling with Hamilton's bass pedals mid-set, leading the bassist to whack him with the neck of his instrument. Eventually the singer tumbled off the stage entirely, and the remainder of the show was canceled. Afterward, Collins smoothed over the fiasco by giving angry ticket holders free copies of *Aerosmith's Greatest Hits*.

Financially at least, the jaunt was an undeniable success. Ticket and T-shirt prices had increased exponentially since Aerosmith's '70s heyday, and even with playing considerably smaller halls, the band grossed $5 million in receipts, which, through a bit of fancy accounting work, they were able to shield from Leber-Krebs. "We set up a different legal entity each night for each concert so we could stay one step ahead of the sheriff," Kramer explained in *Hit Hard*. "Some nights we were performing under the auspices of Large Penis, Inc. Other nights it was Big Belly Productions. After a while Krebs gave up and left us alone."

The tour's success also brought them to the attention of John Kalodner, who, with his Sufi-like beard and sparkling track record, was known within the industry as an A&R guru of sorts. Having made his name at Atlantic Records, where his signings included Foreigner and AC/DC, Kalodner was now at Geffen, where, several years earlier, he had passed on the final lineup of the Joe

Navy Island, St. Paul, Minnesota.

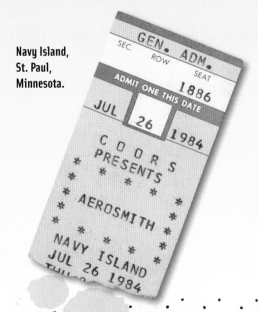

Perry Project, telling Collins the demo he had sent "sucked." But Kalodner saw potential in the revitalized Aerosmith and made it known that Geffen was ready to get onboard—provided the band was free from Leber-Krebs and Columbia. Collins got to work, and after much legal wrangling, convinced Columbia head Walter Yetnikoff to release the band for a quarter-million dollars and an override; Leber-Krebs, with whom lawsuits dragged on for years, eventually walked away with an increased chunk of catalog and publishing royalties. (The managers would further antagonize the band over the next few years by releasing Aerosmith live albums through Columbia: 1986's *Classics Live!*, rumored to feature studio touchups from Crespo, and 1987's more respectable *Classics Live! II*, largely culled, with some input from the band, from the '84 New Year's Eve show at the Orpheum.)

Finally free agents, in late 1984—a dozen years after Clive Davis signed them to Columbia—Aerosmith inked a new recording contract. "We decided to sign with Geffen because we liked John Kalodner's beard," Perry joked to *Rock Scene* in 1986. Added Tyler, "We figured that so many other people found refuge and nested in it, why not us?" The bearded one's first order of business was to put the band in the studio. Intent on dragging Aerosmith firmly

© ROCK 'N' ROLL COMICS, REVOLUTIONARY COMICS, MAY 11, 1990. COURTESY JAY ALLEN SANFORD

into the '80s, Kalodner paired them with ace Van Halen producer Ted Templeman, at the time riding high for his work on their *1984* album. But beyond Templeman, Aerosmith was resistant to Kalodner's suggestions, in particular bringing in outside songwriters to work with them on new material. And so the *Done with Mirrors* sessions at Fantasy Studios in Berkeley, California, saw the band revert back to their old ways, indulging in drugs and alcohol and working with less-than-finished material. "We went into the studio and winged it," Perry told *Musician's* Charles Young in 1990. Furthermore, Templeman held his own misguided ideas about how to approach the recording. With a mind toward capturing Aerosmith raw and loose, he discreetly ran tape during what the band assumed were practice runs, and used the tracks as finished takes.

Released on November 9, 1985, *Done with Mirrors* was hardly the comeback everyone had in mind.

Other than leadoff track "Let the Music Do the Talking," their rewrite of the five-year-old Perry tune, and the mildly rocking "My Fist Your Face," the new material was altogether uninspired. *Rolling Stone* in particular gave the effort a scathing review, writing, "Aerosmith's unawaited reunion LP is the work of burned-out lugheads whose lack of musical imagination rivals their repugnant lyrics." But even those who had been eagerly anticipating a new 'Smith album may not have been able to find it in the racks—in keeping with the mirror theme, the band's name (sans recognizable logo) and the album's title were printed backward on the cover. To further confuse the message, the band counterintuitively asserted that, despite its obvious drug reference, the title was a statement that Aerosmith's music was the real deal (i.e., not "done with mirrors").

And yet, as part of the promotional campaign, band and

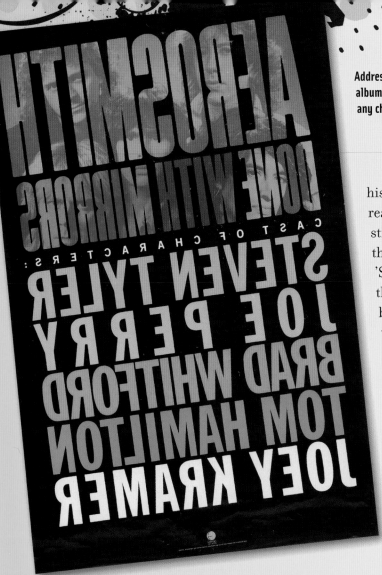

AEROSMITH
DONE WITH MIRRORS

CAST OF CHARACTERS:

STEVEN TYLER
JOE PERRY
BRAD WHITFORD
TOM HAMILTON
JOEY KRAMER

Addressing the title of their reunion album, members of Aerosmith denied any cheeky drug double entendres.

his mind, obviously realizing that it might strike me as going against the new, clean-living 'Smith image." Despite their best efforts, the band's attempts to prove they were "done with mirrors" were readily transparent as nothing more than "done with mirrors"–style trickery. As Whitford admitted to *Screamer* magazine in 1989, "The band members were still involved in certain things that they shouldn't have been. And it took

a while to come around to realizing that if we wanted to do what we wanted to do, we weren't going about it the right way."

Indeed, in August 1985 Aerosmith headed out on the *Done*

with Mirrors tour, and, despite the inclusion of several new songs in the set, it was largely the same old song and dance—right down to the band's opener for many of the dates, Ted Nugent. By this time, the crowds were filled with young Mötley Crüe and Van Halen fans, but Aerosmith held fast to the line that they had little need to change with the times. "They get Steven's scarves right," Perry scoffed to *CREEM*'s Chuck Eddy of the newer generation of bands. "But as far as the soul that we try to put into it, they just don't have the roots that go back that far." Boasted Tyler to Malcolm Dome, "I still maintain that this is essentially a live band and there are few outfits around that can match us." But with the shows reportedly lackluster, this proved to be so much lip service, as was Tyler's contention that the band didn't harbor desires to be accepted by MTV. "We all feel like pandering to stations like MTV restricts the fans' ability to make

album were trotted out to the press as the new, improved Aerosmith, with a drug-free storyline to boot. Perry even went so far as to tell *Rolling Stone*'s Steve Pond, "Just to make the record clear, I went someplace for a while, had my blood changed and got cleaned out." But while he and Tyler had by this point visited their fair share of treatment facilities, the two were far from clean and sober. In an October 1985 profile in *Kerrang!*, journalist Malcolm Dome commented, "I doubt very much that Perry and Tyler are either totally drug-free or teetotal. Indeed, at one stage during this afternoon Perry actually orders a beer, then changes

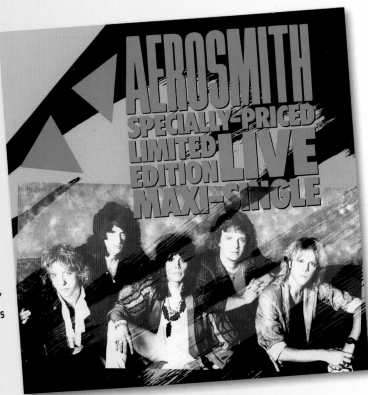

This limited edition 12-inch single for "Darkness" featured live takes of "She's on Fire," "The Hop," and "My Fist Your Face" as B-sides. U.S., 1986.

AEROSMITH
SPECIALLY-PRICED
LIMITED EDITION
LIVE MAXI-SINGLE

Done with Mirrors **tour, State Fairgrounds, Des Moines, Iowa, May 26, 1986.** © FRANK WHITE

STROKE BOX

DONE WITH MIRRORS TOUR 1986

GEFFEN RECORDS

OTTO

self-oriented judgments on a song's meaning," Tyler told Dome, with more than a bit of artistic gravitas. And yet, that November, Aerosmith and director Jerry Kramer filmed two dates at the Orpheum in Boston for later use in a video for "Let the Music Do the Talking"—a clip that, tellingly, MTV didn't bother to air.

But the music channel would in fact soon come to the table, and in a big way. In early 1986, Collins received a phone call from Rick Rubin, a white, Jewish, heavy metal fan from Long Island, New York, who, a few years earlier, had launched the Def Jam rap label out of his New York University dorm room. In the process, he'd helped bring artists like LL Cool J, Run-DMC, and the Beastie Boys to national

AEROSMITH SHELA

"Shela" b/w "Gypsy Boots," U.S., 1985.

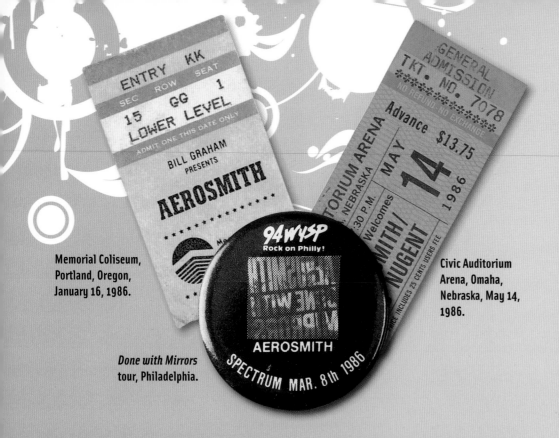

Memorial Coliseum, Portland, Oregon, January 16, 1986.

Done with Mirrors tour, Philadelphia.

Civic Auditorium Arena, Omaha, Nebraska, May 14, 1986.

prominence. Rubin had been in the studio producing Run-DMC's third album, *Raising Hell*, when the rappers brought to his attention an old rock beat that they used to freestyle over as kids in Hollis, Queens. That beat was Kramer's opening drum salvo to "Walk This Way." In 2006, Darryl McDaniels, a.k.a. DMC, told *Classic Rock*'s Greg Prato, "Before rap records were made, we used to have to find beats to rap over, and 'Walk This Way' was one of our favorites." That said, the rappers were so unaware of Aerosmith's history as to believe the name of the band that wrote the song was "Toys in the Attic." "They were about as much into Aerosmith as we were into rap back then," Tyler told *Blender*'s Ben Mitchell in 2002. Collins was likewise unfamiliar with the rappers when Rubin called to inquire about a collaboration on a new version of "Walk This Way." But the manager agreed after getting the go-ahead

from Kalodner—as well as securing $8,000 for a day's studio work.

On March 9, 1986, Tyler and Perry arrived at Manhattan's Magic Ventures Studios to lay down new guitars and vocals on one of their biggest hits. "Joe Perry didn't say one word. But Steven was very friendly and inquisitive, like, Wow, do the DJ thing. Show me how to DJ," McDaniels told Prato. Perry re-cut his famous four-note guitar riff to a prerecorded drum track, as Tyler shouted the chorus and Run-DMC worked their way through Tyler's tongue-twisting lyrics—proto-rap at its finest. Of the rap-rock hybrid, Perry told *Classic Rock*'s Ian Fortnam in 2002, "To me rap sounded like an offshoot of the blues, so it seemed like a very natural thing for us to come in and play on it. Especially when we saw how they were using bits and pieces of rock records to rap over." Two weeks later, the two parties met again at the Park Theater

in Union City, New Jersey, where they filmed what would become an iconic video (with Tyler and Perry backed, somewhat inexplicitly, not by the rest of Aerosmith but rather local New York rockers Smashed Gladys), in which the wall between rap and rock was literally brought crumbling down.

The new "Walk This Way" was issued as the first single from Run-DMC's *Raising Hell* in July 1986, and, fueled by much press as a groundbreaking fusion of rock and hip-hop, quickly became a massive crossover hit on the urban and rock charts; on the latter, it made it all the way to No. 4—Aerosmith's first Top 10 hit since, ironically, "Walk This Way," ten years earlier. MTV entered the video into heavy rotation, playing the clip as much as twice an hour, and Aerosmith and Run-DMC were hailed by the media as music trailblazers. The stage was set for an Aerosmith comeback of epic proportions, but the band wasn't quite ready to take advantage of it—yet.

Even as "Walk This Way" scaled the charts and wormed its way into mainstream cultural consciousness, Aerosmith continued to tour, unspectacularly, behind *Done with Mirrors*. The album stalled on the charts, ultimately selling a disappointing 400,000 copies, and the performances were spotty. "I remember not remembering anything from the night before," Perry recalled of the tour to *Musician*'s Charles Young. "I used to drink to blackout and it wouldn't be any big deal, but it got to be every night. I'd have to call somebody to find out how I played." With tensions again at a high and drug and alcohol abuse running rampant, the band pinned the blame for their troubles on everyone from Geffen to Ted Templeman to Collins. In the summer of '86, with yet more live dates on the horizon, including legs in Europe and the Far East, Collins, sensing imminent disaster, abruptly pulled the plug on the tour. All work stopped, and Aerosmith went on hold. Observed Kramer in *Hit Hard*, "Not even getting a miracle second chance like Run-DMC recording 'Walk This Way' was going to solve our problems. . . . Until we got clean and sober, our effort to resuscitate the band seemed to be just so much pissing in the wind."

In 1986, Rick Rubin was a twenty-three-year-old punk rock fan and hip-hop producer who paired Aerosmith with Run-DMC for a cover of "Walk This Way."

Perry and Tyler's 1986 collaboration with Run-DMC became Aerosmith's first Top 10 hit since the original version of "Walk This Way" was released ten years earlier. It also set the stage for a comeback of epic proportions and laid the groundwork for future rock/hip-hop fusions.

Done with Mirrors

by Chuck Eddy

Done with Mirrors, besides being the last uncompromisingly hard-rocking album Aerosmith made, is also almost definitely the least commercially successful studio album of their lifespan. It never got higher than No. 36 in *Billboard*, and while one Aerosmith album—*Get Your Wings*, from 1974—peaked lower (No. 74), that one has gone triple-platinum over the decades. *Done with Mirrors* (like 1982's No. 32-peaking *Rock in a Hard Place* before it) never climbed past gold. In fact, the RIAA didn't even award *Mirrors* that certification until 1993. At eight songs in its original vinyl version, none exceeding four and a half minutes, *Mirrors* is also Aerosmith's *shortest* LP. Truth is, when all's said and done, its most historically pivotal distinction may be that I wrote a review about it once.

If that sounds like an insane delusion on my part, bear with me. *Done with Mirrors* hit the stores November 9, 1985. Two months later—January 7, 1986—I reviewed it in New York's *Village Voice*; with the band's career clearly on the skids, sundry other publications ignored the release entirely. On the way to praising it as a better comeback album than those that Tina Turner, Aretha Franklin, Stevie Wonder, John Fogerty, Bob Dylan, or the Clash had managed in those past couple of years, I reminded readers how ahead-of-their-time Aerosmith had been back in the '70s. "Maybe calling Aerosmith proto-rappers is a bit much," I wrote. "But a decade before (Run-DMC's) 'Rock Box,' they made a fairly good living harnessing James-Brownian bass-and-drum thrusts to cosmic-sloppy axe raunch, and overlaying the fonky mess with both some outrageous boasts (what Bronx emcee wouldn't envy 'Lord of the Thighs'?), and some pretty awesome toasts, like the very fresh one in 'Walk This Way,' their 1975 def jam of adolescent psychosexual discovery." See what I'm getting at yet? So here's John Leland, in the June 17, 1986, *Voice*, reviewing Run-DMC's *Raising Hell*: "It's safer to remake 'Walk This Way' than to write

According to *Rolling Stone*, "the work of burned-out lugheads whose lack of musical imagination rivals their repugnant lyrics." Chuck Eddy liked the album just fine. Still does.

an original, especially after the failure of most of the guitar songs on [their previous album] *King of Rock*. [Rick] Rubin suggested the collaboration after reading Chuck Eddy's Aerosmith review in the *Voice*." And of course, once Rubin got Run-DMC together with Steve Tyler and Joe Perry to revive their masterpiece, Aerosmith was introduced to a whole new generation on MTV. And for a good long time, as nobody in 1985 would ever have predicted, they stayed there. Their next album, 1987's *Permanent Vacation*, went quintuple platinum; the two after that have each sold at least seven million copies in the U.S.—and my *Done with Mirrors* review set the wheels in motion!

Then again, if *Mirrors* wasn't real good in the first place, I never would've acknowledged it myself. But even though it was the album where guitarists Perry and Brad Whitford rejoined after six and four respective years in absentia, not much time passed before Aerosmith was apologizing for the album. Perry, when I interviewed him and Tyler for *CREEM* while they were in the studio recording *Permanent Vacation* in 1987, said "it was, like, finding our place again as far as writing and the direction we wanted to take the band . . . *Done with Mirrors* was the best record we could do at the time, but it wasn't the best record we can do. We should have had a month with those tracks as they sit on that record, instead of having one week, which is what we had."

Thing is, I *was* an Aerosmith fan. So I liked it just fine, and still do. In fact, I recently sampled it back-to-back with *Rock in a Hard Place* (which, despite the superb "Lightning Strikes," relies too much on torch schmaltz), and *Mirrors* won by a mile—maybe partly because it's almost entirely the guitarists' and the rhythm section's record, all big, fat chunky funky boxy boogie riffs. The songs are too concise to get complicated, and they don't need to. There may be no other Aerosmith album that so fully opts for rhythm over melody. Which isn't to say

the songs aren't catchy, just that the band's Beatles-pomp side is nowhere to be found. The first two tracks are the best. After that, nothing's absolutely earthshaking, but the record just keeps on punching.

So why is it so ignored? Is it the title's kick-the-coke-habit pun? Or maybe it was the fact a remake of a five-year-old Joe Perry Project song, "Let the Music Do the Talking," was the leadoff track and the first single. But Aerosmith's version tightened the tune up and gave it more vocal personality, while still appropriately letting Joe's guitar talk—like an elephant, no less—while Tyler discussed somebody being his "brand-new drug," Huey Lewis be damned. From there they go into "My Fist Your Face," in which Tyler delivers what may well be the last undeniably crazed jive-talk tongue-twisting of his pre–*American Idol* career, all Betty Boop and Julio Afrokeluchie and thirteen-year-old hookers and east house pinball wizards. The first side's rounded out with "Shame on You" (nose-powdering Lolitas and Joe Perry buzzing like a killer bee to a "Back in Black"-ish groove) and "The Reason a Dog" (tail-wagging canines teaching male-nagging spouses life lessons to a tune that faintly echoes "Invisible Sun" by the Police.)

Side two starts with the syncopated workout "Shela," which almost goes disco, at least in the mid-1980s, ZZ Top sense of the word, before being followed by "Gypsy Boots," the AC/DC-like riff and teen-runaway-on-drugs motif of which align it with "Shame on You," at least until it adopts a sort of "Shakedown Street" (Grateful Dead)/"Nighttime in the Switching Yard" (Warren Zevon)/proto-"Need You Tonight" (INXS) bass vamp toward the end. The album bows out with the quivery Sahara blues undulations of "She's on Fire" and finally "The Hop," straightforward and comparatively speedy rattlesnake shake R&B with a blues harp. "Darkness," omitted from the vinyl LP but included as a cassette and CD bonus, is a slick sort of dirge that heavies up at the end; maybe think of it as a hidden hallway connecting foreboding old Aerosmith alley crawls like "Seasons of Wither" with more lucrative Tin Pan Alley moves to come. Those were right around the corner—yet with *Done with Mirrors*, still nowhere in sight. ◣

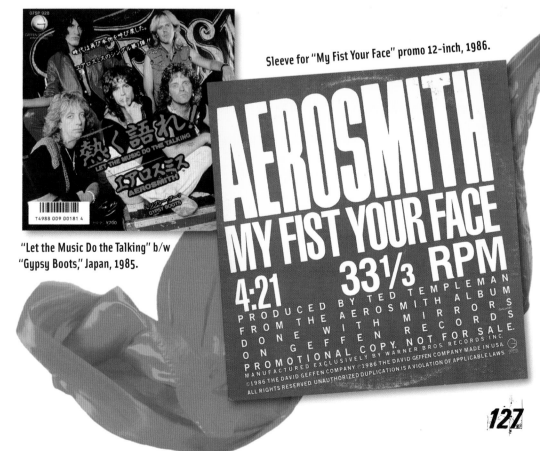

"Let the Music Do the Talking" b/w "Gypsy Boots," Japan, 1985.

Sleeve for "My Fist Your Face" promo 12-inch, 1986.

chapter 11

Done with Mirrors (Pun Intended)

Indeed, Aerosmith's first years back together had done little to restore their faded glory. Remarked Hamilton to journalist Roy Trakin in 1994, "We really thought we'd put out *Done with Mirrors* and Aerosmith would be a huge band again. And we found out that didn't happen." Rather, they fell back into the same patterns of drug abuse and dysfunction, with a failed album and largely lackluster performances to show for their efforts. But the Run-DMC collaboration was a sign of something greater on the horizon, and it was Collins who determined that the only way forward was with the entire band cleaned up. Electing to cut the snake off at the head, so to speak, he set his sights on Tyler first, speculating that if the singer submitted to rehab, his bandmates would follow.

In the fall of 1986, Collins, with the help of New York–based psychiatrist Lou Cox, enlisted Perry, Kramer, Whitford, and Hamilton in staging an intervention. Though the four bandmates were hardly sober themselves, Perry, at least, had agreed to enter a rehab facility following the imminent birth of his son. "For years, I was thinking, 'Poor Steve, he has to go to rehab,'" Perry told *Musician*'s Charles Young. "Or I'd

"We crawled out from under our problems and got in touch with ourselves. It was a wonderful experience because after all that abuse you go dead inside. You go dead musically, too."

—Brad Whitford, quoted by Charles Young in *Musician*, January 1990

Facing page: **Permanent Vacation** tour, Giants Stadium, East Rutherford, New Jersey, August 16, 1988. © FRANK WHITE

Facing page, inset: **January 23, 1988, Reno, Nevada.**

say to my manager, 'Steven's terrible. He's got to go away. I'm going to the Cayman Islands to have a vacation to get away from my dealer.' That's what I was gonna do, 'cause I didn't have a problem as bad as Steven. But what you find out is, everyone's problem is just as bad, whether Brad with his alcohol, or Joe with his cocaine, or Steven with his pills. Everyone was fucked."

Convincing his Toxic Twin to take the plunge would be a harder proposition. The band determined their best chance of catching the singer in a somewhat sober state was to confront him first thing in the morning, and so Collins summoned Tyler to his office at six a.m., under the pretext of a scheduled interview with Britain's BBC. When Tyler arrived, he found his manager, bandmates, and Cox waiting for him.

The singer was livid. He recalled on VH1's *Behind the Music*, "The band had the intervention and it was me, me, me. Why are *you* nodding out at the piano? Let me see . . . because you gave me a Dilaudid, Joe? What about you?" "The irony is that the rest of us *were* fucked up," Kramer confirmed in *Hit Hard*. "But I'm relatively sure Tim believed that if Steven didn't get clean, it wouldn't have really mattered much what the rest of us did." Despite his objections to the manner in which he was approached, Tyler told VH1, "It worked, because I went away."

The singer was sent to Chit Chat Farms, a treatment facility in Wernersville, Pennsylvania, where he underwent an intense forty-five-day detox program. At the same time Perry, following the birth of his son Tony, completed a stint at

Bournewood Hospital in Brookline, Massachusetts. It wasn't either member's first attempt to kick his addictions, but it was the first time it took. And Whitford, who had taken it upon himself to enroll in Alcoholics Anonymous, soon joined them. Kramer and Hamilton followed within a year. "We crawled out from under our problems and got in touch with ourselves," Whitford told Charles Young. "It was a wonderful experience because after all that abuse you go dead inside. You go dead musically, too."

But Aerosmith was about to be resurrected. In early 1987, they began work on what would prove to be their true comeback album, *Permanent Vacation*. This time, however, they followed the advice of John Kalodner, who insisted on bringing in outside songwriters. Kalodner first paired Tyler and Perry with Desmond Child, who had recently cowritten two smash hits for Bon Jovi, "You Give Love a Bad Name" and "Livin' on a Prayer." Together, they completed an idea Tyler and Perry had worked up from a Perry riff and a hook the singer had crafted after fiddling with the presets on a Korg keyboard. The working title was "Cruisin' for a Lady." Tyler told VH1's *Behind the Music*, "I had the song, I just didn't have the first verse. And [Child] came up with *Cruised into a bar on the shore*. And I went, *Her picture graced the grime on the door*. It was at that moment that I realized, there may be another career here for me. There may be something else other than the frustration of writing with the band."

That spring, Kalodner dispatched the band to Little Mountain Sound

COURTESY WYCO VINTAGE

Studios in Vancouver to work with producer Bruce Fairbairn, whose track record for turning out slick, commercially viable hard rock for acts like Loverboy and Bon Jovi made him ideal to helm Aerosmith's comeback. Key to the recording would also be engineer Bob Rock, who had a particular talent for crafting massive guitar sounds, a defining trait of his later work with Mötley Crüe and Metallica. "Bob was a big element in what was going on soundwise," Whitford told *Guitar World*'s Alan di Perna in 1997.

All along, Kalodner kept the band working with outside writers. In addition to the song that would become "Dude (Looks Like a Lady)" (by some accounts, the title was a nod to Tyler's observation, while hanging with the members of Mötley Crüe, of their fondness for the word *dude*), the band collaborated with Child on two more tracks, "Heart's Done Time" and the grandiose power ballad "Angel." Additionally, in Vancouver, Fairbairn brought in an associate, Jim Vallance, with whom he had played in the '70s-era Canadian band Prism. Vallance had since established a career as a for-hire songwriter, making a name for himself cowriting hits like "Cuts Like a Knife" and "Summer of '69" for Bryan Adams. He worked with Tyler and Perry on four cuts, including the Delta-blues influenced "Hangman Jury" (for which the band would later be sued, successfully, by the estate of Leadbelly, who claimed the song's refrain too closely mirrored the bluesman's "Can't You Line 'Em") and the brassy rocker "Rag Doll."

"Angel" b/w "Girl Keeps Coming Apart," U.S., 1987.

"Angel" b/w "Girl Keeps Coming Apart," Ecuador, 1988.

"I think [Perry's] been brainwashed by engineers and producers and his own ego and by all the fallacies that equate rock 'n' roll with fancy licks, neatfreak-perfection and an absence of surface noise. And I think he's full of baloney—who rocks harder, Oscar Madison or Felix Unger?"

—Chuck Eddy, *CREEM*, October 1987

"Dude (Looks Like a Lady)" picture disc b/w "Monkey on My Back," U.K., released 1990.

The view from the press box for Texxas World Music Festival (a.k.a. Texxas Jam) at the Cotton Bowl in Dallas, June 20, 1987. Aerosmith was second on a bill that also included Boston, Whitesnake, Poison, and Tesla. © BOB LEAFE

In a posting to his official website, Vallance recalled crafting the latter tune at his first meeting with Tyler and Perry: "Bruce brought Steven and Joe to my studio, along with their bodyguard, Bob Dowd, a six-foot-six former cop whose primary function was to ensure that no drugs came within a Minnesota mile of the recently rehabbed Aero-guys. . . . By the time Bruce returned, just before dinner, we'd completed the basic structure of the song, including the temporary title 'Rag Time,' inspired by the track's New Orleans feel. That title stuck for a few more weeks, but it would prove to be problematic."

Indeed, Kalodner hated the song's name and brought in Holly Knight, who had previously worked with KISS, Tina Turner, and Pat Benatar, for further input. Reportedly, after several days of

Texxas World Music Festival (a.k.a. Texxas Jam), the Cotton Bowl, Dallas, June 20, 1987. ALL © BOB LEAFE

Aerosmith launched the *Permanent Vacation* tour in October 1987, staying on the road for close to a year and firing on all cylinders.

brainstorming, Knight reread Tyler's lyric that began *I'm rippin' up a rag doll*, and suggested the new title. For her efforts she received credit as a cowriter, an acknowledgment Tyler deemed excessive.

Regardless, Kalodner's tactics proved successful. "[He] made some suggestions that worked for us," Hamilton told Roy Trakin. "He just threw a constant stream of ideas at us. We definitely wanted to build the band back up. We wanted radio airplay. We wanted to survive the cut. There were a lot of new bands coming along and it took us a while to realize, if we wanted to continue doing this, we needed a hit single."

They would get far more than that. Released on September 5, 1987, *Permanent Vacation*, all big hooks, glossy guitars, and radio-ready choruses, was a bona fide smash, going platinum within four months and reaching No. 11 on *Billboard*. The record's lead single, "Dude (Looks Like a Lady)," made it to No. 14 and was paired with a big-budget performance video (with a cameo by Kalodner, dressed as a bride-to-be) by director Marty Callner, who would go on to have a long and fruitful relationship with the band. The clip went into immediate heavy rotation on MTV and was nominated for two Video Music Awards, including

Best Group Video—a 180-degree turnaround from the network's longtime disregard of the band. Two more radio and MTV hits followed: "Angel" and "Rag Doll," the latter with a video featuring a memorable final thirty seconds of Tyler sucking face with what appeared to be another man's wife. Amazingly, not only had Aerosmith finally been accepted by the MTV generation, but the band, its members now pushing forty, were quickly becoming among the channel's biggest and most recognizable stars.

And if they had to make some concessions to get there, so be it. Over the years the band would

Permanent Vacation tour, 1988.
© DANA FRANK/RETNA LTD.

alternately praise and damn the writing and recording approach they employed on *Permanent Vacation*—and would continue to use in the years following—in particular the use of outside songwriters. "Some songs were real high points and I think they get close to what Aerosmith is about," Perry reasoned to *Guitar World*'s Richard Grula in 1990. "On other cuts I think we kind of went in the wrong direction because we were trying to change our songwriting." But, he added, "We'd been writing together for years and years, so it was good to have somebody come in and go, 'Why don't you just try this?' People put us

down for that, but I wonder how an AC/DC record would sound if they'd pull somebody like Jim Vallance into the songwriting process."

The song that would continually serve as a flashpoint for the new, sleeker Aerosmith was "Angel," viewed by hardcore fans, and in some cases the band members themselves, as bending too much to the will of radio and MTV. "It's definitely got that big, wet production," Perry told *Guitar World*'s Alan di Perna in 1997. "You can probably name dozens of power ballads from that era that typify what that was. Whitesnake had one, Bon Jovi had one. . . ." Added Tyler in the same interview, "That

The Spectrum, Philadelphia, August 4, 1988. Promoting their debut album, Guns N' Roses opened for Aerosmith on most of the July–September *Permanent Vacation* dates, during which Tyler and Perry presented their young acolytes with Toxic Twins T-shirts like the one Perry is wearing here. Reportedly, at the end of the tour, they also gave each member of GN'R a Halliburton suitcase, having taken pity on them for the ramshackle condition of their luggage. © BOB LEAFE

record, I'm scared of it today. We wrote the chorus. But others took that chorus and put it on a silver platter. There are other ways to do it." Speaking to *Behind the Music* several years later, Hamilton laid out his feelings about the song in no uncertain terms: "I thought 'Angel' crossed the line," he said. "The song's just too wimpy. Too corny."

And yet, the results were undeniable. Aerosmith launched the *Permanent Vacation* tour on October 16, 1987, and stayed out on the road for close to a year, selling out arenas across the U.S. and embarking on a brief but successful Japanese leg. The band was firing on all cylinders, with a set list that mixed classics like "Toys in the Attic" and "Back in the Saddle" with new hits like "Dude" and "Angel." Furthermore, they were in peak physical condition. "We stopped drinking. We stopped taking drugs. We started to work out and get back in shape until it seemed like we were training for some competition—or a war," Perry recalled in *Walk This Way*.

Support on the tour came from Aerosmith-influenced acts like White Lion, Dokken, and, in the summer of 1988, Guns N' Roses, perhaps the most 'Smith-like—in sound, appearance, and drug intake— of all the 1980s hard rockers. Though Aerosmith, in particular Perry, were professed fans of the Gunners (likewise, GN'R guitarist Slash has repeatedly gone on record about the impact *Rocks* had on him as a teen), Collins was hesitant to bring them onboard, particularly as it was known that several members dabbled in heroin. A plan was hatched whereby

GN'R would perform and then retreat to their dressing room before Aerosmith arrived on site. This setup led to an oft-repeated story in the press that the elder band had attempted to impose their clean-as-a-whistle lifestyle on the young act—a move hardly in keeping with the rebellious, anarchic spirit of rock 'n' roll. But as Tyler clarified to *Blender*'s Ben Mitchell in 2002, "I told those guys, 'This is my dressing room, and if you whip out the coke I'm going to have to leave. That was it. Then it was printed that we banned them from drinking backstage. Never."

That said, there were reportedly some uneasy moments. In his book *WAR: The Unauthorized Biography of William Axl Rose*, author Mick Wall recounted a tale in which Slash entered his own dressing room only to find Tyler rooting around in his things. "Gesturing to the two bottles of Jack Daniels on the table, one of which was already empty, the other half-full," Wall wrote, "Tyler asked Slash reproachfully, 'Did you drink all that today?'" But any uneasiness between the two bands soon dissipated, with Perry and Tyler even presenting their acolytes with custom-made Toxic Twins T-shirts, a list of their rehab stints—rather than tour dates—printed on the back.

Furthermore, the pairing was gangbusters at the gate. Though the rejuvenated Aerosmith was clearly the main event, by the summer of '88 Guns N' Roses' Geffen debut, *Appetite for Destruction*, was a massive hit, and the album's second single, "Sweet Child O' Mine," was steadily climbing the charts. The dates with Aerosmith included a massive blowout gig at

"But when you get to being about 14 you start to discover your own stuff. So it was 'Back in the Saddle' by Aerosmith. That was off *Rocks*— the album that set me in the direction that I'm in. I first heard it in about 1978 and it just changed my life."

—Slash, quoted by James Jackson in *The Times*, May 8, 2010

Giants Stadium in New Jersey on August 16, filmed for eventual use in the video for another *Appetite* smash, "Paradise City." By the end of the year, Guns N' Roses was arguably the hottest new act in rock.

Aerosmith, of course, wasn't doing so bad either. By the time they came off the road in September 1988, *Permanent Vacation* had pushed past

the two million mark and spawned three hit singles. The contentious "Angel" made it all the way to No. 3 and in the process became their highest-charting song to date. Clean, lean, and playing like a well-oiled machine, Aerosmith was, officially, back in the saddle.

Permanent Vacation

by Bill Holdship

It couldn't have been easy to be Aerosmith in 1987. They were a band stuck in the middle of what looked to be a long and difficult rebound. It's hard to think of another band that had reached the same heights in terms of rock stardom, only to fall as far, the victims of excess and drug addiction of epic proportions.

Ironically, there wasn't a band in the pop-metal/hard-rock scene that dominated the American charts at that time that didn't tip their hat (or poodle hairdos) to Aerosmith. Watching these inferior young upstarts take their respective places in the rock 'n' roll food chain surely made everything that much harder.

Their collaboration with producer Rick Rubin and Run-DMC the year before on the groundbreaking rock-rap mash-up version of "Walk This Way" had given them newfound credibility and even some critical revaluation and revision. But the much-ballyhooed "reunion" album, *Done with Mirrors*, from 1985, had been a relatively bland hit-and-miss affair. Geffen Records A&R executive John Kalodner decided to take advantage of the band's incredible influence on the pop-metal scene this time out, recruiting producer Bruce Fairbairn, who'd recently hit multi-platinum pay dirt with Bon Jovi, yet another band that had built a career around a faded variation of Aerosmith's East Coast hard-rock "bar band" sound and ethos.

Permanent Vacation was also the controversial disc on which Kalodner teamed the band with outside songwriters, including rock-ballad hitmaker Desmond Child. And while the executive may have given the pop universe other horribly antiseptic music, damn if he didn't work with Aerosmith to deliver, well, an *Aerosmith* album. And a mighty terrific one on top of it all.

Initial fears may have even seemed wellfounded given the record's two opening cuts. "Hearts Done Time" is *so* pop-metal in its slickness that it wouldn't have sounded out of place on a Dokken album. And the equally slick "Magic Touch" might well be the best Bon Jovi song that Bon Jovi never recorded.

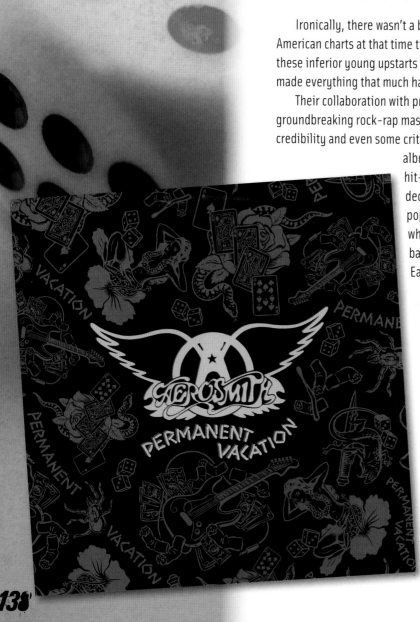

The disc on which Geffen A&R executive John Kalodner controversially teamed the band with outside songwriters, including rock-ballad hitmaker Desmond Child.

Throughout the album, Tyler demonstrated that David Lee Roth had nothing on his still-potent vocal tics, squeals, and squawks, while Perry, Whitford, and the rhythm team displayed that none of the young bucks had anything on their chops, either, which gave equal emphasis to emotion and the technique-is-king philosophy that still dominated *rawk* in 1987.

It's the tracks that follow the somewhat lumbering opening ones, however, that revealed that when it came to tunes, fans of the "old" Aerosmith had little cause for concern. "Rag Doll" and "Dude (Looks Like a Lady)" are both very familiar to rock fans now, but both came on like gangbusters and musical revelations upon their release. The first song, featuring Tyler's rapping and scat singing about yet another "bad girl," has the horns, synths, and 1980s production sheen blended well enough into the overall mix for the guitar hooks to stand out with timeless Aerosmith raunch. Even the mythology behind "Dude" is legendary: Tyler claims the idea originated while hanging with Mötley Crüe during which time every other word seemed to be *dude*. A defensive Vince Neil later argued that it referenced an afternoon he and Tyler spent together in a female impersonator bar. Nikki Sixx later claimed that the song was specifically about Vince Neil. Whatever the case, the band delivered a hook-laden, pop-metal delight that surpassed anything all those imitators had recorded thus far. More amazingly, the song perfectly captured a cultural zeitgeist and managed to appeal to both lovers *and* detractors of the hair-metal scene. It was a win-win situation.

Likewise, none of those Hollywood poseurs ever seemed capable of recognizing a *real* blues riff even if it hit them in the face, and *Permanent Vacation* finds Aerosmith upping the ante by offering up not one but two fine examples of the form via their own "St. John" and "Hangman Jury," the latter of which is positively Zeppelin-esque, not only

in its arrangement and Tyler's exemplary vocals and harp-playing, but also in its history of litigation: The band got permission from bluesman Taj Mahal to adapt parts of a traditional blues-based song he performed, but Aerosmith was then sued by Leadbelly's estate for copyright infringement. Still, neither Taj nor Leadbelly ever did a version with a refrain as melodically poppy as the one Tyler, Perry, and outside writer Jim Vallance (who also contributed to "Rag Doll") brought to this incarnation. As if to drive the Zeppelin-like aspects in Aerosmith's sound all the way home, the album closes with "The Movie," a pseudo-psychedelic, atmospheric instrumental that owes at least a major nod to Page-Plant-Jones-Bonham (and once again, shows the youngsters how it should be done).

Aerosmith practically invented what was by now termed the "power ballad" with 1973's "Dream On" (a much better tune than anything being called a power ballad at the time, by the way). So it seemed absolutely mandatory for "Angel" to be here. Written

with Child (who also contributed to "Dude"), and opening with a lift from Lou Reed's "Sweet Jane" as applied to symphonic strings, it's the one song Tyler has said is often difficult for him to sing live. But it's also the one that set the stage for future "grand" MTV moments, including videos starring Alicia Silverstone and daughter Liv Tyler for songs that a generation young enough to be Aerosmith's, well, daughters nursed broken hearts to. Throw in "Girl Keeps Coming Apart," a Tyler-Perry composition that ranges from Beatlesque to metal-esque—and makes it all work—and a salute to the quintessential pop-rock band via a faithful cover of the Fabs' "I'm Down" that's superior to their 1978 cover of "Come Together" (the band's last hit single . . . no one said there wasn't a formula at work here), and you have one fine Aerosmith LP.

It may not exactly be as earth-shattering as Elvis' 1968 comeback spectacular. But in terms of rock 'n' roll revivals, *Permanent Vacation* stands pretty damn monumental.

"Dude (Looks Like a Lady)" b/w "Simoriah," U.S., 1987.

"Rag Doll" b/w "St. John," U.S., 1987.

chapter 12

Aero Force

Following the remarkable success of *Permanent Vacation*, Aerosmith barely stopped to take a breath. By December 1988, they had begun rehearsals for their next record at Rik Tinory Productions in Cohasset, roughly a half-hour south of Boston. Working through the winter, they fleshed out the skeletons of the songs that would form the core of what would become *Pump*, including "Monkey on My Back," Tyler's chronicle of his emergence from the depths of drug addiction, and the two tracks that would come to define the album, "Love in an Elevator" and "Janie's Got a Gun."

"[L]ast year we were doing a gig and I remember thinking, Well, we're ready for the Nineties, no one can deny us that."

—Steven Tyler, quoted by Christie Eliezer in *Juke*, September 1990

In February 1989, the band returned to Little Mountain Sound to begin recording with Bruce Fairbairn. There, they again employed the services of Jim Vallance, who had a hand in "Young Lust" and "The Other Side," and Desmond Child, who contributed to the rollicking "F.I.N.E.*" and the country-ish ballad "What It Takes."

But despite the similar working arrangement, *Pump* proved to be a very different beast from *Permanent Vacation*. The band was stronger and more focused, and if they were now

Facing page: Get a Grip tour, Wembley Arena, London, December 7–8, 1993. MICK HUTSON/REDFERNS/GETTY IMAGES

GET A GRIP
TOUR '93-95

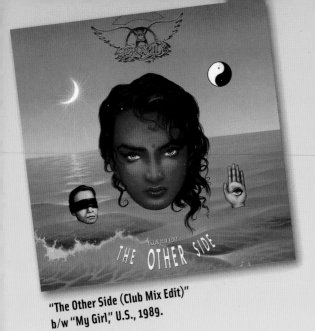

"The Other Side (Club Mix Edit)" b/w "My Girl," U.S., 1989.

Pump 1989 tour.

Münsterland Halle, Münster West Germany.

fully accepting of using outside collaborators, they were also more in control of the process, employing Child and Vallance somewhat sparingly and as co-conspirators rather than crutches. "It just makes it better to have other people in there sometimes," Perry explained to *Guitar World*'s Alan di Perna. "They put their slant on what they think an Aerosmith album should sound like. And it's great. They hear different stuff than we do." Furthermore, they also recaptured a certain rawness that had been glossed over on their previous effort. Remarked Perry to *RIP*'s Katherine Turman in 1990, "*Permanent Vacation* was a great record, but I think it was a little more commercial than we would have liked it to have been. This record, I think, is a way more real, true, flailing, Aerosmith album."

Indeed, *Pump* was a loud and aggressive record, both in spirit and sonics—it sounded as if the whole thing was recorded in the red. The band virtually detonated from the outset, kicking off with the raucous one-two punch of "Young

Lust" and "F.I.N.E.*," whose title was Tyler shorthand for the words *Fucked up, Insecure, Neurotic*, and *Emotional*—"my constant state!" as he told Turman. From there, it was on to the Tyler/Perry collaborations "Love in an Elevator" and "Monkey on My Back," followed by the album's centerpiece, the Tyler/Hamilton cut, "Janie's Got a Gun." Together, these five songs made for the strongest side of Aerosmith music in more than a decade—if not, arguably, their entire career. The album's back end boasted several more first-rate cuts in "Don't Get Mad, Get Even," another Tyler/Perry job, and the album closing "What It Takes." Additionally, the entire production was held together by risqué spoken-word skits and evocative musical interludes, the latter played on indigenous instruments from the collection of Vancouver-based folklorist Randy Raine-Reusch. "Joe and I went to his place and tried everything," Tyler told *Musician*'s

Facing page: Pump tour, Nassau Coliseum, Uniondale, New York, January 15, 1990. © FRANK WHITE

142

KONTR.-ABRISS

BY THE TIME WE WERE RECORDING "PUMP", ALL OF US HAD GOTTEN OUR **HEADS** TOGETHER.

AND HAVING ALL GONE THROUGH **DRUG REHAB**, WE WERE DETERMINED TO KEEP OURSELVES TOGETHER... (MENTALLY **AND** PHYSICALLY)

WE RETURNED TO THE REMOTE CANADIAN STUDIO WHERE WE'D RECORDED OUR **LAST** ALBUM...

I LOVE THIS PLACE. IT'S SO **INSPIRATIONAL!**

Y-YEAH... MAYBE NEXT TIME WE CAN GET INSPIRED IN SOMEPLACE **WARM!**

© ROCK 'N' ROLL COMICS NO. 57, REVOLUTIONARY COMICS, 1993. COURTESY JAY ALLEN SANFORD

Charles Young in 1990. "Everything except the drum made out of a human skull. We didn't want the karma. I didn't want to be banging away on some P.O.W."

With *Pump*, it seemed as if Aerosmith's cleaned-up lifestyle had the effect of rousing a long-dormant musical power in the band. A side effect of this, also in evidence on the record, was what appeared to be an almost hypersexual reawakening in Tyler. The singer admitted in *RIP* magazine that he believed his years of heavy drug use had led him to miss out on reaping the abundant feminine fruits of his labors: "Most of the Seventies, I was in the closet, snorting cocaine instead of fucking," Tyler lamented to Turman. "So many nights . . . missed opportunities." Now he was committed to making up for lost time, so to speak, and this reshuffling of his extracurricular energies came to the fore in his lyrics, which, particularly on *Pump*'s first three tracks, were among his most rude and lewd since "Walk This Way"—perhaps even more so, as in some cases he was clearly speaking from first-hand experience. As the singer exclaimed to Paul Elliott of *Sounds*, "Love in an elevator? Yeah, I've done it!"

Tyler was somewhat more philosophical on the subject when asked by Charles Young in *Musician* how he would respond to a mother offended by lyrics like *You better keep your daughter inside / Or she's gonna get a dose of my pride*, from "Young Lust": "What do you want to be telling your child?" the singer reasoned. "That lust is bad? Get

Pump tour luggage tag, 1990.

Pump tour, 1990. GEORGE DE SOTA/REDFERNS/GETTY IMAGES

ALL AREA ACCESS

outta here. That's the holy wars." In a humorous twist, later in the same story Young solicited the opinion of an actual mother— Perry's mom, Mary—in regard to the same song. "As an aerobics teacher I love the rhythm. It makes me want to move," Mary Perry responded. "I'm just glad I can't understand the words."

Released on September 12, 1989, *Pump* shipped platinum and garnered some of the best reviews of the band's career (*Rolling Stone*: "[It] transports the listener right back to the gilt-edged grunge of Aerosmith's wonder years"). The album's first single, "Love in an Elevator," complete with a tongue-in-cheek Marty Callner–directed video, reached No. 5 on the *Billboard* singles charts and No. 1 on the Mainstream Rock charts. But it was the follow-up single, "Janie's Got a Gun," for which the band shot a stylishly noir video with Hollywood filmmaker David Fincher, that would take them to new heights. The song itself was unlike anything in Aerosmith's canon—hardly a ballad, but not quite a rocker—with a moody atmosphere and unique instrumentation, including a Perry guitar solo played on a Chet Atkins acoustic-electric with an incredibly

harsh, biting tone, and an intro piece—dubbed "Water Song"—that featured various exotic instruments from Raine-Reusch's collection.

But the greatest departure in "Janie's" was its lyric, for which Tyler spun a frank and affecting tale of child abuse and incest. "It took me nine months to write," the singer told Alan di Perna in 1997. "I came up with the first line and then got stuck. Then I picked up an issue of *Newsweek*, and it had an article on all the people who'd died of gunshot

wounds that particular week. I put it together with the abuse issues in America. Drug addiction isn't the only thing that's swept under the carpet. There's child molestation, and fathers going ape on their daughters. So I went with the child abuse theme."

The song proved to have incredible resonance with the public at large, reaching No. 4 on the *Billboard* singles chart and becoming one of the most requested videos of its day on MTV. It went on to win the Best Rock Video and Viewer's Choice categories at the network's Video Music Awards that year, and in 1991 earned a Grammy—the band's first—for Best Rock Performance by a Duo or Group with Vocal.

The *Pump* world tour, launched in October 1989, was another mammoth and hugely successful undertaking. Augmented by keyboardist Thom Gimbel, the band stayed on the road a full year, crisscrossing the U.S. with Skid Row and the Black Crowes, returning to Japan, spending significant time in Europe—their first visit since 1977—and making their maiden voyage to Australia. Many of these miles were covered in the band's private plane, a converted Cessna Citation II formerly owned by recently deceased

Maxi single issued for an eight-date tour of Australia in September and October 1990—the band's maiden voyage Down Under. The A-side, "Walk This Way," was backed with "Sweet Emotion" and "Back in the Saddle."

Philippine dictator Ferdinand Marcos, which they christened Aero Force One. High in the air en route to a show in Glens Falls, New York, Tyler, sitting in the plane's cabin, recalled his previous history with private aircrafts: "I owned a plane once upon a time," he commented to *Rolling Stone*'s David Wild. "But I snorted it away.

Special Australian TOUR SOUVENIR

I snorted my Porsche. I snorted my house. It all went bye-bye."

The long tour was filled with highlights. In February 1990, they performed "Monkey on My Back" and "Janie's Got a Gun" for a national audience on *Saturday Night Live*, and also appeared in a memorable "Wayne's World" skit, jamming the titular theme song alongside Wayne (Mike Myers) and Garth (Dana Carvey) with a bespectacled Tom Hanks playing the part of an Aerosmith roadie. On August 11, the band stopped by the Ed Sullivan Theater in New York to tape what would become a highly regarded performance for *MTV Unplugged*. August 18, they appeared before 80,000 fans at the massive Monsters of Rock festival at England's Donington Park; two days later they gave a sweaty, incendiary performance for a packed 850-capacity house at London's Marquee Club, where they were joined onstage by Jimmy Page

THE FUTURE OF AEROSMITH:

A PUMP TOUR IS GOING TO FOLLOW AFTER THE SUCCESS OF THE RECORD. AFTER SO LONG IN THE MUSIC BUSINESS, ARE YOU GUYS TIRED OF TOURING?

Janine Janine Janine

NO WAY! NOT A CHANCE! WE LOVE IT! IN FACT, WE CAN'T WAIT TO HIT THE ROAD AGAIN! AEROSMITH HAS ALWAYS BEEN A GREAT LIVE BAND. TOURING IS AN ESSENTIAL PART OF AEROSMITH!

© ROCK 'N' ROLL COMICS NO. 57, REVOLUTIONARY COMICS, 1993. COURTESY JAY ALLEN SANFORD

Saturday Night Live, Studio 8H, Rockefeller Plaza, New York City, February 17, 1990. The band performed "Monkey on My Back" and "Janie's Got a Gun," and also appeared in a memorable "Wayne's World" skit. ALAN SINGER/NBCU PHOTO BANK VIA AP IMAGES

PUMP
WORLD TOUR
1989 - 1991

AEROSMITH

FOOD DRIVE

for a blistering five-song mini-set that included romps through the Yardbirds' "Think About It" and Led Zeppelin's "Immigrant Song," and closed with an electrifying "Train Kept a Rollin'."

By the time the *Pump* tour came to a close, the album had posted two more hit singles—"What It Takes" (No. 9) and "The Other Side" (No. 22)—and sold upwards of four million copies. Aerosmith had performed to more than a million fans around the world, and things were only about to get bigger. Speaking of their arc in an interview

with *Juke* magazine, Tyler recalled that after Perry left the band in 1979, the guitarist had commented to a journalist, "Aerosmith isn't ready for the Eighties." Said the singer, "It hurt, because in the back of my head I knew he was right. But last year we were doing a gig and I remember thinking, Well, we're ready for the Nineties, no one can deny us that. It's a nice feeling."

Indeed, no one could have anticipated their next feat. In the fall of 1991, with three albums still left on their Geffen contract, Tim Collins had a falling-out with label

head David Geffen during contract renegotiations for the band. The manager went looking for a better deal, and found one—at Sony. The numbers offered were staggering: a minimum guarantee of $30 million, consisting of a $25 million

Pump 1990 tour, the Forum, Inglewood, California. ARTIST: DANNY GARRETT/DANNYGARRETT.COM

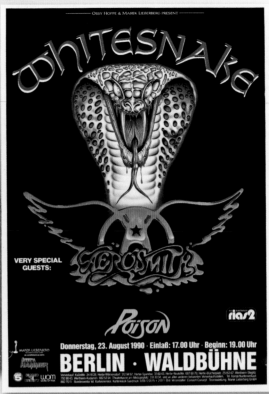

The band added several Monsters of Rock festival dates to their 1990 *Pump* tour.

MTV Unplugged, Ed Sullivan Theater, New York City, August 11, 1990. © GARY GERSHOFF/RETNA LTD.

commitment for a multi-album deal, and roughly $5 million more in renegotiated royalties on their back catalog. In addition, the band received a "superstar" royalty rate of close to 25 percent on all albums recorded for the label, putting Aerosmith in the same league as top-tier artists like the Rolling Stones and Michael Jackson.

It was hard to argue that the money wasn't well deserved: At the time, Aerosmith was among the most successful, respected, and recognizable acts in rock 'n' roll. Their last two albums had moved more than seven million units combined in the U.S. alone, and the band was a blockbuster at the gate. And yet, there was a segment of the industry that believed Sony had grossly overpaid for a "heritage act" whose best days—once again—were considered to be behind them. In a report announcing the deal in the October 3, 1991, issue of *Rolling Stone*, journalist Michael Goldberg commented, "Aerosmith will not begin recording for Sony until it has delivered two new studio albums, plus a greatest-hits anthology, to Geffen. As a result, it is unlikely that Sony will receive its first new Aerosmith album before 1995." By that time, Goldberg went on to point out, "lead singer Steven Tyler will be nearly fifty years old."

Tyler, at least, was confident they'd prove any naysayers wrong. "When critics talk about the age thing in rock and roll, they're reduced to other people's clichés," the singer told Roy Trakin. "The music still gets me higher than any dope I ever thought of doing. It's

got nothing to do with age. In my mind, I'm only 19 or 20." Perry was, as always, unshakeable and suitably blunt on the matter: "We're going to start getting some shots about our age, I'm sure," he told *Guitar World's* di Perna. "But who gives a shit? People like the music."

On their end, Sony immediately set to work pushing out product, issuing the three-CD retrospective, *Pandora's Box*, through Columbia in late 1991. (In a twist, Sony had three years earlier absorbed the CBS Records Group, including Columbia Records, meaning that all Aerosmith releases would once again bear the imprint of their old label.) The expansive set collected the band's history through *Rock in a Hard Place*, offering album cuts, rarities, outtakes, and live performances, as well as one track each from the Joe Perry Project and Whitford/ St. Holmes and a true gem, the 1966 Chain Reaction single "When I Needed You." To promote the box, Columbia released a remixed version of "Sweet Emotion"; in a nice touch, the accompanying video showed the present-day band performing in the basement of their old stomping grounds at 1325 Commonwealth Avenue in Boston.

At the same time Columbia was promoting *Pandora's Box*, Aerosmith commenced work on their next studio album for Geffen. In January 1992, the band rejoined Bruce Fairbairn, this time at Hollywood's A&M Studios. There, they worked up the beginnings of several new songs, including "Eat the Rich," a chugging riff-rocker, and two ballads, "Crazy" and "Amazing," the latter a poignant

redemptive tale penned by Tyler and old cohort Richie Supa. In contrast to *Pump*, the sessions this time were slow going—at one point their Geffen A&R man, John Kalodner, discouraged with the material that was coming together, went so far as to threaten to remove his name from the record. Recalled Tyler to journalist John Stix in 1993, "I heard Kalodner say, 'It's not as good as "Janie,"' or, 'Do you have a "Janie" on there?'"

Furthermore, relations between Collins and the band had taken a distressing turn: The manager, ever fearful of someone falling off the wagon and putting the sobriety— and success—of the entire unit in jeopardy, began pushing hard for individual members to undergo additional in-patient rehab stints. In early 1991, Tyler, at Collins' behest, was sent to Sierra Tucson in Arizona for sex addiction therapy; later that year, Perry, Hamilton, and Whitford were dispatched to the same hospital for what was, in Hamilton's words, a "recharge." But, he explained in *Walk This Way*, "It was Tim's fear of the always-impending relapse. . . . Tim said, 'If you're not in recovery, I can't be your manager, and I won't sell Columbia a bill of goods.' He was playing a heavy card: Either you do what I say or I'll blow off the Sony deal."

With an atmosphere of uneasiness all around, the band eventually split Hollywood and returned, once again, to Vancouver's Little Mountain Sound. Throughout the fall and winter of 1992 they continued to write material and also tracked the remainder of the album. When Fairbairn encountered

Nº 07978

Strictly Limited Edition Numbered 12" Picture Disc

Livin' on the Edge

Limited edition 12-inch picture disc featuring "Livin' on the Edge" b/w "Don't Stop" and "Flesh," U.K., 1993.

FEVER

PRO-CD-4692

Sleeve art for "Blind Man" promotional CD, 1993

Sleeve art for "Fever" promotional CD, 1993.

difficulty in constructing a final mix, up-and-coming producer Brendan O'Brien, then making a name for himself for his work with the Black Crowes, was brought in to remix the entire effort at the eleventh hour.

Finally, after many stressful months, *Get a Grip* was released to the world in April 1993. With its long gestation period and incredibly layered sound—"We did 8,000 overdubs," Perry told Alan di Perna, "way over the top"—and various guest appearances (Don Henley on "Amazing," Lenny Kravitz on "Line Up"), the album certainly bore all the marks of a big-budget, superstar effort. It also came with a long list of outside songwriters: Child and Vallance made multiple appearances each—"Flesh" and "Crazy" for the former, "Eat the Rich," "Boogie

Man," and the title track for the latter—while new names included Taylor Rhodes ("Cryin'"), Damn Yankees' Jack Blades and Tommy Shaw ("Shut Up and Dance"), Kravitz ("Line Up"), and producer and writer Mark Hudson ("Gotta Love It" and "Livin' on the Edge"). When di Perna pointed out the larger pool of collaborators onboard this time around, a somewhat exasperated Tyler responded, "So sue me. As someone once said, 'If this was easy, everybody would be doing it.'" Released at a moment when grunge dominated the airwaves and alternative rock was just beginning to ascend as the music of choice for '90s youth, *Get a Grip*, with its glossy, uptempo rockers and sweeping power ballads, seemed almost anachronistic. But Aerosmith's

strength and momentum was undeniable, so much so that the effort became their first to reach No. 1 on the *Billboard* album charts, and went on to spawn five hit singles: "Livin' on the Edge," "Eat the Rich," and a trio of ballads—"Cryin'," "Amazing," and "Crazy"—whose impact would be as much visual as musical. The latter three songs each were paired with a cinematic—and steamy—clip from director Marty Callner, all starring teenage sexpot actress Alicia Silverstone; furthermore, for "Crazy," Callner and the band introduced a Sapphic undercurrent in the relationship between Silverstone and a schoolgirl friend. That friend, in a subversive twist, was played by a young model—Tyler's daughter Liv, the girl he had sired with Bebe Buell in 1977, and who for much

of her young life was raised believing Todd Rundgren to be her biological father. Following Tyler's emergence from his drug haze in the late '80s, Buell had seen fit to begin slowly reintroducing father and daughter. Finally, in 1991, Tyler went so far as to legally establish his paternity via a blood test. When the results came back, Tyler recalled in *Walk This Way*, "I offered Liv my name. 'Use it,' I told her. 'Liv Tyler.'"

As *Get a Grip* dominated the charts and MTV, Aerosmith was cleaning up on the road. The *Get a Grip* tour launched on June 2, 1993, in Topeka, Kansas, and over the course of eighteen months took the band through the U.S., Canada, Europe, and Japan, as well as their first stops in Central and South America and almost a dozen countries, including Romania, Poland, Russia, Israel, and Spain. There were a few personal snags—in March

Monsters of Rock, Donington Park, England, June 4, 1994. MICK HUTSON/REDFERNS/GETTY IMAGES

Eleventh Annual MTV Video Music Awards, Radio City Music Hall, New York City, September 8, 1994. AP PHOTO/BEBETO MATTHEWS

1994, Kramer's father passed away, and that May, Whitford missed several Japanese dates to return home to visit his ailing father (his responsibilities were handled by David Minehan, guitarist in the Boston band Neighborhoods, whose 1990 album *Hoodwinked* Whitford had co-produced). Otherwise, there was nothing but highs. The band topped the bill at the 1994 Monsters of Rock festival at Donington Park, and on August 13 of that year—a quarter-century after Tyler and Kramer ran into one another at the original—headlined the second night of the Woodstock 1994 festival in

Saugerties, New York, playing before 350,000 during a set that began amid an early-morning rainstorm and ended with a fireworks display at 3:30 a.m. "The first one I showed up as a spectator," Tyler recalled to *Q*'s Mat Snow in 1995. "But this one I was the carrot on the end of the stick."

The *Get a Grip* tour wrapped on December 19, 1994, with a celebratory gig at Mama Kin Music Hall, a new, 600-capacity club on Boston's Lansdowne Street in which Aerosmith were part owners. The hometown venue was merely another notch in the band's collective belt. By this time, *Get a Grip* had sold

more than twelve million copies worldwide, launched four Top 40 singles, and earned numerous awards, including multiple Grammys and MTV VMAs. *Big Ones*, a compilation album of Geffen-era hits issued that November, was another smash, reaching No. 6 on *Billboard* and going on to move more than four million units in the U.S. Furthermore, domestically, *Permanent Vacation* was approaching the five million mark, while *Pump* was hovering in the range of seven million copies sold.

Visually, the band was everywhere. Between sold-out arena and stadium gigs, they had appeared on *Saturday Night Live*, the *MTV Video Music Awards* and *Europe Music Awards*, the *Grammy Awards*, the *Late Show with David Letterman*, and numerous other television programs. The band's ubiquity was such that in June 1994, they were honored with their own arcade game, *Revolution X*, a Midway shoot-'em-up that saw players gunning down bad guys to the sounds of "Sweet Emotion" and "Toys in the Attic" in an effort to save Tyler & Co. from a cadre of corrupt government and military forces that had taken them hostage. Coupled with their participation in a guitar simulation game, *Quest for Fame*, it seemed as if Aerosmith had at this point actually transcended the physical realm. But Tyler's goals were set still higher. "People ask me, 'What do you have left to do, Steven?'" he commented to *Rolling Stone*'s David Fricke in 1994. The singer, of course, had an answer at the ready: "Fuck you. I'm looking to be the lounge act on the space shuttle so I can sing 'Walk This Way' on the ceiling. That's the kind of guy I am."

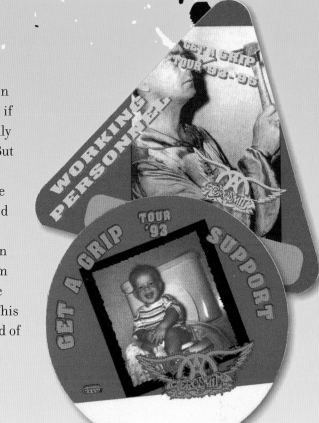

Get a Grip tour, Wembley Arena, London, December 7–8, 1993. MICK HUTSON/REDFERNS/GETTY IMAGES

Pump
by Bill Holdship

Depending on how one looks at it, Aerosmith had either nothing or everything left to prove—and perhaps lose—when they entered the studio in November 1988 to begin work on *Pump*, their tenth studio album. It was only two months after the final leg of their *Permanent Vacation* tour, one of the most successful rock treks of the year and their first ever clean-and-sober tour.

The tour had concluded with Guns N' Roses as the opening act just as that band exploded to become one of the biggest rock bands in the world. Headlines were written regarding the irony of a bunch of new-kid-on-the-block heroin addicts, known for debauchery and nonstop partying, touring with the now-former Toxic Twins. (On the final night of the tour, GN'R joined their hosts onstage to jam on "Mama Kin," which they had covered on their debut EP.)

With *Vacation* now one of the most phenomenal comebacks in the history of rock—hit singles and heavy MTV play making them some of the oldest dudes on the airwaves—Aerosmith had transformed from screw-ups into elder statesmen of rock in just a few years' time. The band reinstalled *Vacation* producer Bruce Fairbairn behind the mixing board and decided to shoot for the sky . . . and then some.

Whether or not the band wrestled more control over this album away from A&R man John Kalodner—there is some debate on the subject—is irrelevant. But it's true that two of the best songs here (and one of the biggest hits) are solely Tyler-Perry compositions, while a third (and yet another hit single) was created solely by Tyler and Brad Whitford. Not only that, but *Pump* feels more like a *genuine* album in its flow than *Vacation*, which had some filler here and there. Indeed, critics of the era compared *Pump* to *Toys in the Attic*—and, indeed, various tracks are sometimes connected via brief snippets of dulcimer-based hillbilly, hoodoo blues, or other experimental music, just the way genuine concept albums of yore once were. And whereas *Vacation* kicked off with a track that seemed perhaps too intent on approximating the popular big hair-metal sound of the time, *Pump*'s opening track, "Young

A number of outside collaborators, as with its two predecessors, gave *Pump* added dimension and opened the band's sound to more influences.

Lust," has a roar, rhythm, and raunch that brings to mind Aerosmith at their 1970s best.

So what does a clean-and-sober pop-metal band sing about after years of mainly celebrating good times? Well, in the band's autobiography, Tyler confesses that he spent a year "going wild with women," making up for time lost when opiates had destroyed his libido. This was not an unfortunate development, however, since the pop-metal of the time was about nothing if not sex, even if most of the lunkheads of the genre lacked anything that could even be described as subtlety. Yet even when Tyler squawks "I'll shove my tongue right between your cheeks" on "F.I.N.E.*" (the title's an acronym for *Fucked up, Insecure, Neurotic, and Emotional*), there is a cleverness on display in the wordplay, including a, um, tongue-in-cheek reference to PRMC music censorship group head and future vice-presidential wife Tipper Gore.

It was interesting and even endearing to find these forty-year-old rockers still addressing youthful concerns; the bluesy "Don't Get Mad, Get Even" repeats John Belushi's mantra from *Animal House*. And sex *is* universal, after all, and so the raunch continues on songs like the stompin' "My Girl" and, of course, the hit single "Love in an Elevator," which Tyler claims is based on firsthand experience. On the album version, the song kicks off with the wink-wink, nudge-nudge sexy voice of a female elevator operator asking "Mr. Tyler" if he wants to "go down."

But for all the juvenile "boys will be boys" nonsense of that intro, the song proved to be one of the most ambitious, atmospheric, and experimental musical numbers the band had achieved to that date—modern-sounding yet completely and identifiably Aerosmith. Ditto the album's second hit single, "Janie's Got a Gun," which, like its predecessor, went top five on the *Billboard* charts (it later scored a Grammy Award) and also featured a like-minded

experimental musical feel. "Janie" was also unique in that it was the first Aerosmith song to ever address an important social issue: incest and child rape, an interesting concept on an album that mostly deals with lust and sex, although that might make the message even more powerful in the end.

Elsewhere, the band brings the *pop* and the *rawk* in equal doses. "The Other Side" is so pop, in fact, it got the band sued by Motown songwriters Holland, Dozier, and Holland for sounding *too much* like their "Standing in the Shadows of Love." While there's a similar melodic line, it's not the same song but actually a pretty fine one in its own right. Desmond Child joins up with Tyler again for the hit power ballad "What It Takes," which closes *Pump* and at the very least demonstrates why in 2010 Tyler was chosen to be a judge on TV's *American Idol*. Instrumentally, "Voodoo Medicine Man," with its opening *masturbating with a noose* and *kick out the jams* lyrical lines, illustrates that the five members of the band are in as

fine form here as any hard-rock band on the planet at the time.

Earlier on *Pump*, the band rocks especially hard on the powerful "Monkey on My Back," *Pump*'s other tune that goes beyond just sex, this one addressing drug abuse and addiction. Of course, just the very existence of an album this good from a newly clearheaded band is probably as powerful an anti-drug statement as there is.

Combined with the artistry and success of *Permanent Vacation*, *Pump* is exactly where Aerosmith began to achieve iconic rock status. The album presents everything Aerosmith ever was, as well as everything it would or could ever be. No longer would critics refer to them as "a poor man's Rolling Stones," which never seemed all that accurate or fair. From here on out, Aerosmith would be on a level of their own and in absolutely nobody's shadow.

"Love in an Elevator (Edit)" b/w "Young Lust," 1989.

Seven-inch picture disc featuring "Janie's Got a Gun" b/w "Voodoo Medicine Man," 1989.

Get a Grip

by Neil Daniels

Aerosmith's eleventh studio album was unleashed in 1993, four years after their mega-successful, Grammy Award–winning opus *Pump*. By the end of 1995 *Get a Grip* had sold a very healthy seven million copies in the United States alone—just as many as its predecessor. Worldwide, *Get a Grip* has since achieved sales of more than 20 million, making it one of the top-selling rock albums of all time. Suffice it to say, with *Get a Grip*, Aerosmith cemented their status as the biggest, most popular American rock band in the world. Their drug- and booze-addled days were apparently behind them as they produced a steady stream of terrific hard-rock albums that not only pleased their enthusiastic fan base but also the reluctant rock press too.

GET A GRIP

Get a Grip, Aerosmith's fourth and last LP on Geffen Records, was produced by the late, great Bruce Fairbairn, whose previous production credits included *Pump*, Bon Jovi's *Slippery When Wet* and *New Jersey*, and albums by AC/DC and Poison. Recorded at A&M Studios in Los Angeles and Little Mountain Sound Studio in Vancouver during two periods—December 1991 to March 1992 and October 1992 to March 1993, respectively—*Get a Grip* features a number of outside collaborators, just like its two predecessors. This gave the album an added dimension, opening up the band's sound to more influences. It was a shrewd move and it obviously worked to the band's advantage. Don Henley contributed vocals to "Amazing," while guitarist Lenny Kravitz added some funk to "Line Up." Other notable guests included Jim Vallance, Mark Hudson, Desmond Child, Jack Blades, Tommy Shaw, Richard Supa, and Taylor Rhodes.

The American release featured fourteen songs (the international version was beefed up by inserting "Can't Stop Messin'" as the thirteenth track before "Amazing" and "Boogie Man." Following the twenty-three-second "Intro," the underrated gem "Eat the Rich" kicks the LP into action with a fast pace and feisty guitars. The song found little success as the album's second single, but fans loved it and it found its way onto the band's set list.

Opening the band's sound to outside influences was a shrewd move that worked to the band's advantage.

The slightly underwhelming title track follows "Eat the Rich" and precedes "Fever," the latter being the only song on the album written by Steven Tyler and Joe Perry without an external collaborator; "Fever" was also the album's fifth single and one of the LP's hardest rockin' efforts. The apparently (at least) semiautobiographical lyrics relate the story of a band that has given up the druggin' for somewhat safer vices, mainly sex.

"Livin' on the Edge" follows. The first single lifted from the album, and a hit in both the United States and the U.K., the song has been noted for its socially aware observations and infectious melody. It went on to become a permanent fixture in the band's live set in addition to earning a Grammy Award (Best Rock Performance by a Duo or Group with Vocal) in 1993.

Cowritten by Desmond Child, "Flesh" is a smooth five-minute track that precedes the Joe Perry–sung "Walk on Down." One of the album's heaviest tracks follows. With a thumping rhythm section and the mighty twin-guitar attack of Perry and Brad Whitford, "Shut Up and Dance," cowritten by Jack Blades of Night Ranger and Tommy Shaw of Styx, reached No. 24 on the U.K. charts but failed to chart in the U.S. despite its inclusion in the 1993 Mike Myers movie Wayne's World 2.

"Cryin'" took on a life of its own when it was released as Get a Grip's third single in the summer of 1993, aided and abetted by a video featuring a young Alicia Silverstone. The song has become one of Aerosmith's best-known ballads.

The seventh and final song released as a single from Get a Grip, "Crazy" follows the mostly forgettable "Gotta Give Love." Co-penned by Desmond Child, "Crazy" was accompanied by another memorable video featuring Silverstone (her third video appearance for the band) and Tyler's teenaged daughter Liv. The song is also notable as the album's second Grammy winner for Best Rock Performance by a Duo or Group with Vocal, this time in 1994.

"Line Up" stands out for its funky groove, while the emotionally charged fourth single, "Amazing," shows the band's prowess in full stead (and another video featuring Silverstone). "Boogie Man" closes the album with a stellar example of the band's musicianship.

When Get a Grip was released in the United States in April 1993, the critical praise was unanimous. Even the revered "dean of rock critics" Robert Christgau gave the album undying

praise along with an A- rating in the Village Voice. For many diehard fans, Get a Grip was what an Aerosmith album should sound like: the band had cleaned themselves up and rocked from start to finish. Power ballads complement hard-rock tracks, and lyrics range from cheeky teenaged themes to social commentary.

There are also melodies galore, the band proving that, with the passing of grunge, there was room for a good old-fashioned rock band that still sounded modern and vital. With Get a Grip, Aerosmith injected some much-needed excitement, charisma, and a relentless energy into the American rock scene of the mid-'90s. The album reached No. 1 on the North American Billboard 200 album chart, while eight singles reached the top 10. Perhaps in its modernity the album was too far removed from Aerosmith's blues-rock roots for some longstanding fans, but on the whole, more than fifteen years later, it remains one of the band's strongest albums and stands the test of time. Like its predecessor Pump, Get a Grip excelled both as an artistically successful and commercially viable album. The band had, indeed, gotten a grip.

CD sleeve for "Eat the Rich" EP, Japan, 1993. The CD also featured the LP versions of "Love in an Elevator," "Janie's Got a Gun," and "Dude (Looks Like a Lady)."

Sleeve art for "Cryin'" promotional CD, 1993.

CD sleeve for "Crazy" EP, U.S., 1993. The CD also featured "orchestral" and "acoustic" versions of the title track, the "orchestral" version of "Amazing," and the LP version of "Gotta Love It."

chapter 13

Feelin' F.I.N.E.

Nineteen ninety-five opened with another milestone moment, with Perry and Tyler delivering the induction speech welcoming Led Zeppelin into the Rock and Roll Hall of Fame at a January 12 ceremony at the Waldorf-Astoria in Manhattan. Afterward, the two joined Page, Robert Plant, John Paul Jones, and Jason Bonham onstage, where they jammed for a half-hour on classics like Zeppelin's "Bring It On Home," the Yardbirds' "For Your Love," and the steadfast "Train Kept a Rollin'."

In an interview with journalist Mat Snow that same year, Tyler took a moment to reflect on Aerosmith's extraordinary second coming: "The last eight years," the singer noted, "were what the first ten years were supposed to be like." And yet, Aerosmith was about to enter a period in which, much like in the early '80s, their very survival would be threatened.

That spring, Perry and Tyler convened at the guitarist's basement home studio outside Boston to begin working up songs for the follow-up to *Get a Grip*. The album would be their first effort for Sony under the terms of their new multimillion-dollar deal, and the pressure was on. "It [felt] like our first record, ever," Hamilton remarked to Alan di Perna in

"[Their] musicianship is improved, like, tenfold. But, the energy that they had in the beginning—that they manage to sustain—I think is the key to their longevity."

—Producer Jack Douglas, quoted by R. Scott Bolton and Lou Moreau at roughedge.com

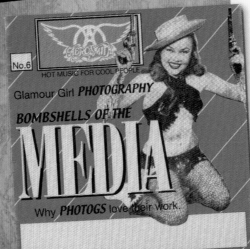

Facing page: Nine Lives tour, Madison Square Garden, New York City, August 6, 1997. KEVIN MAZUR/WIREIMAGE/ GETTY IMAGES

The *Nine Lives* tour was a globetrotting affair that kept the band on the road for two years. Ahoy Stadium, Rotterdam, May 27, 1997. PAUL BERGEN/REDFERNS/GETTY IMAGES

a 1997 interview for *Guitar World*. Over the next few months the two collaborated with an array of outside writers, including musician Marti Frederiksen, Stone Temple Pilots bassist Robert DeLeo, Janet Jackson producers Jimmy Jam and Terry Lewis, and old standbys Taylor Rhodes and Mark Hudson. They also partnered with Glen Ballard, who had worked as a staff producer for Quincy Jones and would soon find incredible success helming Alanis Morissette's *Jagged Little Pill*. Forging an immediate bond with the producer, the three decamped to Miami in early 1996 to begin work on the album in earnest.

There, things would begin to unravel for the band. From the start John Kalodner, who had followed the band to Columbia, was rather inexplicably sidelined from the project at the behest of Tim Collins—effectively estranging from the band the man who had served as their guiding force for several years. Then, just as recording was about to get underway at Criteria Studios, Kramer, in an apparent delayed reaction to his father's passing two years earlier, was gripped by a deep depression and found himself unable to contribute to the sessions. He soon fled Miami for Southern California, where he checked into the Steps rehabilitation center. In a 1997 interview with *Metal Edge*'s Gerri Miller, Kramer referred to his condition as the "Deep Blue Funk." He explained: "There were a lot of personal issues that were coming up for me . . . and I was incapacitated to the point where I couldn't even play. I had to go away."

Down their A&R man and now their drummer, Aerosmith forged ahead, continuing to write songs with Ballard, Desmond Child, Richie Supa, and others, and picking up ex–Average White Band sticksman and session ace Steve Ferrone to fill in for Kramer in the studio. It was, to say the least, a new way of working for the band: Ferrone was a considerably more refined and nuanced player than Kramer, while Ballard, unlike Jack Douglas or even Bruce Fairbairn, was a thoroughly modern producer who fully embraced digital recording techniques. "He had top of the line ADAT's with the new Apogee converters, and we were fuckin' up and running with 50,000 tracks," Tyler told di Perna of the producer. "Glen's vibe was, 'You want it? You got it. Can you do that? You can do anything.'" But, as Perry recalled in *Walk This Way*, "We did a lot of experimenting. . . . Then we began hearing from other people that it didn't sound as rock as it could have. It didn't sound like Aerosmith."

Possibly compounding their problems were rumors that, after engineering Kalodner's dismissal, Collins began fomenting unrest within the band. In particular, Kramer believed the manager was working to isolate the drummer, away at Steps, from the rest of the members. "He told [them] I needed to be by myself," Kramer told *Mojo*'s Phil Sutcliffe in 1999, "when the reality was I needed to hear from them to know I had their support." Essentially, Kramer said, "Tim lied to my partners. He told them the record company was putting pressure on them to get the album done. This

Nine Lives **promo photo.** AP PHOTO/ARCHIV

was not true. He was trying to get rid of me."

Indeed, on the band's end, Tyler confirmed to di Perna, "We were getting reports that [Joey] didn't know if he wanted to stay in the band or when he was coming back." But Kramer did in fact return to Aerosmith, in the spring of 1996, just as they were wrapping up sessions at Criteria. With tracking complete, the band returned to Boston and prepared to reconvene with Ballard in L.A. to mix the album.

They would never get there. Back in Boston, Collins called a meeting with Perry, Hamilton, Whitford, and Kramer and unloaded a litany of accusations against Tyler: that he had reason to believe the singer had relapsed with drugs, had designs

on firing the bassist and drummer, and had been acting out sexually in Miami. (Collins went so far as to call the singer's wife, Teresa, at home where she was tending to the couple's two young children, Chelsea and Taj, to report on her husband's alleged infidelity.) In the end, the manager convinced the four members to draft a joint letter to Tyler threatening, in the face of this supposed behavior, his termination from the band.

Truth be told, Tyler had professed to living it up in Miami. "I loved it. Sylvester Stallone came to my birthday party," he told *Metal Edge*'s Miller. "I was hanging with Jack [Nicholson], Oliver Stone, Michael Caine, Quincy Jones. I had a blast." But, he continued, "Tim had told the band that I was getting high, having

GERARD DROUOT PRESENTE

Nine Lives
TOUR '97

SAMEDI 7 JUIN : LYON-HALLE TONY GARNIER
MERCREDI 11 JUIN
PARIS BERCY
CONCERTS À 20H
1ère partie : **KULA SHAKER**

LOCATIONS LYON : FNAC, 3615 FNAC, TICKET+ 01 49 87 50 50, FRANCE BILLET 01 42 31 31 31.
LOCATIONS PARIS : FNAC, VIRGIN MEGASTORE, CARREFOUR, GALERIES LAFAYETTE,
FRANCE BILLET 01 42 31 31 31, BERCY 01 44 68 44 68,
3615 RESERV, 3615 FUN RADIO, 3615 M6.

HARD N HEAVY   COLUMBIA   GUITARIST

Nine Lives 1997 tour.

BLOCK 103
LOWER TIER   ROW   H   SEAT   10
NYNEX ARENA MANCHESTER
MCP PRESENTS
THE NINE LIVES TOUR
* AEROSMITH *
PLUS SHED SEVEN
SAT 10 MAY 97 7 30PM

PRGM 17.50
£   17.50

May 10, 1997, Manchester, England.

a good old time with Sly Stallone and the models, and that I wanted another drummer and bass player. All those things [were] not true. The band sent me a letter, and I said, 'What the fuck are you talking about? I just got finished writing the best album we got!'"

The letter drove a stake through Aerosmith and froze Tyler out of the band for close to two months. It wasn't until the summer of '96, when all five members retreated to Steps in an attempt at reconciliation, that light was shed on the situation. There, as the band members compared notes, Collins' machinations became apparent.

In more recent years, Kramer, for one, made efforts to explain Collins'

behavior at the time. "Like the rest of us, Tim's insecurities ran deep," the drummer wrote in *Hit Hard*. "[He] was a control addict with an insatiable appetite for ruling the world and the people around him, using fear, shame and what felt like a twisted version of the principles of 12-step recovery as his tools for manipulation." Ironically, the drummer added, "Tim had been so worried about losing control of the band that he came close to breaking it up altogether."

In the end, however, the manager merely engineered his own exit. In late July 1996, the band called an early-morning meeting with Collins at the Four Seasons hotel in Boston and officially ended their twelve-year partnership.

Collins, for his part, did not go quietly, taking his allegations public within days of his dismissal. A report by John Colapinto and Matt Hendrickson in the October 3, 1996, issue of *Rolling Stone* laid bare the turmoil that had enveloped Aerosmith over the preceding

months. The journalists quoted Collins as stating he had received "phone calls from literally 20 different people when [Tyler] was in Florida, saying that they either saw or knew he was using drugs." Tyler countered in an interview for the same story, stating, "I haven't had a drink or drug in 10 years, and I'm really fucking proud of it."

In the aftermath, Tyler best summed up his feelings regarding Collins to Gerri Miller: "He was the best manager we could have in the beginning because he had the same problems we had and we worked through them together. We went to meetings together, we talked things out. But he owes a lot of apologies to a lot of people, me being first and foremost." Regardless, the singer added, "The band was around before Tim Collins, and it will be around after Tim Collins."

But Aerosmith wasn't out of the woods yet. At the same time they were battling Collins, representatives at Sony informed them their new label was unhappy with the Miami material and believed it to be unrepresentative of the band's sound. Sony insisted they return to the studio to recut the album and record additional tracks. By this time however, Ballard was no longer available to helm the sessions. In his place Kalodner, now reinstated on the project, suggested South African–born producer Kevin "Caveman" Shirley, whose reputation as an analog aficionado made him in many ways Ballard's opposite. In September 1996, the band and Shirley commenced recording anew at Avatar Studios in New York City; if nothing else, Kramer was pleased by this turn of events, as he was now able to be fully present in the process. "It was great news to me," he told di Perna in *Guitar World*. "By this time I'd fought my way out of the blue funk, and I was ready to go."

Finally, in April 1997, almost four years after *Get a Grip*, Columbia issued *Nine Lives*, Aerosmith's twelfth studio effort and first under their Sony deal. Boasting thirteen tracks and running in excess of an hour, the album was a sprawling, raging affair, packed with flat-out rockers ("Falling in Love [Is Hard on the Knees]" and "Nine Lives"), elaborate ballads ("Hole in My Soul" and "Full Circle"), lush pop-rock tunes ("Pink" and "Kiss Your Past Goodbye"), and the odd exotic excursion ("Taste of India," the intro to "Fallen Angels"). By all indications,

in the years since *Get a Grip*, the band had indeed been missed: *Nine Lives* debuted at No. 1 on *Billboard*—their second chart-topper in a row—went platinum within weeks of release, and spawned three hit singles in "Falling in Love (Is Hard on the Knees)," "Hole in My Soul," and "Pink," which earned the band another Grammy (Best Rock Performance by a Duo or Group with Vocal) and MTV Video Music Award (Best Rock Video).

The *Nine Lives* tour was another globetrotting affair, kicking off in the U.K. on May 8 and keeping the band on the road more than two full years. They logged upwards of two hundred shows over the course of the tour, though there were several hiccups. At a gig in Anchorage, Alaska, on April 29, 1998, Tyler brought his

special guest **Kenny Wayne Shepherd**

SATURDAY JANUARY 3rd
US AIRWAYS ARENA

Tickets available at all TicketMaster outlets or charge by phone 410.481.SEAT. Use your *VISA* card to purchase tickets.
A CELLAR DOOR EVENT

Nine Lives 1998 tour, Landover, Maryland.

microphone stand down hard on his knee during "Mama Kin," tearing a ligament and leading to the cancellation and postponement of close to three months of dates. Just as the band was set to go back out that August, Kramer was involved in a freak accident at a gas station in Boston when his Ferrari caught on fire. The drummer suffered minor burns across his body, resulting in another month of pushed-back gigs.

When Aerosmith finally returned to the road in September '98, they were no longer promoting only the *Nine Lives* album. Earlier that spring, the band had contributed several songs—including two newly recorded numbers—to the soundtrack of the Michael Bay action flick *Armageddon*, which starred, among others, Tyler's

Nine Lives tour, Madison Square
Garden, New York City, August 6, 1997.

KEVIN MAZUR/WIREIMAGE/GETTY IMAGES

164

Nine Lives tour, PNC Bank Arts Center, Holmdel, New Jersey, October 17, 1998.
© FRANK WHITE

daughter Liv. One of these new tunes, "I Don't Want to Miss a Thing," was a syrupy, sentimental ballad penned by songwriter Diane Warren, best known for composing similar material for the likes of Toni Braxton and Celine Dion (the song, in fact, was originally slated for the latter artist). Though hardly standard Aerosmith fare—"Angel" sounded like a bare-bones rocker in comparison—"I Don't Want to Miss a Thing" was an absolute smash, debuting at No. 1 on the *Billboard* singles chart upon its release on September 1 (and remaining there for four weeks), and topping the charts in numerous countries around the world.

The track's success brought Aerosmith a new level of public recognition—including an Academy Award nomination in 1999 for Best Song—while again igniting the argument of whether they had veered too far off course in search of mainstream glories. Not for the first time in their career, the band found itself in defensive mode. "There's always going to be the little boys club that loves to kick ass and wants nothing except testosterone-charged rock 'n' roll," Perry told this writer in 2002. "But there's a broader picture: we make music for everybody, and doing songs like 'I Don't Want to Miss a Thing' makes sure that we don't miss anyone." That same year, Tyler told *Blender*'s Ben Mitchell, "Is it a soppy ballad that I hate? No, I like the song." What's more, he added, "My daughter was in the movie, and it's a great fucking movie."

Tyler performs "I Don't Want to Miss a Thing" during the 41st Annual Grammy Awards, Shrine Auditorium, Los Angeles, February 24, 1999. AP PHOTO/KEVORK DJANSEZIAN

AEROSMITH
a LITTLE SOUTH of SANITY

STARK, RAVING LIVE!
23 LARGER THAN LIVE TRACKS!
From the band that put rock 'n' roll insanity on the map!

Departure Date October 20

The final Aerosmith product under their Geffen contract was a two-disc live album that saw the band reunited with producer Jack Douglas.

Regardless, the song's ubiquity brought in greater numbers on the road, where the still-ongoing *Nine Lives* dates were rechristened the *Little South of Sanity* tour to coincide with the October release of a double live album of the same name. The final Aerosmith product under their Geffen contract, the two-disc set saw the band reunited with producer Jack Douglas, who had last worked with them on 1982's *Rock in a Hard Place*. In an interview with roughedge .com, Douglas noted that, more than fifteen years on, "the [*band's*] musicianship is improved, like, tenfold. But, the energy that they had in the beginning—that they manage to sustain—I think is the key to their longevity. And I think that has to do with the fact that they're still having fun. And you can tell."

Indeed, the band would have a bit more fun to ride out the rest of the millennium. After coming off tour in July 1999, they helped open the Rock 'n' Roller Coaster at Walt Disney World Resort in Orlando, Florida. The Aerosmith-themed attraction, which featured filmed segments and voiceovers from the members, as well as plenty of the band's music, saw passengers embark on a "limo

ride"—albeit one that went from zero to sixty in 2.8 seconds—that ended at the backstage door of a concert venue. That September, Tyler and Perry reunited with Run-DMC onstage at the MTV Video Music Awards, where they were joined by Kid Rock for a run-through of "Walk This Way." Finally, the band closed out the year with a short tour dubbed Roar of the Dragon, consisting of six Japanese dates, including a New Year's Eve gig at the Osaka Dome. All in all, almost three decades in, Aerosmith was at the top of their game and enjoying every minute of it. "There's always something new, and it's those things that keep it going for us," Perry told journalist Ian Fortnam. "If there's more shit like this coming down, who knows what it's going to be? I just plan to be here when it does."

Nine Lives 1999 tour.

Nine Lives **tour, Wembley Stadium, London, June 26, 1999.** ROBERTA PARKIN/REDFERNS/GETTY IMAGES

Nine Lives

by Phil Sutcliffe

Nine Lives emerged from a world of confusion. Aerosmith's manager, Tim Collins, who'd led them out of addiction hell, was suddenly caught out seeding false rumors that ten-years-clean Steven Tyler had fallen off the wagon—"Back on drugs, out of my mind, and chasing 'round Florida with Sylvester Stallone, fucking all these women," as the singer sarcastically told this writer in a 1998 *Mojo* interview.

Meanwhile, further Collins maneuvering had ousted ever-present drummer Joey Kramer from the Glenn Ballard–produced spring 1996 *Nine Lives* sessions in Florida. Suffering a deep depression after his father's death, Kramer found himself a remote, pained onlooker while session ace Steve Ferrone replaced him.

But then the band fired Collins, and their "new" label, Columbia, rejected the album. At least the remake gave Aerosmith the chance to bring back their old friend. "To find an Aerosmith record couldn't get done without me, that felt good!" Kramer told me. "I wasn't fully recuperated, but I had to go in and dig down deep. I think my partners gained respect for me, observing me come back as strong as I was able."

If he didn't feel strong, he certainly played strong. The opening title track hammered out the message: Joey's back. Nicely crazy from the

Perry and Tyler wrote the title track (with Marti Frederiksen) after seeing AC/DC live. It shows.

When the band learned that the original cover art was offensive to some Hindus, Columbia apologized and issued a new cover.

first moment, it slings out a big, howling guitar swerve and drops in some meows from an unconvincing feline impersonator, then Kramer lets rip with an almighty rockin' thunder that Zeus, Thor, and all the other ancient gods of celestial uproar would have applauded.

Perry and Tyler wrote "Nine Lives" (with Marti Frederiksen) after seeing AC/DC live. It shows. Hard guitars and Tyler at his franticfunmost—it's wondrous under the circumstances how spontaneous his lyrics feel, like a mad improv, inventing words where orthodox vocabulary comes up short. *There's a new cool / Some kind verbooty*. Eh? When exactly did we board this ship? Er, join this army?

No matter, "Nine Lives" starts a run of four brain-shaking rib-ticklers. Slowish "Falling in Love (Is Hard on the Knees)" sounds sort of serious, but even the title's a gag. So self-mockery and the gut thrill of Perry firing sour guitar lines alongside Tyler's voice—the Teetotal Twins, familiar yet inspired.

"You mention the Beatles and my insides get all cheery," Tyler once told me. Well, George Harrison being Aerosmith's fave Moptop, "Hole in My Soul" has the Perry–Whitford guitars gently weeping, except during the rather calculated "Is it over?"

dramatics of the chorus (cowriter Desmond Child's fingerprint?). And "Taste of India" features Ravi Shankar student, Ramesh Mishra, delivering bendy bhaji sounds on a sarangi, while Tyler provides aromatic allusions and the spice, the sauce, the sensual, and the sexual *lingers on the tip of my tongue*.

The rest of *Nine Lives*, although less consistent, still sports plenty of midlife-teen rowdiness. "Ain't That a Bitch" takes those turmeric strings from "A Taste of India"—arranged by Beck's father, David Campbell—and comes up with something new to Aerosmith. Suddenly it's the cabaret, a muted trumpet, a wonky orchestra, and Tyler singing like Sinatra's grandfather, all "set 'em up, Joe" weary regret, in violent contrast to the stomping chorus.

It's worth raising another *Nine Lives* characteristic here: interesting outros all over the place. "Ain't That a Bitch" slow-fades with the strings surging around *yeah-yeahs* and guitar snippets. On "The Farm," it's more strings, strange vocal harmonies, and a closing clip from *The Wizard of Oz*, where the Tin Man and friends long for the brain, heart, and nerve they lack. Not coincidentally, it's a (very retrospective) drug song, working adroitly on the notion that the sweet movie characters are more self-aware than the

squalling rock star—until the hollers of *I got terminal uniqueness / I'm an egocentric man* subside into the resigned hook line *Take me to the farm* (as in rehab).

Surprisingly, given the relapse rumor imbroglio, "The Farm" leads into another tale of heroin and the teetering edge of insanity (Aerosmith refusing to deny their past, or recognizing its market value, or both). Thrashing "Crash" feels totally Perry/Tyler at their most unhinged—*Doin' tons of colon blow / Stuffing it in every hole*. Add "Kiss Your Past Goodbye" to the list of substantial satisfactions too: grit and flair combined in the crunching grind of it and Perry's brief outbursts of sour discord, keep the emotions real when the story starts from *I saw you on the avenue / While other men were having you*.

Which leaves the tooth-suckers and brow-furrowers. "Pink," sleazy-by-numbers, is only okay pop-rock; "Attitude Adjustment," angry by rote, is only okay hard rock. Despite touches of '60s Brit R&B, "Something's Gotta Give" charges along shapelessly (nice outro, mind). And "Full Circle" is a stolid trudge, dragged down by un-Aerosmith clichéd, advice-giving sentiments (*Time / Don't let it slip away . . .*).

Nine Lives is a big album, though; play it soup-to-nuts and it feels good. Footnote for newcomers: buy an edition that includes the 1998 *Armageddon* soundtrack hit single "I Don't Want to Miss a Thing." Diane Warren wrote it, and a massive orchestra mostly played it, with Tyler the only conspicuous band presence—but it might be the best "rock ballad" ever (yeah, eat Aerosmith's dust, Whitney, Brian, and Celine!). Tyler overcame his own prejudices to tackle it, but then he found the heart of the matter, as he told Ian Fortnum for *Kerrang!*: *I could lie awake just to watch you sleep*; I mean how much in love with someone do you have to be to do that? *. . . That's one of the most precious opening lines of any song I've ever heard.*

"Hole in My Soul" b/w "Falling Off," 1997.

Seven-inch picture disc featuring "Hole in My Soul" b/w "Falling Off," 1997.

chapter 14

Rocksimus Maximus

Aerosmith entered the new century firmly ensconced as a rock 'n' roll institution. They kicked off 2000 by contributing a new song, "Angel's Eye," to the film version of *Charlie's Angels*. But the first of many big 'Smith moments in the decade came on January 28, 2001, when the band performed at Raymond James Stadium in Tampa, Florida, for the Super Bowl XXXV halftime show.

Assuming the role of rock elder statesmen, they shared the stage with *N Sync, Mary J. Blige, Nelly, and, wrapped in a barely-there Aerosmith shirt, Britney Spears. For the grand finale, the entire cast joined the band for a set closing run-through of "Walk This Way," marking yet another genre-bounding take on the classic song. In a 2004 interview with *Blender*, Tyler recalled his attempt to procure Spears' shredded Aerosmith top after the show: "I wish I could tell you she gave me the shirt off her back, but she was a lot younger than she is today," he remarked, before turning serious—almost. "Everyone loves to take the piss out of her, but she brings joy to a lot of people. And she's got a nice ass."

"Through all the noise, this band allows me the freedom to do what I want. I can write a song as stupid as 'Just Press Play' [*sic*] or 'Dude (Looks Like a Lady)'; I can get my ya-yas out and get away with it! Then the press take the p*** out of it, and then it's Number One the next day. It's a beautiful thing, man! You can't keep it down!"

—Steven Tyler, quoted by Chris Roberts in *Uncut*, May 2001

Facing page: Route of All Evil tour, Hollywood Bowl, Hollywood, California, November 7, 2006. © KEVIN ESTRADA/KEVINESTRADA.COM

Inset: Route of All Evil tour with Mötley Crüe, 2006.

Sixteenth Annual Rock and Roll Hall of Fame induction, Waldorf-Astoria, New York City, March 19, 2001. KEVIN MAZUR/WIREIMAGE/GETTY IMAGES

In March, the band was bestowed with a Diamond award from the Recording Industry Association of America (RIAA), signifying 10 million units sold for 1980's *Aerosmith's Greatest Hits*. The RIAA also announced quadruple platinum status for *Rocks*, as well as triple platinum sales for *Get Your Wings*. By this time, *Toys in the Attic* was inching close to eight times platinum, while both *Pump* and *Get a Grip* had each surpassed the seven million mark. The new certifications brought the band's total sales to 59.5 million units in the U.S. alone, with worldwide numbers hovering in the 100 million range.

That same month, the band was on hand at New York City's Waldorf-Astoria to be honored—alongside Michael Jackson, Steely Dan, Queen, and Paul Simon—with entry into the Rock and Roll Hall of Fame. Following an induction speech by Kid Rock, who welcomed them to the hall as the "greatest rock 'n' roll band in American history," Aerosmith took the stage for a mini-set highlighted by a duet with Rock on "Sweet Emotion" and a romp through the classic "Train Kept a Rollin'." A triumphant moment to be sure, though Tyler expressed some trepidation toward the distinction. He told Alan di Perna in a 2001 interview with *Guitar World*, "We frowned upon the Rock and Roll Hall of Fame thing. 'Cause we're not done! That's almost like saying, 'Your career's over. Good boy. Here's your gold watch. See you later. Bye!'"

Aerosmith was far from finished. In fact, just weeks earlier on March 9, after more than a year of work, they had unveiled their thirteenth studio album, *Just Push Play*. The album was their first recorded without the aid of an outside producer; as Perry told *Rolling Stone*'s Tom Moon, "To have someone come in, and us turn over control again, it didn't feel right." Rather, in an effort to avoid some of the issues that marred the *Nine Lives* sessions, Tyler and Perry assumed production duties alongside trusted collaborators Mark Hudson and Marti Frederiksen (the pair also helped cowrite much of the material). Furthermore, the majority of the album was tracked in Perry's basement studio, the Boneyard, at his home in the Boston suburbs.

Which is not to say that *Just Push Play* was a stripped-down affair. To the contrary, the effort featured some of the band's most lush and layered recordings to date, incorporating heavy use of Pro Tools and plug-ins, as well as orchestration. "The average song on the album has between 80 and 90 tracks on it," Perry told di Perna. "The ones with an orchestra have as many as 120." In addition, several songs were constructed using loops, with live instruments added later in the process. "You beat yourself to death trying to get a good live take with the whole band," Perry explained. "Then you go back and replace all the parts. So what are you really going for? A good drum take? Well, there's a better way to do that. Start with loops, get the song 90 percent done, then have the drummer play along to it like he's playing the real song. Instead of trying to build the song from the ground up, you're just putting in some details."

The result was an album that, while featuring the customary mix of rockers ("Light Inside," "Beyond Beautiful") and ballads ("Fly Away from Here," "Luv Lies") also included such un-'Smith-like fare as the electronic flourishes of the title track and "Outta Your Head," the acoustic psychedelia of "Avant Garden," and the odd—and oddly titled—"Trip Hoppin'." Reviews were mixed (*Rolling Stone*: "The least self-consciously commercial record Aerosmith have made since their Eighties return from Smacked-Out City"; *Blender*: "The cover looks hopelessly out of date, and the music is mediocre at best"), but the record was nonetheless a hit, quickly going platinum and boasting one truly great single, the gorgeously Beatle-esque "Jaded."

Though Perry and the band at the time stood firmly behind their efforts—"This is the first record in a long time that I feel like we *own*," the guitarist told *Rolling Stone*'s Rob Sheffield in 2001—in the ensuing years several members came to view *Just Push Play* as something of a misstep. The guitarist told this writer in 2010, "I liked a couple of the songs on it; I just wasn't happy with the way it was recorded, in bits and pieces and glued together in Pro Tools. It left out the biggest asset Aerosmith has, which is playing live. And then there are some songs that I can't even believe we did. A song like 'Trip Hoppin'' is not a song I would . . . I just don't see us like that. But you get deep into recording and you lose sight of what you're doing sometimes."

To promote the record the band once again hit the road, launching the *Just Push Play* tour on June 6, 2001, in Hartford, Connecticut, with alternative rockers Fuel in support on many of the dates. That fall, several performances were cancelled in the wake of the September 11 terrorist attacks, and on October 21, the band made a detour to RFK Stadium in Washington, D.C., to take part in the United We Stand benefit concert alongside Michael Jackson, Mariah Carey, and others, to aid victims of the attacks. Overall, the jaunt was far from their longest—it wrapped in February 2002 in Japan (their only destination outside North America)—but across just over eighty shows the band pulled in close to $50 million at the gate.

"We frowned upon the Rock and Roll Hall of Fame thing. 'Cause we're not done! That's almost like saying, 'Your career's over. Good boy. Here's your gold watch. See you later. Bye!'"

—Steven Tyler, quoted by Alan di Perna in *Guitar World*, May 2001

That spring brought more honors, with the entire band on hand in L.A. to be celebrated as the recipients of the second mtvICON award. Filmed for network broadcast, the gala featured testimonials from the likes of Metallica and Janet Jackson, as well as performances from a range of artists, including Kid Rock ("Mama Kin"), Pink ("Janie's Got a Gun"), Shakira ("Dude [Looks Like a Lady]"), and Train ("Dream On"), before ending with a five-song set from Aerosmith themselves. Commented then-MTV entertainment president Brian Graden in a statement, "They have become a fixture at the network"—how times had changed.

In May, the band contributed a version of "Theme from Spider-Man" to the soundtrack of the live-action blockbuster of the same name; in July came another greatest hits package, *O, Yeah! Ultimate Aerosmith Hits*, a two-disc joint effort between Columbia and Geffen that collected thirty tracks across the band's entire career, as well as two new songs: "Lay It Down" and the sun-drenched, incredibly slick—even for latter-day Aerosmith—"Girls of Summer." (This release followed only a year after another two-disc comp, *Young Lust: The Aerosmith Anthology*, a Geffen set that fulfilled their obligation to the label.) Per usual, the band backed up the collection by taking to the road for the Girls of Summer tour with Kid Rock and Run-DMC in support. For each stop on the outing, which ran from August through December, the three acts joined together for an encore performance of "Walk This Way."

Bristow, Virginia, show rescheduled for September 25, 2001, in the wake of the 9/11 attacks.

"United We Stand: What More Can I Give?" benefit concert, RFK Stadium, Washington, D.C., October 21, 2001. Tens of thousands of fans gathered to see an array of acts at a marathon concert raising money for victims of the 9/11 terrorist attacks. AP PHOTO/PABLO MARTINEZ MONSIVAIS

Girls of Summer 2002 tour, East Troy, Wisconsin.
ARTIST: DAVID GINK/SHADOWLANDSTUDIOS.COM

Girls of Summer 2002 tour.
ARTIST: SCOTT BENGE (FGX)

Just six months later, in the summer of 2003, they were back out again, this time co-headlining with KISS on the Rocksimus Maximus tour (oddly, the KISS camp titled the outing "World Domination"). Another August–December excursion, the jaunt was highlighted by several shows at which Perry, wobbling out in Starchild-approved knee-high, stack-heeled boots, joined KISS onstage for a run-through of their classic "Strutter."

In these years Aerosmith had begun to transform, despite offering up the odd new song to greatest hits compilations and movie soundtracks (another new cut, "Lizard Love," appeared in the 2003 animated kids' flick *Rugrats Go Wild*), into what was primarily a steadfast touring unit: rock 'n' roll standard-bearers consistently churning out the hits—to great success—in sheds and arenas across the country. "We're all a bunch of carnies, man," was how Tyler described it to *Rolling Stone*'s

On the Rocksimus Maximus tour, Perry routinely joined KISS for a run through the latter's 1974 classic, "Strutter." The Forum, Inglewood, California, December 18, 2003. © KELLY A. SWIFT/RETNA LTD.

Rocksimus Maximus 2003 tour, Greenwood Village, Colorado.

Austin Scaggs on the eve of the Rocksimus Maximus outing.

But by March 2004, the band had readied a complete album of newly recorded music. The effort that resulted, however, was something of a curveball: a collection of covers of blues standards—Bo Diddley's "Road Runner," Muddy Waters' "I'm Ready," Big Joe Williams' "Baby, Please Don't Go"—as well as one 12-bar-derived original, "The Grind." Produced by Jack Douglas and titled *Honkin' on Bobo* (Perry: "It's a phrase that sounds jazzish, nasty-ish"), the album functioned in the dual roles of revealing some of the band's early influences—or, more accurately, the artists that *influenced* their true influences, e.g., British greats like the Yardbirds, Fleetwood Mac, and Led Zeppelin—and also (somewhat) satiating longtime fans who had grown weary of their increasingly pop-oriented recent output. Perry touched on the latter point in an interview with *Billboard*: "I listen to some of these tracks, and I'm like, I can't believe this is the same band that did 'I Don't Want to Miss a Thing.'"

The *Honkin' on Bobo* tour kicked off two weeks before the album's release, on March 11, in Lubbock, Texas, with Aerosmith performing on a stage designed to resemble an old blues club. With Cheap Trick in support, the jaunt took the band across the U.S. and Canada, ending four months later, much like the *Just Push Play* outing, with a spate of Japanese dates. That November, Sony issued a live DVD culled largely from an April 3 tour stop in Sunrise, Florida, titled

Aerosmith performed a private sound check for 2,000 fans who each donated a bag of food items before their December 18, 2003, show at the Forum in Inglewood, California. © KELLY A. SWIFT/RETNA LTD.

You Gotta Move, which eventually garnered multiplatinum sales.

Early 2005 saw the band—if not all the members—take a break. In March, Tyler popped up on the silver screen with a small role in the John Travolta/Uma Thurman film *Be Cool*. Perry, meanwhile, took advantage of the band's uncharacteristic downtime by issuing, on May 3, an eponymously titled solo album for which he assumed all guitar, bass, and keyboard duties, as well as lead vocals. The effort, co-produced by Perry and Paul Caruso, who also

contributed drums, was tracked at the Boneyard and featured eleven Perry originals and covers of the Doors' "Crystal Ship" and Woody Guthrie's "Vigilante Man."

A bluesy, guitar-heavy effort, *Joe Perry* was, according to the guitarist, "as honest a record as you're gonna get." As for why he released it under his own name

Honkin' on Bobo tour, Philips Arena, Atlanta, April 9, 2004. © COOKIE ROSENBERG/RETNA LTD.

Honkin' on Bobo tour, Tokyo Dome, July 20, 2004. AP PHOTO/SHIZUO KAMBAYASHI

rather than resurrecting the Joe Perry Project moniker, he explained to *Guitar Player*'s Jude Gold: "Back then there was a lot of anger, a lot of *fuck you* toward the other guys. That's why I didn't want to call this a Joe Perry Project album. It's a different time, a different place, and the album was recorded for different reasons." (In addition to the solo release, the guitarist now had his hand in several endeavors outside Aerosmith, including his own record label, Roman, named for his second son with wife Billie, and a line of hot

sauces, dubbed Joe Perry's Rock Your World.)

In October, Aerosmith reconvened for yet another round of dates, this time behind a live set, *Rockin' the Joint*, culled from a 2002 performance at the Joint, at the Hard Rock Hotel in Las Vegas, on the *Just Push Play* tour. With Lenny Kravitz in tow, they toured arenas in the U.S. through February, after which Cheap Trick came aboard for another month of shows in the South and Canada. But in early March, the band began canceling dates as Tyler experienced

complications with his voice. The singer was advised to undergo immediate surgery to tend to a throat ailment, and the remainder of the tour was scrapped. The sudden cancellation sparked rumors that Tyler was seriously ill, which gained traction after it was disclosed he had also undergone chemotherapy treatments for hepatitis C. "Everybody was saying it was cancer,"

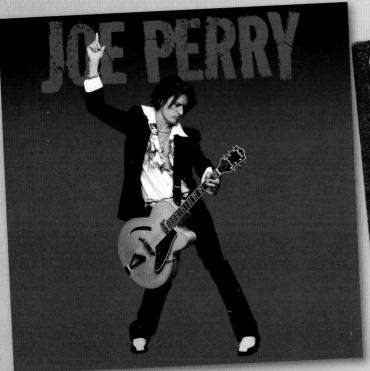

JOE PERRY

Perry assumed all guitar, bass, and keyboard duties on his eponymously titled solo album, issued in May 2005.

Tyler told U.K. journalist Peter Makowski in 2007. "The press love to play up on that shit. It was just nodules that had to be scraped. No big deal. I get fuckin' nodules every time I tour, 'cos I sing so hard."

And yet it wasn't long before Aerosmith announced a September co-headlining outing with Mötley Crüe, dubbed The Route of All Evil. A month prior to the official kickoff, however, throat cancer did in fact rear its head in the Aerosmith camp, though it was Hamilton, not Tyler, who received the diagnosis. In August 2006, the bassist revealed that he had recently completed a seven-week course of radiation and chemotherapy to combat the disease, and as a result would sit out much of the jaunt. In his place the band drafted David Hull, Perry's former bass man in the Project, who stayed

Joe Perry Project collaborator David Hull filled in on the Route of All Evil tour after Tom Hamilton announced he was undergoing treatment for throat cancer. Hollywood Bowl, Hollywood, California, November 7, 2006. © KEVIN ESTRADA/
KEVINESTRADA.COM

on through early December, after which Hamilton came back aboard for the last two weeks of shows.

Halfway through the Route of All Evil dates, Columbia issued yet another greatest hits package, this one titled *Devil's Got a New Disguise: The Very Best of Aerosmith*, essentially a condensed, single-disc repeat of the *O, Yeah!* collection. Tacked on to the end of the eighteen-song set were two "new/old" cuts, "Sedona Sunrise" and the titular "Devil's Got a New Disguise," both culled from the 1989 *Pump* sessions. Ostensibly another in what seemed a long line of compilations, the disc was, in fact, something of a stopgap to remedy the fact that the band had been forced to scrap plans for a new studio album— their first of new material since 2001—in the wake of Tyler's and Hamilton's ailments, not to mention their practically incessant live work. "We were working on getting a studio record out, but we just couldn't do it," Perry explained to *Billboard*. "There wasn't enough time." As for how the new album, now pushed back for a proposed early 2007 release, might sound, he hinted, "There's a lot of songs there that I think have the grit and the meat of what a lot of people expect from Aerosmith. We thought we'd take another look at that stuff, and that's what's going to be the backbone of this record."

Come the new year, however, the band still wasn't any closer to readying fresh material. Instead they once again hit the road for the

World Tour 2007, Palace Grounds, Bangalore, India, June 2, 2007. AP PHOTO/AIJAZ RAHI

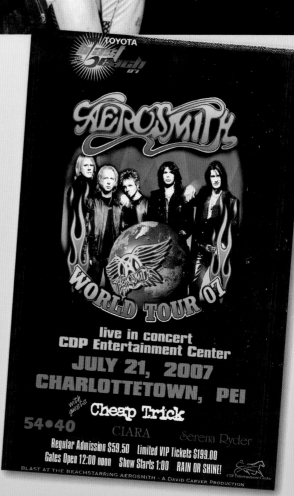

aptly—if rather bluntly—titled World Tour 2007. True to its name, the jaunt saw the band make their first journeys outside North America and Japan in almost a decade, including maiden trips to India, the United Arab Emirates, Russia, and other nations, as well as their first shows in Europe since the *Nine Lives* outing. Beginning with a spate of massive stadium gigs in Latin America that April and finishing up in the U.S. in September, the band hit close to twenty

Facing page: Route of All Evil tour, Hyundai Pavilion, Devore, California, November 11, 2006.
© KEVIN ESTRADA/KEVINESTRADA.COM

World Tour 2007, Prince Edward Island, Canada.

World Tour 2007, Tweeter Center, Mansfield, Massachusetts, September 14, 2007. AP PHOTO/ROBERT E. KLEIN

countries and, though playing less than forty dates, posted big numbers, registering one of the highest-grossing outings of the year.

But the years of heavy road work—and perhaps just the years in general—were beginning to take their toll. In February 2007, prior to the World Tour kickoff, Aerosmith visited London for an intimate gig at the Hard Rock Café for select fans and media types in an effort to stoke excitement for their upcoming shows. Speaking to the U.K.'s *Classic Rock*, Tyler commented on the spate of injuries that had plagued the band in recent years. "Our problem is that when you're a relevant band and you're still doing albums, singles, radio, movies, getting Oscars, Grammys, et cetera, you don't have time to go to the doctors or the dentist, and life gets put on the back burner," he told Peter Makowski. The singer also lamented his recent split from second wife Teresa Barrick: "[She] left me because I wasn't at home for the kids' birthdays or graduations," he said, adding, "It's a rough life."

When Makowski caught up with Perry for the same story, the guitarist sounded similarly weary: "My enthusiasm comes and goes," he admitted. "The music part is a no-brainer, but keeping it together personality-wise, it's tough. Just putting up with everybody else's bullshit. There's four other guys I've been hanging around with in a really intimate situation for thirty-seven years. Sometimes you think, *Is it time? Is it worth it?*" But the guitarist was quick to answer his own question: "Yes, it still is. The fact that there's thirty-seven years makes me wonder what the thirty-eighth year is going to be like—I'm kind of curious to see."

World Tour 2007, Tweeter Center, Mansfield, Massachusetts, September 14, 2007. AP PHOTO/ROBERT E. KLEIN

World Tour 2007. ARTIST: BILLY BISHOP/OBSOLETE-INC.COM

LIVE NATION PRESENTS
AEROSMITH
WITH JOAN JETT & THE BLACKHEARTS
SUNDAY, SEPTEMBER 16, 2007
NISSAN PAVILION

Just Push Play

by Bud Scoppa

As the calendar flipped to 2001, Aerosmith found themselves on yet another roll, even as the world around them took stock of their thirty-year roller-coaster career ride. In January, the band had a brand-new cut, "Jaded," blasting out of car radios. They boldly busted out the new single, right alongside the classics, during their Super Bowl halftime performance. Two months later, after the band dropped their thirteenth studio effort, *Just Push Play*, they were inducted into the Rock and Roll Hall of Fame alongside many of their contemporaries, including Queen, Steely Dan, Paul Simon, and Michael Jackson. During his induction speech, Kid Rock called them "the greatest rock 'n' roll band in American history," employing a pop-culture analogy to illustrate their significance: "Aerosmith are to rock 'n' roll what Fonzie was to *Happy Days*." During the performance that followed, the band showed off its undiminished viability by dropping a slice of "Jaded" into their old warhorse "Train Kept A-Rollin'."

The milestones of early 2001 added up to a historic juncture for Aerosmith, and *Just Push Play* was a fitting amalgam of the various phases that had made up the band's studio efforts over the years. At the same time the LP, sonically dense and epic in scale, revealed a veteran crew unafraid to incorporate new elements into their distinctive sound. The first album produced by Tyler and Perry, *Just Push Play* was a collaborative effort pooling the resources of the extended family that had adhered to Aerosmith during the 1990s. Tyler and Perry shared the production credit with a pair of returnees: hard-rock gun for hire Marti Frederiksen and

The first album produced by Tyler and Perry was sonically dense and epic in scale, and revealed a veteran crew unafraid to incorporate new elements into their distinctive sound.

pop-leaning freelancer Mark Hudson. The foursome, who also collaborated on eleven of the twelve songs in various combinations, dubbed themselves the Boneyard Boys. String arranger David Campbell was back for another tour of duty as well. Guests included the Tower of Power horn section and synth player Paul Santo, while actual family members Tony Perry and Liv and Chelsea Tyler turned in cameos.

Sure, that was a lot of personnel to jam into the recording studio, but augmenting the core group with a squad of specialists had been part of the drill since hard rock's song-doctor era back in the hair-band '80s. Also looking over their shoulders was Columbia, which had been waiting three years for another glossy power ballad along the lines of the band's one and only chart-topper, the Dianne Warren–concocted melodrama "I Don't Want to Miss a Thing." Beyond that, Tyler, Perry, and their teammates were apparently determined to demonstrate that their musical muscle was still rock hard, while also making it clear that they were keeping up with the times.

The resulting album is resolutely front-loaded, opening with the lavishly ornamented pomp-rocker "Beyond Beautiful." The track's stabs at psychedelia and power pop expand the basic Aerosmith recipe of jubilant overkill, as *Rolling Stone*'s David Fricke accurately described it, and set the table for the myriad stylistic moves to follow. The title track, which follows, throws itself into contemporary currents with a vengeance. Over a robotic groove formed by a drum loop and a synthesized churn, Tyler's incantatory, FX-treated vocal borrows from hip-hop and Jamaican toasting, while Perry cranks out one of his indelible cast-iron riffs—thus going for street-level currency while also tipping a fedora to Run-DMC's ghetto-izing of "Walk This Way." The repeated phrase *Fuckin' A!* in the choruses completes the sense of aggro delirium.

"Jaded" stands as *Just Push Play*'s most appealingly inventive track, seamlessly weaving a chiming, bittersweet riff reminiscent of the Smashing Pumpkins' "1979" with Raspberries-style stacked harmonies and sawing strings. All of these melodic fireworks shimmer over a groove as close to swinging as Kramer and Hamilton have ever delivered. It gives way to the album's designated power ballad, "Fly Away from Here," penned by Frederiksen and Paul Chapman. Aerosmith had invented the power ballad with "Dream On" in 1973, and it had served them well (commercially if not always artistically) over the years. But "Miss a Thing" had taken the band so far from its rockin' sweet spot that it demanded a counter-thrust, and you can hear the band pushing against expectations here, as the massive soundscape explodes into Technicolor in the "Hey Jude"–referencing bridge and final chorus.

From there, the band and their support team playfully roll out a series of hybrid genre studies that shudder with vitality, though the material itself is generally less intriguing than what they've done with it. Among the more engaging tracks are the Revolver-meets-Cheap Trick hard-pop rave-up "Sunshine," the Stonesy, horn-bleating rocker "Trip Hoppin'," the melodic metal workout "Under My Skin," and the Perry-sung bruiser "Outta Your Head." Only on "Light Inside" do they play it straight, gleefully dipping into their 1970s bag of tricks. At the other extreme is "Drop Dead Gorgeous," an attempt at rap-rock that collides with "Kashmir"-style Bedouin orchestrations. But even the flawed tracks have redeeming features, like the furious Perry/Whitford volleying in the middle of "Light Inside," and Tyler's heroically over-the-top vocal performance on the closer "Avant Garden."

In 2010, Perry distanced himself from *Just Push Play*—or more accurately, he ripped it to shreds. "I don't think we've made a decent album in years," he said. "*Just Push Play* is my least favorite. When we recorded it, there was never a point where all five members were in the room at the same time, and Aerosmith's major strength is playing together. It was a learning experience for me: it showed me how not to make an Aerosmith record."

Perry's vehement putdown of what was the previous decade's lone album of Aerosmith originals (uttered as the band presumably labored over the studio album they'd reportedly begun in late 2007) only served to ramp up anticipation for what the men of Aerosmith might have up their sleeves on the long-awaited follow-up.

Limited edition 7-inch picture disc featuring "Jaded" b/w "Angel's Eyes," 2001.

Honkin' on Bobo

by Phil Sutcliffe

Seems nobody knows what the title means.* In 2004 when Aerosmith's long-mooted album of blues/R&B covers finally emerged, Joe Perry couldn't be more specific than "nastyish, jazzish." As titles go, it's like it or lump it.

This writer does like it, though: enigmatic, evocative, euphonious. Job done! The only trouble is it fills you with anticipation and then, frankly, the opening track neither honks nor bobos. "Road Runner" should have launched the whole wangdangdoodle with a whoopdedoo. Written by Bo Diddley (Elias McDaniel for the publishing credits) and covered by Tyler's British Beat Boom heroes the Pretty Things, it looks a natural winner.

The first sound you hear, a distorted, swelling guitar drone, gets your attention. But then Tyler hollers fairground barker-style, "Ladies and gentlemen, step right up!" and from that moment the track feels like pantomime R&B, straining for effect. It's almost as if a nervous Aerosmith is apologizing to their fans, assuring them, "Don't worry, it's not really a blues album—it's rockin', it's *us*." The true grit—the earth and sex, the song's Southern black strangeness—gets lost along with most of the lyrics.

So it's a great relief that whatever doubts undermined "Road Runner" are cast aside forthwith. "Shame, Shame, Shame" feels like the real get-go, a boogie-gallop full of ZZ Top insouciance and muscle booting open the saloon doors. Perry's and Brad Whitford's guitars are a tearaway team, loose and unrehearsed (apart from the previous thirty years), Tyler complaining so bitterly about how Miss Roxie treats him that he can hardly keep from laughing his socks off. Phew. Cool and sweaty Aerosmith have got it after all, genuine R&B heart and soul—even though "Shame, Shame, Shame" is an odd hybrid to come out sounding so right for them. Composed by movie and TV songwriters Ruby Fisher and Kenyon Hopkins, it first appeared in the *Baby Doll* movie soundtrack (1956), authenticity infused by New Orleans bluesman Smiley Lewis' vocals.

But Aerosmith never claimed even a smidgen of purism in their "Like it? Grab it!" approach. White Londoner and

Enigmatic, evocative, euphonious—done! The only trouble is it fills you with anticipation and then, frankly, the opening track neither honks nor bobos.

*Do tell, if you do.

Fleetwood Mac founder Peter Green's Chicago/Delta–inspired "Rattlesnake Shake" brought them together when Tyler saw Perry and Tom Hamilton's band play it at the Barn in Sunapee, 1970. And Fleetwood Mac are still right there in the limber strut of Green's "Stop Messin' Around" (listed cowriter Cliff Adams was the Mac's manager). Perry sings it hard over tight guitar lines audibly finger-wagging at the errant lady, while Tyler howls through and around his harmonica in now-nostalgia heaven. (A year later Perry told Ted Drodzowski for rocksbackpages .com, "[Steven]'s not a technical player. . . . He just lets it rip and he's great. Ripping is what we do best.")

Aerosmith's lifelong love of the old right stuff brings that ripping, rowdy spirit to track after track. They stomp and shout through their takes on chestnuts like "Eyesight to the Blind," "Baby, Please Don't Go," "I'm Ready," and "You Gotta Move" (needless to say, *I was hangin' with the Devil when we made a pact / I'm drinkin' welfare whiskey, smokin' food-stamp crack* is a Tyler addition to Fred McDowell and Reverend Gary Davis' original lyric). Tear-along songs about sex, love, loss, madness, chain gangs, drugs, booze, death, and the Devil, all played flat-out wild and powerfully disciplined at the same time.

Honkin' on Bobo draws an improbable line between white New England circa 1970 and black Mississippi, 1900–1940. Not only were Bo Diddley and Aerosmith's R&B exemplar Muddy Waters born or based there, but so were the authors of the songs noted in the previous paragraph: respectively, Sonny Boy Williamson II, Big Joe Williams, Willie Dixon, and the aforementioned McDowell (Davis hailed from South Carolina).

Mississippi Fred became Aerosmith's dusty rural route to the roots; *Honkin'* includes three songs from the *Amazing Grace* album McDowell recorded with the Hunter's Chapel Singers of Como, Mississippi (his hometown). Although they transformed "You

Honkin' on Bobo tour, 2004. ARTIST: DAVID GINK/SHADOWLANDSTUDIOS.COM

Gotta Move" from the original gospel moan —faithfully emulated by the Rolling Stones on *Sticky Fingers*—into a Diddley-beat rave at death's door, they let "Back Back Train" and "Jesus Is on the Mainline" take them right down to north Mississippi. Perry sings the secular "Back Back Train" with dignity and a hint of tremor (unsure whether he's headed for home in the fireside or graveyard

sense), as they pour on swampy menace with slide, dobro, Hamilton's bendy bass notes, and Tyler's hellfire howls. But for "Mainline," Aerosmith relocate their souls to a tin-shack church, wailing raw spirit, Tyler the hoarse hectoring preacher, band and friends yelling the responses, true believers right now, if never before: *If you're sick and you can't get well, just tell Him what you want.* McDowell would surely have been proud.

And it's hard to imagine Aretha Franklin disdaining "Never Loved a Girl," Tyler's unbridled male version of her "I Never Loved a Man (The Way I Love You)" (written in 1967 by Ronnie Shannon, the masculine variant was originally devised by obscure psychedelic band Freedom). Untypically, Aerosmith just hold steady on the slow soul drag, horns and organ snarling tight-lipped, while Tyler roars out love, rage, and self-disgust: *You're a liar and you're a cheat / I don't know why I let you do these things to me.*

The remaining cover, "Temperature," is a more emotionally basic choice, a one-image song of heat and lust, which Aerosmith's lewd hilarity rescues from its archival location as a rather lamely performed 1957 Chess single by harmonica genius Little Walter. Why Aerosmith threw their own song "The Grind" into the mix remains unclear. It's pretty good in their rockin'-verse/rather-disconnected-pop-chorus mode, but it doesn't fit the album.

However, in sum, *Honkin' on Bobo* certainly fits Willie Dixon's sagacious axiom: "The blues are the roots and the other musics are the fruits." ⌐

chapter 15

Train Kept a Rollin'

For Perry and the band, Year 38—or, to non-Aerosmith members, 2008—brought more triumphs and trials. In February, Perry played several East Coast dates with TAB the Band, a rock act featuring his two eldest sons, Adrian and Tony, on vocals/bass and guitar respectively. Together they ripped through TAB originals, Perry solo tunes, and harder-edged Aerosmith deep cuts like "Combination" and "Bright Light Fright," ending their joint sets with Tony and proud papa trading licks on the *Joe Perry* track "Shakin' My Cage."

All along Aerosmith continued to move forward with plans for a new studio album. Perry told *Billboard* they hoped to ready the effort for a March release, while also noting, "I don't think we've ever delivered a record on time since the first one." This time would be no different: In March, Perry underwent reconstructive surgery on his knee, and two months later Tyler entered a rehab facility to attend to lingering foot injuries aggravated by years of vigorous live performances. Of his bandmates' physical ailments, Whitford commented to *Billboard*, "You'd think it was a football team or something."

"The f***-yous run deep in a band like Aerosmith, and the best part about it is the make-up. We live to be on stage with each other and play—because we don't really know what else to do, to be honest with you!"

—Steven Tyler, quoted in *Billboard*

Facing page: **Cocked, Locked, Ready to Rock tour, O2 Arena, London, June 15, 2010.** CHRISTIE GOODWIN/REDFERNS/GETTY IMAGES

That June the entire band was on hand at the Hard Rock Café in New York City to unveil *Guitar Hero: Aerosmith*, the first iteration of the Activision franchise centered on an individual act or artist. The game tracked the close to forty-year career of the band, from Nipmuc High to the Super Bowl, and featured more than thirty Aerosmith songs; in addition, all five members underwent extensive motion-capture sessions to bring their likenesses to animated life. As Perry told this writer in 2008, the decision to pair with Activision was easy: "The record

Root root rooting for the home team. Tyler finishes "God Bless America" during the seventh-inning stretch on opening day at Fenway Park in Boston, April 8, 2008. AP PHOTO/CHARLES KRUPA

labels, and the music industry in general, aren't what they once were. So this is really a great medium to get the music out there."

But even Perry couldn't have predicted just how tremendous a vehicle the video game would prove to be. In its first week of release, *Guitar Hero: Aerosmith* sold upwards of 500,000 copies and grossed more than $25 million—in comparison, pointed out *Rolling Stone*'s Brian Hiatt, their most recent studio album, *Honkin' on Bobo*, had moved 160,500 copies and grossed $2 million in a similar span of time. Furthermore, the mix of Aerosmith hits and deep cuts presented in the game had the effect of turning on yet another new generation to the veteran act. In the wake of the popularity of *Guitar Hero:*

In June 2008, the band unveiled *Guitar Hero: Aerosmith*, the first iteration of the immensely popular Activision franchise centered on an individual act or artist. AP PHOTO/ACTIVISION

Aerosmith, the band saw an incredible 40 percent spike in catalog sales of its albums.

As for adding a new effort to that catalog, in early 2009 the band announced they had brought on board Brendan O'Brien, who had last worked with them as a young engineer on *Get a Grip*, to helm the long-in-the-works project. Soon enough, however, sessions were once again delayed as Perry underwent another surgery related to his knee replacement, and Tyler came down with pneumonia. By the time the band was set to commence work with O'Brien another tour loomed, this time a summer jaunt with ZZ Top. In what seemed to be a pattern, Perry told *Billboard*, "We realized there wasn't any chance of getting it finished before we hit the road for the summer. So basically we had to push [the album] back."

In time, however, it was revealed that deeper issues were also at play within the band, particularly in regard to Tyler. In a December 2009 story in *Rolling Stone*, Whitford stated that the singer ultimately bailed

ARTIST: LINDSEY KUHN/SWAMPCO.COM

Guitar Hero tour, Fiddler's Green Amphitheatre, Greenwood Village, Colorado, **August 1, 2009.** © SCOTT D. SMITH/RETNA LTD.

on the sessions. "We were very excited to work with Brendan—he was number one on our wish list," the guitarist told Andy Greene. "He bent over backward to do whatever he could to make Steven feel comfortable, but he still walked out after two or three weeks."

From the outside, at least, things appeared to be status quo within the band. The Aerosmith/ZZ Top outing got off to an auspicious start, with the band announcing they would for the first time perform one of their classic albums—*Toys in the Attic*—in full (though closing track "You See Me Crying," proving difficult for Tyler to sing, was only added to the set some two weeks in). In addition, they hinted that later shows would see a full-scale rendition of *Rocks*.

But the tour was plagued with difficulties from the outset. Just days prior to the June 10 kickoff in Missouri, Whitford suffered a head injury exiting his Ferrari, requiring surgery after he was found to have internal bleeding. In his place the band drafted Bobby Schneck, who had worked with Weezer and Green Day, to fill in on rhythm guitar. Less than a month in, on June 28 at Mohegan Sun casino in Connecticut, Tyler injured his leg, leading to seven cancelled dates. When the tour picked back up again in Atlanta on July 15, it was with Whitford back in the fold but Hamilton sidelined, again replaced by David Hull, as the bassist underwent noninvasive surgery related to his cancer treatment. The series of health setbacks led *Rolling Stone* to quip, "The Rock and Roll Hall of Famers have seemingly gone from 'America's Greatest Rock and Roll Band' to 'America's Most Injury Prone Rock and Roll Band.'"

The tour finally went off the rails for good in Sturgis, South Dakota, on August 5, when Tyler, dancing across the catwalk during "Love in an Elevator," fell from the stage and had to be airlifted to a local hospital. The singer sustained head and neck injuries and a broken shoulder, and the remainder of the dates were scrapped. In the aftermath, the band expressed concern for their frontman while also bringing growing resentments to the fore. In September, speaking to the Associated Press of the cancelled shows, Perry commented, "The tour was building up to be a great tour, and I was pretty [upset]." He went on to reveal that he hadn't spoken to Tyler in more than a month, and, he said, "All I know is [he's] got to get his act together. I mean, he and I haven't written a song together alone in the same room in over ten years, so there's been some changes in the paradigm of what Aerosmith is."

Tyler, for his part, spoke with *Rolling Stone* in the days following the Sturgis fiasco. In an interview with David Browne, he attested to his health and also denied growing reports that his fall was the result of his having taken to abusing drugs again. "Someone is leaking stuff, pretending to know, and you know, I don't even care," he told Browne, adding that onstage that night he was "as sober as you can be." (In early 2011, however, Tyler spoke to the contrary, revealing to David Letterman that on that night he had in fact been snorting the prescription medication Lunesta as a means of dealing with orthopedic pain associated with a condition known as Morton's neuroma.)

Regardless, one point not open for debate was that the cancelled tour

Unused ticket for St. Paul, Minnesota, show cancelled after the Sturgis mishap.

Tyler strikes a pose for fans at the Sturgis Motorcycle Rally in Deadwood, South Dakota, on August 3, 2009. Two nights later, he fell off the stage in Sturgis, thus scrapping the rest of the tour and bringing growing intraband resentment to a head. AP PHOTO/STEVE McENROE

had opened a wide chasm within Aerosmith (compounding the rift was the fact that Tyler had recently taken on management separate from the rest of the band), and the tensions and hostilities that lay within were about to spill out in the press. That October, the band reconvened for two shows in Hawaii, as well as a November 1 gig in the United Arab Emirates as part of the Abu Dhabi Grand Prix. Speaking with *Classic Rock*'s Peter Makowski in Abu Dhabi, Tyler dropped the news that his plans for the near future did not involve his Aerosmith bandmates: "I don't know what I'm doing yet, but it's definitely going to be something Steven Tyler," he told Makowski. "Working on the brand of myself—Brand Tyler."

Perry, for one, made it clear that the rest of the band wasn't going to wait around for the frontman. Earlier that October, the guitarist had resurrected the Joe Perry Project moniker and issued a new album, *Have Guitar, Will Travel*; upon Aerosmith's return from Abu Dhabi he gathered the reconstituted Project (with original bassist Hull) and hit the road for a tour of U.S. clubs and small theaters. Then, on November 9, he fired a shot across the bow, taking to his Twitter feed to declare: "Aerosmith is positively looking for a new singer to work with. You just can't take 40 years of experience and throw it in the bin!"

Tyler, however, quickly countered. The following night, he turned up, to Perry's surprise, at a Project gig at Irving Plaza in New York City and joined the band onstage for a run-through of "Walk This Way." Prior to the song's start, he issued his own statement, announcing to the crowd that he was not leaving Aerosmith. He then turned to his bandmate of close to forty years and asserted, rather enigmatically, "Joe Perry, you are a man of many colors. But *I*, motherfucker, am the rainbow!" Following a performance that saw some uneasy interaction between the singer and guitarist, Tyler vanished as quickly as he had appeared. Perry recalled to this writer, "He showed up backstage, came up, and sang the one song and that was the last I saw of him."

Weeks later an article appeared in *Rolling Stone* that chronicled the band's fracturing over the past several months, and in which various members vented their frustrations publicly. Kramer restated their intention to push forward in the wake of their singer's focus on Brand Tyler: "[Steven's] management contacted us recently and told us that he wanted to take two years off," the drummer said. "We aren't

Official Aero Force One membership card, 2009.

waiting two years for him, so we've been talking to some famous singers." Whitford, meanwhile, while stopping short of confirming that Tyler had indeed fallen off the wagon, practically stated as much, commenting, "He doesn't act like a sober person."

In fact, while chatter from Tyler's camp hinted at the imminent release of a solo album and a memoir, in late December an announcement came that the singer had instead checked into an undisclosed rehabilitation center in California to deal with an addiction to prescription painkillers. (This was followed by some bizarre turns: While undergoing treatment, Tyler emerged at a Palm Desert karaoke bar, where he treated patrons to an impromptu performance of "I Don't Want To Miss a Thing." Several days later he was spotted at a nearby Home Depot, crooning "Dude [Looks Like a Lady]" over the loudspeaker system.)

Perry, meanwhile, busied himself touring North America and Europe in support of *Have Guitar, Will Travel*, as well as firming up plans to proceed with a Tyler-less Aerosmith. In January 2010, on the eve of a Project stint as the support act for Mötley Crüe on a Canadian tour, the guitarist told Canada's QMI Agency that, following the tour, Aerosmith would "start having some auditions, making some phone calls. Hopefully, we'll have found a new singer by the summer, and Aerosmith will be able to go back out on the road." At the same time, he left the door open for Tyler to return: "I'm ready to write with him, to play onstage with him anytime he's physically ready and wants to do it. But it's really up to him." All the while, the story gained steam in the press. High-profile names like Lenny Kravitz, Paul Rodgers, Billy Idol, and Chris Cornell, among others, were reported on as possible Tyler replacements, and during this time it also surfaced that, in 2008, Tyler had secretly auditioned to fill Robert Plant's shoes for the aborted Led Zeppelin reunion tour.

By late January, the situation had become heated enough to turn litigious. An attorney for Tyler drafted a letter to Aerosmith's management demanding the band "immediately cease and desist from

engaging in acts and conduct to the harm and detriment of your own client, Aerosmith, and our client who is one of its members." The document went on to threaten to pursue legal remedies for damages incurred if these actions were not halted.

But circumstances would never reach that point. In mid-February, with new tour dates looming—including several South American gigs and a number of European festival stops—Tyler and the band met in Boston and laid down their weapons. "We all got together with Steven and his manager at our rehearsal space and hammered things out," Perry told this writer. Soon after, they announced a full-scale tour, Cocked, Locked, Ready to Rock, which, in addition to the South American and European dates, also included a summer run through the U.S. highlighted by a triumphant hometown blowout gig

with fellow native sons the J. Geils Band at Boston's Fenway Park. In an interview with *Billboard*, Tyler casually brushed aside the band's contentious few months: "The *fuck-yous* run deep in a band like Aerosmith, and the best part about it is the make-up. We live to be on stage with each other and play—because we don't really know what else to do, to be honest with you!"

The Cocked, Locked, Ready to Rock tour kicked off on May 17, 2010, in Caracas, Venezuela, and ran smoothly through the spring, taking the band through more than a dozen

countries. By the time they hit the U.S., however, cracks began to show. At Long Island's Jones Beach Theater on August 12, Tyler, launching himself off the drum riser at the conclusion of "Sweet Emotion," accidentally brought his microphone stand down hard on Perry's head; gathering himself from the blow, the guitarist removed his instrument, hurled it at a wall of amps, and walking offstage. After several tense minutes he returned, somewhat bloodied, to finish the set.

Five days later, at Toronto's Air Canada Centre, Perry seemingly took

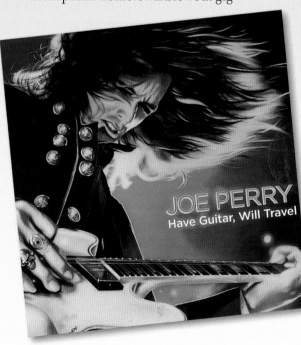

Right: In late 2009, Perry busied himself touring North America and Europe behind the new Joe Perry Project album *Have Guitar, Will Travel.* ARTIST: ADAM TURKEL FOR ALTAMONT RECORDS

SATURDAY DECEMBER 5th
ST.PETERSBURG, FLORIDA
DOORS 7PM

STATETHEATRECONCERTS.COM

POSTER BY ADAM T.

revenge. Standing opposite Tyler on a catwalk during "Love in an Elevator," Perry appeared to slowly back into the singer, nudging him off the platform and sending him tumbling into the audience. After being helped back onstage by several fans, Tyler retook the microphone and, in a reference to his Sturgis fall, announced, "It ain't gonna happen again, baby!" before telling Perry, "You will pay for that, my brother."

Afterward, Tyler and Perry commented separately on the incident to Canada's *Globe and Mail*. By the singer's account, "I had bumped into Joe. I kind of strafe him—that's what we do night after night. We've done it for forty

years. In return, he gave me a hit that I feel was a bit out of place." Countered the guitarist, "If you watch the film, he backed into me hard. And I was also standing on the edge. All I did was brush against him. Basically he had a choice: he could have kept his balance and not gone into the audience, or he could have dropped in, which he did. None of it was planned—it's a contact sport. The week before, he hit me over the head with a mic stand. But did you read anything about that?"

But while Perry went on to dismiss the uproar over the incident as "typical Aerosmith mumbo jumbo," there was in fact a new storm brewing with Tyler. Several weeks earlier, a report had surfaced in the media that the singer would be replacing the departing Simon Cowell at the judge's table for the upcoming season of *American Idol*—and much like his "Brand Tyler" comment the previous year, the

Cocked, Locked, Ready to Rock tour, Explanada Monumental, Lima, Peru, May 22, 2010. AP PHOTO/KAREL NAVARRO

news apparently caught the rest of Aerosmith by surprise. On August 3, a livid Perry told the *Boston Herald*, "I found out on the Internet, like the rest of the world. None of us in the band knew anything about it." The guitarist went on to vent, "I mean, after forty years he couldn't tell me about this? Why so secretive? We're told [the *American Idol* gig is] a done deal—but if Steven is committed to a TV show, that kinda affects the rest of us. We'd like to plan our lives."

Indeed, on September 22, little more than a month after the Cocked, Locked, Ready to Rock tour wrapped, Tyler was officially announced as one of two new judges, along with Jennifer Lopez, for *American Idol*. The news was not exactly met with across-the-board enthusiasm. Longtime fan and friend Kid Rock told *Entertainment Weekly*, "I think it's the stupidest thing he's ever done in his life. He's a sacred American institution of rock 'n' roll, and he just threw it all out the window. Just stomped on it and set it on fire." (Countered Tyler: "He's just jealous.")

Surprisingly however, tempers within Aerosmith's ranks remained in check this time, with Perry telling spinner.com in October he hoped Tyler was "really happy doing it." His bandmates followed suit: Kramer expressed the belief that the show would expose the veteran band to yet another new generation of fans, while Hamilton told the *Boston Herald*, "Steven's been very emphatic in saying that the way his time is arranged on the show leaves room to work on a record. He's been taking great pains to remind everybody of

that, so hopefully that's the way it will come out."

In November, Whitford, on the road with the Experience Hendrix tour, told *Billboard* that he envisioned Aerosmith perhaps performing on the program: "I haven't heard anything yet, but my guess is . . . certainly if I was a producer on that show, I'd want to see that happen." The guitarist went on to speak on the band's future, and hinted that they would soon resume work on the long-stalled follow-up to *Just Push Play*. "Obviously we'll have to work a little bit around Steven's television schedule, but he's ready to do it and he's pretty confident he can do this record, so hopefully we can get some of that new music out next year." Furthermore, Whitford declared, 2011 would see yet another world tour from the band (hardly surprising in light of the fact that, in the first decade of the new millennium, Aerosmith

had, according to *Billboard*, cleared an astonishing $292 million on the road, making them the fourteenth highest-grossing act of the 2000s).

And so as the band planned for a future that, not for the first time in their long career, appeared somewhat shaky, Tyler, by now 62, embarked on his maiden solo outing. In the fall, he issued his debut solo single, "Love Lives," a swelling piano ballad very much in the Diane Warren vein and written as the theme song to the Japanese science fiction film *Space Battleship Yamato*. He also readied for the release of his autobiography, titled *Does the Noise in My Head Bother You?*

When the tenth season of *American Idol* premiered on January 19, 2011, the singer quickly established himself as the breakout star and alpha judge of the rejiggered series. Tyler proved to be a scene-chewing force, as easy with heartfelt criticism as he was with off-the-

Cocked, Locked, Ready to Rock tour, Mid State Fairgrounds, Paso Robles, California, July 26, 2010.
AP PHOTO/MICHAEL A. MARIANT

wall exclamations; in just the first episode, one starry-eyed hopeful's audition was met with the peculiar response, "Hellfire, save matches, fuck a duck and see what hatches!" Though viewers and critics may not have been able to decipher exactly what it was Tyler was trying to say, they apparently liked what they heard. In an early evaluation of the singer's performance, Jon Caramanica of the *New York Times* declared him a "genius" of sorts, commenting, "Mr. Tyler has done much of the heavy lifting for *Idol* this season." Furthermore, as Tyler's star rose in this new realm, Aerosmith's catalog sales followed suit. In the first weeks following *Idol*'s debut, sales of the band's numerous greatest hits collections spiked more than 250 percent, while "I Don't Want to Miss a Thing" and "Dream On" combined to register more than 50,000 digital downloads.

At the end of January, it was reported that Aerosmith had convened at the Los Angeles–area home studio of Marti Frederiksen to begin working up songs for a new album. Noticeably absent from the sessions, however, was Joe Perry, who claimed a previous commitment prevented him from joining his band mates in the studio. Addressing the absence in an interview with Howard Stern, Tyler said of Perry, "I just texted him twenty minutes ago—Hey Joe, where are you? He's angry at me for what? Because I took fucking *Idol*? What a crock of shit!" Tyler also revealed

that since wrapping up the Cocked, Locked, Ready to Rock tour he and Perry had not spoken directly.

For his part, Perry chose to clarify his position via Twitter, where he posted a series of blunt updates in early February that read in part: "I am in Aerosmith. I am not going anywhere . . . Asmith [*sic*] will

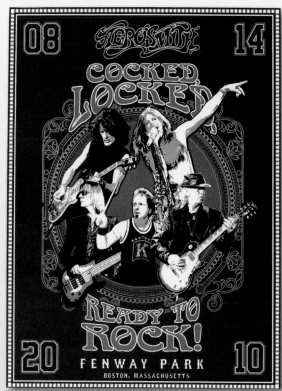

The Cocked, Locked, Ready to Rock tour was highlighted by a triumphant hometown blowout gig at Boston's Fenway Park.

resume in the spring to finish writing the new CD." One month later, Tyler posted a somewhat more hopeful statement to his own Twitter page: "Joe and I sent smoke signals, shot the shit and chewed the fat for the last year, but just smoked the peace pipe for an hour today. On our way to rockin' your fkin [*sic*] worlds this summer by locking ourselves away somewhere w/guitars and drums. . ." Indeed, as Tyler continued to be

beamed into millions of households each week on *Idol*, it was revealed that a new Aerosmith album and tour were on the horizon for late 2011, with South American and Japanese dates already confirmed.

Then in an interview with *Rolling Stone*'s Brian Hiatt published April 29, 2011, Tyler alleged that in 2008, for the first time in seventeen years, he and Perry took drugs together during their ill-fated recording sessions with Brendan O'Brien. "Joe was high and he couldn't play," Tyler told Hiatt. "I couldn't sing, really, because I was snorting everything, and it fucks up your throat." According to *Rolling Stone*, Perry declined the magazine's requests to comment.

In the end, however, the Aerosmith train will keep a rollin', just as it has numerous times in the past. In a 2010 interview with this writer, Perry opined, "There were times in the '70s when people would see us and go, 'They're not gonna live another three months.' But for some reason we've always managed to keep going." Now, forty years in, the guitarist expressed a measure of awe at it all, while also looking ahead. "I wonder about how we've been able to do it," he continued. "So sometimes I just have to shake my head. Because there's not many bands out there who have been around for as long as we have, and who still have all their original members, and that are still doing new and bigger things the way we are. So it's kinda like there's no template for what's to come."

Cocked, Locked, Ready to Rock tour, Fenway Park, Boston, August 14, 2010. MARC ANDREW DELEY/PICTUREGROUP VIA AP IMAGES

Perry and Tyler pictured together in Los Angeles in August 1984, shortly after Perry rejoined the band.
RICHARD E. AARON/REDFERNS/ GETTY IMAGES

Afterword

Advice to Young Bands

by Phil Sutcliffe

Aerosmith having seen it all, *Mojo*'s Phil Sutcliffe asked Steven Tyler and Joe Perry what advice they would give to a young band setting out with long-term intent. A step-by-step manual of do's and don'ts was never in the cards.

STARTING OUT

Steven Tyler: First, if your aspiration is to be a rock star, then you're in trouble. There's gotta be some kind of art, some kind of thought, some kind of something else. I'm not saying "Fake it till you make it" don't work. But sometimes losing an illusion is better than finding a truth. It's been that way for us.

Joe Perry: Yeah, check your motives.

ST: After that it's simple. Grab yourself an old Fleetwood Mac album. Grab the old blues stuff. Listen to it for form. Learn that shit.

JP: We use that stuff as a reset button. We sit back and go, "Why is it making me feel this way? What is it?" It's like when you eat a really good meal, you wanna know what's in there, you try to figure out what it is about the taste you really like.

ST: I was just listening to *Fleetwood Mac at the BBC*. What the fuck? That's a hidden truth, that's a *secret*. Get that record! You'll learn melodic sensibility, you'll learn . . . even a fuck-off, it's really obvious in there.

When I first saw [Perry's Jam Band, circa 1969] they were terrible. They weren't in tune and they weren't in time, but they did "Rattlesnake Shake" and there was a fuckin' energy that all the bands that I'd been in before couldn't do ever. With all the acid and Tuinals we couldn't get to what they had on the natch. What was shining through was the core of Aerosmith, the fact that the horse doesn't want to be ridden with a fuckin' bit in its mouth the whole time, let it go, if you've created this monsterin' animal, let it run!

PUTTING A BAND TOGETHER

ST: It's real simple. You don't get along if you don't talk to each other. And I mean *stuff*. Like, there's a band we're friends with where the lead singer and the guitarist don't speak to each other.

Not about the things that brought them down at times. Not about the *deaths*. It's hushed. So many men don't talk in a group.

JP: And that's gonna stifle their creativity, it's going to come up when they're playing and writing. Somebody says, "I don't like the way you're singing that," and deep inside the singer's saying, "He fucked me over way back when so I'm not gonna listen to him." What's the point of being in a band if you're not building on each other's talents?

Phil Sutcliffe: But could you "talk" when you first came together in Aerosmith?

ST: Well, when I saw Joe playing guitar, I knew he was a goldmine no matter what. But he had a girlfriend and I got jealous. That was Elyssa, his first wife. I was really hurt that he would rather be with her than be with me, especially after we sat on a waterbed and started writing songs, 'cos writing songs was fuckin' . . . I took my *anger* and jealousy and put it into "Sweet Emotion," which I pointed at her directly: [sings] *You talk about things that nobody cares / You're wearin' out things that nobody wears.*

A lot of bands break up because they just don't talk. So this guy's a fuckin' asshole. "Who's a fuckin' asshole?" "You're a fuckin' asshole!" "No, you're a fuckin' asshole!" "You fuckin'. . ." They don't talk it out.

JP: But it isn't just about talking, it's about being able to listen and really hear what someone else has to say and not take it personally. It's hard to do especially when people have big egos, which is what rock 'n' roll is all about. You've got to accept people for what they are, not go, "Let's see if we can get him to be *like this*." That's fucked. We used to run like that. It's fucked.

ST: If I ask Tom Hamilton to play fretless bass and he whines and I say, "Come on, just try it," it's up to him to make the decision whether he's going to do it. If he tries it, then in the long run it's only to his benefit, because he's going to realize whether he can do it or not. In this band, if Joe Perry says, "You're a fuckin' asshole, Steven, to talk like that . . ."

JP: But I would never say that now. I used to say that, but I don't anymore because he's *not*, I love him, he's my brother.

ST: What I'm sayin' is, if I tell you what you're doin' fuckin' pisses me off, you can either change it or not. I'm not saying it works all the time. But it's about how you catch the ball [makes a baseball mitt shape with his right hand]. "I don't wanna fuckin' hear you don't like it, try it! It's my idea and if you don't try it you're disrespecting me and I may take that to heart and hold it against you forever . . ."

JP: And you probably will.

BUSINESS

JP: Don't let anyone tell you that you have to sign something that day. It's been going on since they recorded Robert Johnson in a hotel room and the guy never got any royalties.

PS: What was the worst contract Aerosmith ever signed?

JP: In 1973 when we didn't sign to Columbia Records, although we recorded for them. We signed to our management company Leber and Krebs's production side and they provided the services of the band to Columbia. We didn't realize that until six years later.

ST: That gave the management total control to get the money first. And how about giving them 50 percent of your publishing! We did that. You're eighteen, you go, "Fuck, I just don't wanna play another club," and you sign. But! In that contract there's a clause including the phrase "in perpetuity" which means as long as you fuckin' live your manager gets a piece of you. I'm sorry. We did that.

JP: No matter how desperate you are, and "Aw, I don't wanna look at that" because you think it's hip not to worry about money, it's gonna come around. Hopefully, none of us are in it just for the money, but if somebody's going to make some, you know, it might as well be you. That's all.

DIVIDING THE SPOILS

JP: When we started out as a band we decided to split it all down the middle.

PS: What? Including the publishing?

ST: No, a small percentage goes to the band members who didn't write the song. When Joey Kramer's home driving his Ferrari and Joe and I are in Florida writing songs . . .

JP: . . . he's getting a taste. If you look at the history of the band everyone has written songs.

PS: Did you work that out from the start?

JP: No, that came along in the '80s.

PS: Had it provoked tension before that?

JP: If feathers were ruffled, that's all it was, it's not been something to split up the band.

ST: Certain Beatles that I talk to are pissed about money, the shares they got. In any band, if the money is not fair and you're afraid to say anything, it causes a fucked-up bad vibe when the tape's rolling and then you have to get high on drugs to get rid of that feeling.

FITNESS

ST: I don't like to look fat in my pictures. I look at a lotta people my age and they've let themselves go, they've turned into this distortion with eight years of sedentary fat all over them. Also, when I'm overweight, the way I sing, it hurts up there. I wanna make it look as effortless as I fuckin' can in front of all those kids, so that means eating a certain way, fuckin' boiled owl and essence of cloud and footprint.

JP: One of the big fallacies is that we're a bunch of fuckin' vegetarians. Bunch of shit.

ST: But it feels so good now, after the second week of being on the road. The muscles back here [thighs] and back here [lumbar region] feel right. Suddenly these muscles don't hurt either [diaphragm]. When I was at home my back hurt all the time.

It's about getting up in the morning, breaking a sweat up in the health club and lookin' at the girls and using that as a little incentive. Now I'm fuckin' jumpin' around like a wild man on stage doing shit that I don't even know what it is until I see a picture, but having a grand old time, being my twelve-year-old self.

LOVE, MARRIAGE, CHILDREN, ETC.

JP: We wrote the book. It's a tough one because a young band is like a gang and there's so much all-for-one one-for-all that when one person gets a relationship everyone else is going to feel the loss. It's important for that person to be aware of it. I never recognized that in the early days. It's one of the things that helped tear the band apart. I'm a really selfish person, very hedonistic. We all are, we took drugs to the max because it felt good. I found a relationship that made me feel good to the point where I really shut off from the band.

We give a hundred percent to the band. But how can you give a hundred percent to the band and a hundred percent to your family? It's a constant battle, but it's one we're all in together now. We've gone through hell figuring that out.

ST: I just have to think that if . . . John Lennon's saying to the rest of the guys, "I'm lost." Say if he *knew*. "I have a mother complex because my mother left me and then she died. And I love Yoko so much that it's a piece that was missing in my life even though I'm in the best band in the world." If he told that to the rest of the guys would things have worked out different? With George, who still holds a fuckin' grudge about not being allowed into the writing process? With Paul and John? Instead it was behind John's back, "That fucking cunt, what is she doing in the studio? How *dare* she come in here?"

JP: Because one day she's sitting there, as opposed to him laying his soul out and telling the guys what was going on inside him.

ST: "I'm fuckin' weak and I really need her with me right now and if you could just see me through this for a while then . . ."

JP: I know we're playing amateur psychologists, but these things happen when people don't lay shit on the table.

PS: So one of your solutions to all this is you bring your families on the road part of the time.

ST: Because when my eight-year-old daughter's fourteen I don't wanna have to go fuckin' back to therapy—"Daddy, you weren't there for me." I don't want her to have that psychological deficit that she missed something of her father when she was growing up and she's pissed off about it.

JP: The other side is, *I* don't wanna miss them growing up. I hate being away for three weeks and having my kids' vocabulary double and not being part of that.

ST: Havin' my fuckin' neighbor teach my daughter how to ride a bike. I mean it's really selfish to write a song. I still think a song is a cute child because it comes from nowhere, either your mind or a little something you steal from the Beatles or the Everly Brothers, but your brain is breathing life into something that wasn't there. When I hear them back on the radio, I remember the time, I remember the orgy of love and fun that I went through, livin' on the edge, the angst, the freak-out.

But you can teach a child how to ride a bike or climb up on a wall and fall down and get back up and you suddenly see little bits and pieces of yourself in there and that's what life is all about for me. And to have a wife who says, "Go on, get the fuck out of here and go on tour." That lets me have my whore, my music, that I can *fuck* until I'm sore and have my way with and do whatever I want with. That's great.

I used to think it would be great to have a wife that was bisexual so that when I got home her girlfriend would be there and I could fuck 'em both. The max. But now, finally, I've met somebody who knows how much I love my music, knows the importance of it to my soul.

There are nights we've come offstage, we've played to 60,000 people and I'm so happy, I'm in the greatest band in the world, and I call my kids and it makes me cry. It's great. I love it.

Appendix A

Toys in the Studio and on the Stage

The Guitars of Joe Perry and Brad Whitford

by Richard Bienstock

Any attempt to take a full accounting of the instruments employed by Joe Perry and Brad Whitford over their forty years in—and out—of Aerosmith is a Herculean, if not downright insurmountable, task. Perry told this writer in 2010 that his collection at present stood at upward of six hundred guitars; an imposing number in and of itself, and one that also didn't begin to acknowledge the many six-strings that had been worked to exhaustion, destroyed, or sold off—either by choice or necessity—over the years. And unlike, say, a Brian May or Angus Young, players whose guitar preferences are famously narrow, or a Jimi Hendrix, whose recording years spanned a short and finite amount of time, Perry and Whitford go deep and long. Furthermore, neither player's collection has been scrutinized to the same obsessive degree as has that of a guitarist like Jimmy Page, for example, whose every instrument used with Led Zeppelin has seemingly been dissected and rebuilt in myriad interviews.

In Burbank, California, taping the *Midnight Special* episode that aired August 16, 1974. The guitars Whitford and Perry played on the show—a Gibson Les Paul Junior and a Fender Stratocaster—were workhorses of the band's early career. MICHAEL OCHS ARCHIVES/GETTY IMAGES

Even so, the information available on Perry and Whitford's guitars is hardly insubstantial, and is in many cases— though much more so for Perry—rather extensive. The following examination, while far from all encompassing, is an effort to gather as much of this data as is possible together in one place, focusing on the notable, and sometimes iconic, pieces that have helped to create and define the Aerosmith sound over four decades. It is the product of much research, as well as this writer's own discussions with both guitarists and various others who were there—onstage, backstage, and in the studio—in the '70s, '80s, and more recent years. Not to mention, of course, knowledge gleaned from a lifetime listening to and observing Perry and Whitford in action.

In Aerosmith's earliest days, Perry leaned heavily on Fender Stratocasters, while Whitford, designated as more of the rhythm man, opted for the chunkier sound of Gibson Les Pauls. Perry told this writer in 2002 that his main guitar on the band's 1973 self-titled debut was indeed a Strat, and in photos and video from 1973 and '74 he can be seen wielding both an early-'70s example in Olympic white, with large headstock and a bullet truss rod; and a black model, with white pickguard and rosewood fretboard, of undetermined year. This latter guitar is believed to have carried the lion's share of the workload on that first album.

Whitford employed a Les Paul goldtop with P-90 pickups for his parts on *Aerosmith*. Soon after the recording, he has said, this guitar's neck "gave up the ghost" and he purchased a second goldtop. This new instrument, along with a one-pickup Les Paul Junior, were staples of his arsenal for the next few years. But as Aerosmith's popularity grew, so did Whitford's

collection. In the mid-'70s he acquired several more Les Pauls of various vintages, including a '57 goldtop with a Bigsby tremolo. He also purchased a Fender Broadcaster, the extremely rare (only a few hundred were produced, from late 1950 to early '51) precursor to the company's Telecaster model.

Perry likewise began to amass more guitars. By the time of *Toys in the Attic* he had obtained several vintage Strats—including a '59 sunburst model, the guitar heard on "Walk This Way"—as well as a '60s Telecaster and a handful of Les Pauls. The most prominent of these Pauls was a "Black Beauty" Custom with the pickguard removed, a Perry mainstay in the mid-'70s. Other notable Perry instruments from this era include a stock Gibson "reverse" Firebird VII and a Fender Bass VI, the latter famously used on "Back in the Saddle."

In 1976 Perry acquired a Les Paul whose story would play out over the course of more than two decades. He purchased

the instrument, a tobacco 'burst of the much-fetishized 1959 vintage, from renowned Nashville dealer George Gruhn for $2,500 (by comparison, '59 'bursts today sell—if one can even be found—for well into the six figures). Perry made heavy use of the guitar, but in the early '80s sold it off—as Whitford did with much of his own gear—to combat dire financial straits. After passing through several hands, the 'burst ultimately wound up in the possession of Aerosmith super-fan and eventual Perry friend Slash, who can be seen playing the guitar in Guns N' Roses' 1992 video for "November Rain." Perry subsequently made several attempts at buying the instrument back; Slash, however, wasn't selling. All was righted in 2000, when Slash, as a surprise fiftieth birthday gift to Perry, returned the guitar to its one-time owner, free of charge.

Back when Perry first purchased the 'burst, in 1976, he and Whitford had just begun to venture beyond the worlds of Gibson and Fender. That same year, Perry acquired an early-model B.C. Rich Mockingbird—reportedly, one of the first twenty ever produced—which can be heard on 1977's *Draw the Line*. This gave way to a heavy period of B.C. Rich use for both guitarists, as well as an endorsement from the company. Among the many B.C. Rich models in their arsenal were Perry's solid rosewood Mockingbird—obtained as part of the endorsement deal—and Whitford's natural-finish Eagle (two, actually). These guitars were each played by their respective owners on the studio version of "Come Together." In addition, both procured incredibly cool-looking Bich 10-strings—Perry in red and Whitford in blue—from which they would simply remove the four extra strings (and often the corresponding machine heads) and play as normal. Perry, on the rare occasion, also wielded a natural-finish Bich double-neck.

Other Perry guitars from this era included a Dan Armstrong Plexi, used onstage with a bass A string in place of the low E for "Draw the Line" (though in the studio this song was recorded on a Tele);

Goldtops have long been a mainstay of Whitford's arsenal. As the band's popularity grew, so did his collection. Detroit, circa 1975. © ROBERT ALFORD

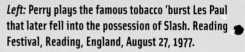

Left: Perry plays the famous tobacco 'burst Les Paul that later fell into the possession of Slash. Reading Festival, Reading, England, August 27, 1977.
PETER STILL/REDFERNS/GETTY IMAGES

Below: The years 1976 and 1977 ushered in a heavy period of B.C. Rich use for both guitarists, as well as an endorsement from the company. Among their many B.C. Rich models were Perry's famous red B.C. Rich Bich and Whitford's two natural-finish Eagles. Detroit, circa 1978. BOTH © ROBERT ALFORD

a '63 Les Paul Junior with custom inlay; and several new and vintage left-handed Strats, which—à la Jimi Hendrix, but opposite—Perry would flip over and play righty. Whitford, in addition to his B.C. Rich models, often employed a 1978 black Les Paul Custom at this time.

A key component of the Aerosmith guitar sound in the late '70s was both players' use of Bill Lawrence pickups, a change enacted in part by then–guitar tech Neil Thompson. All B.C. Rich guitars, and many Les Pauls, including Whitford's '78 Custom, were loaded with Lawrence L-90 humbuckers, while Strats received single-blade L-220s. Perry and Whitford also used Lawrence strings on their instruments and appeared in ads for the company; Bill Lawrence, in turn, acted as a consultant for the guitarists.

By late '79, Perry was out of Aerosmith and fronting the more streamlined Joe Perry Project. He likewise pared his gear down to just a clutch of instruments: a few Strats; two metal-necked Travis Bean 500s in silver and blue (one of which can be heard on "Let the Music Do the Talking"); the red Bich; and a mongrel famously known as the Telerat. Constructed by Thompson, this instrument was the product of a lefty Strat body—black, with the paint belt-sanded off—grafted to a lefty Tele neck. Pickups, per usual, were Lawrence L-200s.

In 1984 Perry and Whitford rejoined Aerosmith, and in their first years back

Left, top: Perry often employed a black Les Paul Custom in the 1970s. World Series of Rock, Municipal Stadium, Cleveland, August 23, 1975.
© ROBERT ALFORD

Left: Fronting the more streamlined Joe Perry Project, Perry likewise pared his gear down to a clutch of instruments, including this mongrel famously known as the Telerat. Constructed by his guitar tech Neil Thompson, this instrument comprised a lefty Strat body—black, with the paint sanded off—grafted to a lefty Tele neck. Pickups, per usual, were Lawrence L-200s. L'amour, Brooklyn, New York, September 30, **1983.** © FRANK WHITE

both men took to trying out guitars current to the era, including various "super-strat" models from Charvel and other manufacturers. Whitford also made use of a white-on-black Hendrick and a black Guild Firebird. Perry employed a blond Schecter emblazoned with the phrase "Protest and Survive" to record his parts on the Run-DMC version of "Walk This Way" in 1986. The video for that song shows the guitarist wielding a downright futuristic-looking black Guild X-100 Bladerunner, with triangular body cutouts and a sharply pointed horn. One of the more bizarre designs of the era, it is also among the most rare; manufactured for just two years, in 1984 and '85, fewer than one hundred of these guitars exist. Perry reportedly owns two.

By the time of *Permanent Vacation*, both guitarists had begun to turn back to the classics. Whitford relied heavily on a stock '65 Strat and a '56 Les Paul Junior for that album, while Perry's main guitars included a Tele-like 1985 Guild T-250 with EMG pickups, a Gretsch Silver Jet, and an ESP Strat-style model known as "the Spoon." This last instrument, a "parts" guitar with an unfinished body, Kahler tremolo, and a Duncan JB pickup with coil-splitter cutter in the lead position, was also his primary workhorse on the road.

From the late '80s on, Gibson and Fender were again the main order of the day. Perry's gear for 1989's *Pump* included '54 and '57 Les Pauls, a '53 goldtop, a Chet Atkins Classical Electric (heard on "Janie's Got a Gun"), an A-tuned Dan Armstrong ("F.I.N.E.*"), and a '57 Strat, his primary guitar for the sessions. Whitford, meanwhile, largely stuck to an '87 goldtop with Seymour Duncan pickups, but also employed a '54 Strat and a stunning '53 goldtop with a black pickguard.

Both guitarists continued to expand their collections throughout the *Get a Grip* era. In 1994, Perry picked up a prized 1960 Les Paul, while Whitford added a '59; each showcased his respective instrument on 1997's *Nine Lives*. Other guitars employed by Whitford on that album included a Parker Fly, Jerry Jones Danelectro copy,

Perry slings the "Bullets and Bones" guitar on opening night of the Cocked, Locked, Ready to Rock tour, Oracle Arena, Oakland, California, July 23, 2010. TIM MOSENFELDER/GETTY IMAGES

and Veillette baritone. Perry, meanwhile, played '57 and '59 Strats, and made much use of his first signature model, the Joe Perry Les Paul, issued by Gibson that same year. Modeled on Perry's '59 and '60 Pauls, the guitar also featured an active mid-boost tone-shaping circuit, "Joe Perry" signature logo on the body, and translucent "Blackburst" finish.

This instrument was discontinued in 2000 and replaced three years later with a new signature model, the Boneyard Les Paul. Inspired by the green-tinted stain on a Gibson Custom Shop guitar commissioned by Perry's wife, Billie, as a Christmas gift to her husband, the Boneyard boasted a striking translucent "Green Tiger" finish, as well as a reverse-wired BurstBucker neck pickup and mother-of-pearl Boneyard headstock logo.

Mrs. Perry would influence another of her husband's more recent guitars,

this one a custom white Gibson B. B. King "Lucille" model with Billie's visage airbrushed across the lower half of the body. Perry has often cited this instrument as one of his favorites, and, indeed, it remains a primary stage guitar to this day. There are, of course, many others. For Aerosmith's 2010 Cocked, Locked, Ready to Rock tour, Perry brought close to fifty guitars on the road, among them almost a dozen Les Pauls (including the Boneyard prototype, a rare Jeff Beck "Oxblood," and a Jimmy Page signature), numerous Strats, several familiar models (the red Bich, the Guild X-100), and some newer custom examples, including a pair of ornately designed one-offs from RS Guitar Works: a metal-topped creation known as "Admiral Perry," and one featuring volume and tone knobs constructed from bullet casings and elk horn, named, appropriately, "Bullets and Bones." These

days, Whitford travels primarily with a selection of vintage and newer Les Pauls, including goldtops, 'bursts, flame tops, and a red model with Bigsby tremolo. He also carries an assortment of Strats, many of which were on display during his 2010 stint on the Experience Hendrix tour.

These numerous and varied instruments represent only a fraction of those Perry and Whitford have recorded with and performed on over the years. It should be noted that the guitar itself embodies only one sonic element in each musician's tonal universe. There are also, for starters, the many amplifiers and effect pedals employed throughout the life of the band. Taking these into account, however, would introduce hundreds of additional pieces of gear into the picture, a move that would no doubt necessitate a separate—though, to be sure, equally fascinating—study altogether.

Appendix B
Just Push Play

An Aerosmith Discography

This compendium encompasses all official Aerosmith audio and visual releases. Studio albums, live recordings, and the many—particularly in the later years—compilations are listed chronologically and with appropriate notes. In the interest of curbing repetition, soundtrack contributions have not been documented, as in almost all cases (save for a small number of instances) this material likewise appears on a band studio effort or collection. Likewise, songwriting credits are referenced only on first mention of each song. Additionally, individual output from primary members has been cataloged when deemed appropriate: specifically, all full-length albums from Joe Perry (with the Joe Perry Project and solo), Brad Whitford's Whitford/St. Holmes outing, and, for their historical significance, Steven Tyler's 45-rpm recordings with Chain Reaction.

ALBUMS

Aerosmith personnel on all albums (unless otherwise noted):

Steven Tyler / Joe Perry / Brad Whitford / Tom Hamilton / Joey Kramer

AEROSMITH

Label: Columbia
Released: January 1973
Produced by: Adrian Barber
Recorded: Intermedia Sound, Boston, MA

Make It (Steven Tyler); Somebody (Tyler, Steven Emspack); Dream On (Tyler); One Way Street (Tyler); Mama Kin (Tyler); Write Me (Tyler); Movin' Out (Tyler, Joe Perry); Walkin' the Dog (Rufus Thomas)

Additional musician:
David Woodford—saxophone on "Mama Kin" and "Write Me"

Note: "Write Me" is alternately referred to as "Write Me a Letter."

GET YOUR WINGS

Label: Columbia
Released: March 1974
Produced by: Jack Douglas, Ray Colcord
Executive Producer: Bob Ezrin
Recorded: Record Plant Studios, New York City

Same Old Song and Dance (Tyler, Perry); Lord of the Thighs (Tyler); Spaced (Tyler, Perry); Woman of the World (Tyler, Don Solomon); S.O.S (Too Bad) (Tyler); Train Kept a Rollin' (Tiny Bradshaw, Lois Mann, Howard Kay); Seasons of Wither (Tyler); Pandora's Box (Tyler, Joey Kramer)

Additional musicians:
Michael Brecker—tenor saxophone on "Same Old Song and Dance" and "Pandora's Box"
Stan Bronstein—baritone saxophone on "Same Old Song and Dance" and "Pandora's Box"
Randy Brecker—trumpet on "Same Old Song and Dance"
Jon Pearson—trombone on "Same Old Song and Dance"
Ray Colcord—keyboards on "Spaced"

TOYS IN THE ATTIC

Label: Columbia
Released: April 1975
Produced by: Jack Douglas
Recorded: Record Plant Studios, New York City

Toys in the Attic (Tyler, Perry); Uncle Salty (Tyler, Tom Hamilton); Adam's Apple (Tyler); Walk This Way (Tyler, Perry); Big Ten Inch Record (Fred Weismantel); Sweet Emotion (Tyler, Hamilton); No More No More (Tyler, Perry); Round and Round (Tyler, Brad Whitford); You See Me Crying (Tyler, Solomon)

Additional musicians:
Scott Cushnie—piano on "Big Ten Inch Record" and "No More No More"
Jay Messina—bass marimba on "Sweet Emotion"

ROCKS

Label: Columbia
Released: May 1976
Produced by: Jack Douglas, Aerosmith
Recorded: The Wherehouse, Waltham, MA; Record Plant Studios, New York City

Back in the Saddle (Tyler, Perry); Last Child (Tyler, Whitford); Rats in the Cellar (Tyler, Perry); Combination (Perry); Sick as a Dog (Tyler, Hamilton); Nobody's Fault (Tyler, Whitford); Get the Lead Out (Tyler, Perry); Lick and a Promise (Tyler, Perry); Home Tonight (Tyler)

Additional musician:
Paul Prestopino—banjo on "Last Child"

DRAW THE LINE

Label: Columbia
Released: December 1977
Produced by: Jack Douglas, Aerosmith
Recorded: The Cenacle, Armonk, NY; Record Plant Studios, New York City

Draw the Line (Tyler, Perry); I Wanna Know Why (Tyler, Perry); Critical Mass (Tyler, Hamilton, Jack Douglas); Get It Up (Tyler, Perry); Bright Light Fright (Perry); Kings and Queens (Tyler, Whitford, Hamilton, Kramer, Douglas); The Hand That Feeds (Tyler, Whitford, Hamilton, Kramer, Douglas); Sight for Sore Eyes (Tyler, Perry, Douglas, David Johansen); Milk Cow Blues (Kokomo Arnold)

Additional musicians:
Stan Bronstein—saxophones on "Bright Light Fright" and "I Wanna Know Why"

Scott Cushnie—piano on "I Wanna Know Why" and "Critical Mass"
Jack Douglas—mandolin on "Kings and Queens"
Karen Lawrence—background vocals on "Get It Up"
Paul Prestopino—banjo on "Kings and Queens"

LIVE! BOOTLEG

Label: Columbia
Released: October 1978
Produced by: Jack Douglas, Aerosmith
Recorded: Various performances 1973, 1977, and 1978

Back in the Saddle (Indianapolis, IN, July 4, 1977); Sweet Emotion (Chicago, IL, March 23, 1978); Lord of the Thighs (Chicago, IL, March 23, 1978); Toys in the Attic (Boston, MA, March 28, 1978); Last Child (The Paradise Club, Boston, MA, August 9, 1978); Come Together (John Lennon, Paul McCartney) (The Wherehouse, Waltham, MA, August 21, 1978); Walk This Way (Detroit, MI, April 2, 1978); Sick as a Dog (Indianapolis, IN, July 4, 1977); Dream On (Louisville, KY, July 3, 1977); Chip Away the Stone (Richard Supa) (Santa Monica, CA, April 8, 1978); Sight for Sore Eyes (Columbus, OH, February 24, 1978); Mama Kin (Indianapolis, IN, July 4, 1977); S.O.S. (Too Bad) (Indianapolis, IN, July 4, 1977); I Ain't Got You (Calvin Carter) (Paul's Mall, Boston, MA, April 23 1973; WBCN-FM radio simulcast); Mother Popcorn (James Brown, Pee Wee Ellis) (Paul's Mall, Boston, MA, April 23, 1973; WBCN-FM radio simulcast); Train Kept a Rollin' (Detroit, MI, April 2, 1978)

Additional musicians:
David Woodford—saxophone on "Mother Popcorn"
Mark Radice—keyboards and backing vocals

Notes: "Draw the Line," recorded at the Tower Theater in Philadelphia, PA, on March 26, 1978, appears as a hidden track following "Mother Popcorn."
    A section of "Strangers in the Night," written by Bert Kaempfert, Charlie Singleton, and Eddie Snyder, is performed during "Train Kept a Rollin'."

NIGHT IN THE RUTS

Label: Columbia
Released: November 1979
Produced by: Gary Lyons, Aerosmith
Recorded: Mediasound Studios, New York City; Record Plant Studios, New York City

No Surprize (Tyler, Perry); Chiquita (Tyler, Perry); Remember (Walking in the Sand) (George

"Shadow" Morton); Cheese Cake (Tyler, Perry); Three Mile Smile (Tyler, Perry); Reefer Head Woman (Lester Melrose, Joe Bennett, William "Jazz" Gillum); Bone to Bone (Coney Island White Fish Boy) (Tyler, Perry); Think About It (Keith Relf, Jim McCarty, Jimmy Page); Mia (Tyler)

Additional musicians:
Richard Supa—additional guitars on "Mia" and "No Surprize"
Neil Thompson—electric guitar on "Mia"
George Young—alto saxophone on "Chiquita"
Lou Delgotto—baritone saxophone on "Chiquita"
Lou Marini—tenor saxophone on "Chiquita"
Barry Rogers—trombone on "Chiquita"

Note: Jimmy Crespo is uncredited for guitar work on "Three Mile Smile."

AEROSMITH'S GREATEST HITS

Label: Columbia
Released: October 1980
Produced by: [see respective studio albums for info]
Recorded: [see respective studio album for info]

Dream On; Same Old Song and Dance; Sweet Emotion; Walk This Way; Last Child; Back in the Saddle; Draw the Line; Kings and Queens; Come Together (from the soundtrack to the film *Sgt. Pepper's Lonely Hearts Club Band*, produced by Jack Douglas and George Martin); Remember (Walking in the Sand)

Additional musicians:
[see respective studio album for info]

Note: "Same Old Song and Dance," "Sweet Emotion," and "Kings and Queens" appear as edited, single-release versions.

ROCK IN A HARD PLACE

Label: Columbia
Released: August 1982
Produced by: Jack Douglas, Steven Tyler, Tony Bongiovi
Recorded: The Power Station, New York City; Criteria Studios, Miami, FL

Jailbait (Tyler, Jimmy Crespo); Lightning Strikes (Supa); Bitch's Brew (Tyler, Crespo); Bolivian Ragamuffin (Tyler, Crespo); Cry Me a River (Arthur Hamilton); Prelude to Joanie (Tyler); Joanie's Butterfly (Tyler, Crespo, Douglas); Rock in a Hard Place (Cheshire Cat) (Tyler, Crespo, Douglas); Jig Is Up (Tyler, Crespo); Push Comes to Shove (Tyler)

Band Personnel:
Steven Tyler / Jimmy Crespo / Rick Dufay / Tom Hamilton / Joey Kramer

Additional musicians:
Brad Whitford—rhythm guitar on "Lightning Strikes"
Paul Harris—piano on "Push Comes to Shove"
John Turi—saxophone on "Rock in a Hard Place (Cheshire Cat)"
Reinhard Straub—violins on "Joanie's Butterfly"
John Lievano—guitar on "Joanie's Butterfly"
Jack Douglas—percussion

DONE WITH MIRRORS

Label: Geffen
Released: November 1985
Produced by: Ted Templeman
Recorded: Fantasy Recording, Berkeley, CA

Let the Music Do the Talking (Tyler, Perry); My Fist Your Face (Tyler, Perry); Shame on You (Tyler); The Reason a Dog (Tyler, Hamilton); Shela (Tyler, Whitford); Gypsy Boots (Tyler, Perry); She's on Fire (Tyler, Perry); The Hop (Tyler, Perry, Whitford, Hamilton, Kramer); Darkness (Tyler)

Note: "Darkness" does not appear on original vinyl LP; cassette and, later, CD only.

CLASSICS LIVE!

Label: Columbia
Released: April 1986
Produced by: Paul O'Neill
Recorded: Various performances, 1977–1983

Train Kept a Rollin'; Kings and Queens; Sweet Emotion; Dream On; Mama Kin; Three Mile Smile / Reefer Head Woman; Lord of the Thighs; Major Barbra (Tyler)

Notes: Some tracks are rumored to contain in-the-studio guitar overdubs from Jimmy Crespo.
"Major Barbra" was an unreleased studio recording, produced by Paul O'Neill and Tony Bongiovi. On 1991's Pandora's Box, the song is listed as "Major Barbara."

CLASSICS LIVE! II

Label: Columbia
Released: June 1987
Produced by: Paul O'Neill, Aerosmith
Recorded: Tracks 1, 2, 3, 5, 6, and 8—Orpheum Theatre, Boston, MA, December 31, 1984; Track 4—Ontario Motor Speedway, Ontario, CA, (California Jam II) March 18, 1978; Track 7—Worcester Centrum, Worcester, MA, March 12, 1986

Back in the Saddle; Walk This Way; Movin' Out; Draw the Line; Same Old Song and Dance; Last Child; Let the Music Do the Talking; Toys in the Attic

PERMANENT VACATION

Label: Geffen
Released: August 1987
Produced by: Bruce Fairbairn
Recorded: Little Mountain Sound Studios, Vancouver, BC, Canada

Heart's Done Time (Perry, Desmond Child); Magic Touch (Tyler, Perry, Jim Vallance); Rag Doll (Tyler, Perry, Vallance, Holly Knight); Simoriah (Tyler, Perry, Vallance); Dude (Looks Like a Lady) (Tyler, Perry, Child); St. John (Tyler); Hangman Jury (Tyler, Perry, Vallance); Girl Keeps Coming Apart (Tyler, Perry); Angel (Tyler, Child); Permanent Vacation (Tyler, Whitford); I'm Down (Lennon, McCartney); The Movie (Tyler, Perry, Whitford, Hamilton, Kramer)

Additional musicians:
Morgan Rael—steel drum on "Permanent Vacation"
Jim Vallance—organ on "Rag Doll" and "Simoriah"
Drew Arnott—Mellotron on "Angel" and "The Movie"
Bruce Fairbairn—cello on "The Movie"
Scott Fairbairn—cello on "The Movie"

The Margarita Horns (on "Dude [Looks Like a Lady]," "Rag Doll," and "Girl Keeps Coming Apart"):
Tom Keenlyside—tenor saxophone, clarinet, arrangements
Ian Putz—baritone saxophone
Bob Rogers—trombone on
Henry Christian—trumpet

GEMS

Label: Columbia
Released: November 1988
Produced by: [see respective studio album for info]
Recorded: [see respective studio album for info]

Rats in the Cellar; Lick and a Promise; Chip Away the Stone; No Surprize; Mama Kin; Adam's Apple; Nobody's Fault; Round and Round; Critical Mass; Lord of the Thighs; Jailbait; Train Kept a Rollin'

Additional musicians:
[see respective studio album for info]

Note: "Chip Away the Stone" is a 1978 single-only studio version, produced by Jack Douglas.

PUMP

Label: Geffen
Released: September 1989
Produced by: Bruce Fairbairn
Recorded: Little Mountain Sound Studios, Vancouver, BC, Canada

Young Lust (Tyler, Perry, Vallance); F.I.N.E.* (Tyler, Perry, Child); Going Down; Love in an Elevator (Tyler, Perry); Monkey on My Back (Tyler, Perry); Water Song; Janie's Got a Gun (Tyler, Hamilton); Dulcimer Stomp; The Other Side (Tyler, Vallance); My Girl (Tyler, Perry); Don't Get Mad, Get Even (Tyler, Perry); Hoodoo; Voodoo Medicine Man (Tyler, Whitford); What It Takes (Tyler, Perry, Child)

Bonus track (Japanese version):
Ain't Enough (Tyler, Perry)

Note: "Going Down" is a seventeen-second skit featuring Catherine Epps in the role of "Elevator Operator."
"Water Song," "Dulcimer Stomp," and "Hoodoo" are short musical interludes performed by Tyler, Perry, Randy Raine-Reusch, and Fairbairn; on releases in certain countries, a fourth instrumental piece appears as a hidden track following "What It Takes."
In the early 1990s, famed Motown songwriting and production team Brian Holland, Edward Holland, Jr., and Lamont Dozier threatened a lawsuit against Aerosmith, claiming the melody in "The Other Side" was similar to that of their song "Standing in the Shadows of Love," originally recorded in 1966 by the Four Tops. As part of a settlement, credits for "The Other Side" were subsequently amended to read "Tyler-Vallance-Holland-Dozier-Holland."

PANDORA'S BOX

Label: Columbia
Released: November 1991
Produced by: [see respective studio album for info]
Recorded: [see respective studio album for info]

Disc 1:
When I Needed You (Tyler) (Steven Tyler, pre-Aerosmith, with Chain Reaction, recorded 1966); Make It; Movin' Out (unreleased alternate version, *Aerosmith* sessions, 1972); One Way Street; On the Road Again (Floyd Jones) (unreleased recording, *Aerosmith* sessions, 1972); Mama Kin; Same Old Song and Dance; Train Kept a Rollin'; Seasons of Wither; Write Me a Letter (unreleased live version, 1976); Dream On; Pandora's Box; Rattlesnake Shake (Peter Green) (live radio broadcast, WKRQ, Cincinnati, OH, 1971); Walkin' the Dog (live radio broadcast, WKRQ, Cincinnati, OH, 1971); Lord of the Thighs (live, Texxas Jam, Dallas, TX, 1978)

Disc 2:
Toys in the Attic; Round and Round; Krawhitham (Kramer, Whitford, Hamilton) (unreleased recording, *Draw the Line* sessions, the Cenacle, Armonk, NY, 1977); You See Me Crying; Sweet Emotion; No More No More; Walk This Way; I Wanna Know Why (live, Texxas Jam, Dallas, TX, 1978); Big Ten Inch Record (live, Texxas Jam, Dallas, TX, 1978); Rats in the Cellar; Last Child (remix of original album version); All Your Love (Otis Rush) (unreleased recording, *Draw the Line* sessions, the Cenacle, Armonk, NY, 1977); Soul Saver (Tyler, Whitford) (unreleased rehearsal recording, *Rocks* sessions, Record Plant Studios, New York City, 1975); Nobody's Fault; Lick and a Promise; Adam's Apple (live, Indianapolis, IN, 1977); Draw the Line (remix of original album version); Critical Mass

Disc 3:
Kings and Queens (unreleased live version, 1978); Milk Cow Blues; I Live in Connecticut (Tyler, Perry) (unreleased rehearsal recording, *Night in the Ruts* sessions, the Wherehouse, Waltham, MA, 1979); Three Mile Smile; Let It Slide (Tyler, Perry) (unreleased recording, *Night in the Ruts* sessions, 1979); Cheese Cake; Bone to Bone (Coney Island White Fish Boy); No Surprize; Come Together; Downtown Charlie (unreleased recording, Record Plant Studios, New York City, 1978); Sharpshooter (Whitford, Derek St. Holmes) (from the 1981 Whitford/St. Holmes self-titled album); Shit House Shuffle (Perry) (unreleased rehearsal recording, *Night in the Ruts* sessions, Record Plant Studios, New York City, 1979); South Station Blues (Perry) (from the 1981 Joe Perry Project album *I've Got the Rock 'n' Rolls Again*); Riff & Roll (Tyler, Crespo) (unreleased recording, *Rock in a Hard Place* sessions, the Power Station, New York City, 1981); Jailbait; Major Barbara (unreleased alternate version, the Power Station, New York City, 1971); Chip Away the Stone (unreleased alternate version, 1978); Helter Skelter (unreleased recording, Great Northern Recording Studios, Boston, MA, 1975); Back in the Saddle

Note: An unlisted instrumental, "Circle Jerk" (Whitford), appears at the end of Disc 3.

GET A GRIP

Label: Geffen
Released: April 1993
Produced by: Bruce Fairbairn
Recorded: Little Mountain Sound Studios, Vancouver, BC, Canada; A&M Studios, Los Angeles, CA

Intro (Tyler, Perry); Eat the Rich (Tyler, Perry, Vallance); Get a Grip (Tyler, Perry, Vallance); Fever (Tyler, Perry); Livin' on the Edge (Tyler, Perry, Mark Hudson); Flesh (Tyler, Perry, Child); Walk On Down (Perry); Shut Up and Dance (Tyler, Perry, Jack Blades, Tommy Shaw); Cryin' (Tyler, Perry, Taylor Rhodes); Gotta Love It (Tyler, Perry, Hudson); Crazy (Tyler, Perry, Child); Line Up (Tyler, Perry, Lenny Kravitz); Amazing (Tyler, Supa); Boogie Man (Tyler, Perry)

Bonus track (international versions):
Can't Stop Messin' (Tyler, Perry, Blades, Shaw)

Additional musicians:
John Webster—keyboards and programming
Richard Supa—keyboards on "Amazing"
Don Henley—background vocals on "Amazing"
Desmond Child—keyboards on "Crazy"
Lenny Kravitz—"Come on Joe" on "Line Up"
Mapuhi T. Tekurio, Melvin Liufau, Wesey Mamea, Liainaiala Tagaloa, Sandy Kanaeholo, and Aladd Alatina Teofilo, Jr.—Polynesian log drums on "Eat the Rich"

The Margarita Horns:
Tom Keenlyside—saxophone
Bob Rogers—trombone
Ian Putz—baritone saxophone
Paul Baron—trumpet
Bruce Fairbairn—trumpet

BIG ONES

Label: Geffen
Released: November 1994
Produced by: [see respective studio album for info, except * by Michael Beinhorn]
Recorded: [see respective studio album for info, except * at the Power Station, New York City, and Capri Digital Studios, Isle of Capri, Italy]

Walk on Water* (Tyler, Perry, Blades, Shaw); Love in an Elevator; Rag Doll; What It Takes; Dude (Looks Like a Lady); Janie's Got a Gun; Cryin'; Amazing; Blind Man* (Tyler, Perry, Rhodes); Deuces Are Wild (Tyler, Vallance); The Other Side; Crazy; Eat the Rich; Angel; Livin' on the Edge

Bonus track (international versions):
Dude (Looks Like a Lady) (live recording from the *Get a Grip* tour)

Notes: "Deuces Are Wild" was recorded in late 1988/early 1989 at Distorto Studios, Vancouver, and Little Mountain Sound Studios for the Pump album. It eventually surfaced on the 1993 compilation, The Beavis and Butt-Head Experience. According to Vallance, the final version featured only himself, Tyler, Perry, and Kramer. He wrote on jimvallance.com: "For reasons I've never fully understood (perhaps they were in the middle of a tour?) Aerosmith decided not to record a new track [for The Beavis and Butt-Head Experience]. Instead, they simply added Steven's vocal and Joe's guitar to the 'Deuces Are Wild' demo I'd recorded in my home studio five years earlier (and some drum overdubs from Joey?)."

Additional musicians:
[see respective studio album for info]

BOX OF FIRE

Label: Columbia
Released: November 1994
Produced by: [see respective album for info]
Recorded: [see respective album for info]

Note: This box set collects remastered versions of all twelve Aerosmith albums originally issued by Columbia, with expanded booklets featuring original liner notes and additional photos and memorabilia. Also includes bonus disc of previously unissued material.

Albums:
Aerosmith (Disc 1)
Get Your Wings (Disc 2)
Toys in the Attic (Disc 3)

Rocks (Disc 4)
Draw the Line (Disc 5)
Live! Bootleg (Disc 6)
Night in the Ruts (Disc 7)
Greatest Hits (Disc 8)
Rock in a Hard Place (Disc 9)
Classics Live! (Disc 10)
Classics Live! II (Disc 11)
Gems (Disc 12)

Bonus disc (Disc 13):
Sweet Emotion (remix); Rockin' Pneumonia and the Boogie Woogie Flu (Huey "Piano" Smith) (outtake from the *Permanent Vacation* sessions, originally released on the soundtrack to the 1987 film *Less Than Zero*); Subway (instrumental) (Whitford, Hamilton, Kramer); Circle Jerk; Dream On (from the MTV tenth anniversary special, recorded October 13, 1991, the Wang Center, Boston, MA)

NINE LIVES

Label: Columbia
Released: March 1997
Produced by: Kevin "Caveman" Shirley; additional production by Aerosmith
Recorded: Avatar Studios, New York City; additional tracks for "The Farm" recorded at the Boneyard, South Shore, MA, by Steven Tyler, Joe Perry, and Mark Hudson

Nine Lives (Tyler, Perry, Marti Frederiksen); Falling in Love (Is Hard on the Knees) (Tyler, Perry, Glen Ballard); Hole in My Soul (Tyler, Perry, Child); Taste of India (Tyler, Perry, Ballard); Full Circle (Tyler, Rhodes); Something's Gotta Give (Tyler, Perry, Frederiksen); Ain't That a Bitch (Tyler, Perry, Child); The Farm (Tyler, Perry, Hudson, Steve Dudas); Crash (Tyler, Perry, Hudson, Dominic Miller); Kiss Your Past Good-bye (Tyler, Hudson); Pink (Tyler, Supa, Ballard); Attitude Adjustment (Tyler, Perry, Frederiksen); Fallen Angels (Tyler, Perry, Supa)

Bonus tracks:
Falling Off (Perry, Tyler, Frederiksen) (international and Japanese versions)
Fall Together (Tyler, Hudson, Greg Wells, Dean Grakal) (Japanese version only)
I Don't Want to Miss a Thing (Diane Warren) (international version; added to 1999 album reissue)

Additional musicians:
John Webster—keyboards
Ramesh Mishra—sarangi

Notes: The original Nine Lives *album cover drew protest from the American Hindu Anti-Defamation Coalition (AHADC) as well as several other Hindu organizations, accusing the band and Sony of, in the words of the AHADC, presenting a "distorted and offensive picture of Hindu God, Shree Krishna." In response, Sony issued a public apology and, beginning in summer 1997, issued* Nine Lives *with revised cover art.*

A LITTLE SOUTH OF SANITY

Label: Geffen
Released: October 1998
Produced by: Jack Douglas
Recorded: culled from various performances on the *Get a Grip* and *Nine Lives* tours

Disc 1:
Eat the Rich; Love in an Elevator; Falling in Love (Is Hard on the Knees); Same Old Song and Dance; Hole in My Soul; Monkey on My Back; Livin' on the Edge; Cryin'; Rag Doll; Angel; Janie's Got a Gun; Amazing

Disc 2:
Back in the Saddle; Last Child; The Other Side; Walk on Down; Dream On; Crazy; Mama Kin; Walk This Way; Dude (Looks Like a Lady); What It Takes; Sweet Emotion

Additional musicians:
Russ Irwin—keyboards, background vocals
Thom Gimbel—keyboards, background Vocals

JUST PUSH PLAY

Label: Columbia
Released: March 2001
Produced by: Steven Tyler, Joe Perry, Mark Hudson, Marti Frederiksen (a.k.a. "The Boneyard Boys")
Recorded: The Boneyard, South Shore, MA; the Bryer Patch, South Shore, MA
Drums recorded: Long View Farms Studio, North Brookfield, MA
Strings recorded: Ocean Way Studios, Los Angeles, CA; Sound Techniques, Boston, MA; Village Recorders, Los Angeles, CA

Beyond Beautiful (Tyler, Perry, Frederiksen); Just Push Play (Tyler, Hudson, Dudas); Jaded (Tyler, Frederiksen); Fly Away from Here (Frederiksen, Todd Chapman); Trip Hoppin' (Tyler, Perry, Frederiksen, Hudson); Sunshine (Tyler, Perry, Frederiksen); Under My Skin (Tyler, Perry, Frederiksen, Hudson); Luv Lies (Tyler, Perry, Frederiksen, Hudson); Outta Your Head (Tyler, Perry, Frederiksen); Drop Dead Gorgeous (Tyler, Perry, Hudson); Light Inside (Tyler, Perry, Frederiksen); Avant Garden (Tyler, Perry, Frederiksen, Hudson); Under My Skin (Reprise)

Bonus tracks:
Face (Tyler, Perry, Frederiksen) (international versions and North American Best Buy exclusive)
Won't Let You Down (Tyler, Perry, Frederiksen)
I Don't Want to Miss a Thing (Japanese version)

Additional musicians:
Tony Perry—scratching on "Just Push Play"
Jim Cox—piano on "Fly Away From Here"
Dan Higgins—clarinet and saxophone on "Trip Hoppin'"
Tower of Power—horns on "Trip Hoppin'"
Chelsea Tyler—background vocals on "Under My Skin"
Paul Caruso—loop programming on "Drop Dead Gorgeous"
Paul Santo—Kurzweil on "Fly Away From Here"; Hammond organ on "Avant Garden"
Liv Tyler—whispers on "Avant Garden"

Note: "Under My Skin (Reprise)" is a hidden track.

YOUNG LUST: THE AEROSMITH ANTHOLOGY

Label: Geffen
Released: November 2001
Produced by: [see respective studio/compilation album for info]
Recorded: [see respective studio/compilation album for info]

Disc 1:
Let the Music Do the Talking; My Fist Your Face; Shame on You; Heart's Done Time; Rag Doll; Dude (Looks Like a Lady); Angel; Hangman Jury; Permanent Vacation; Young Lust; The Other Side; What It Takes; Monkey on My Back; Love in an Elevator; Janie's Got a Gun; Ain't Enough; Walk This Way (Run-DMC version)

Disc 2:
Eat the Rich; Love Me Two Times (Jim Morrison, Robby Krieger, Ray Manzarek, John Densmore) (originally released on the soundtrack to the 1990 film *Air America*); Head First; Livin' on the Edge (acoustic version); Don't Stop; Can't Stop Messin'; Amazing (orchestral version); Cryin'; Crazy; Shut Up and Dance; Deuces Are Wild; Walk on Water; Blind Man; Falling in Love (Is Hard on the Knees) (live); Dream On (live); Hole in My Soul (live); Sweet Emotion (live)

Additional musicians:
[see respective studio/compilation album for info]

Notes: In 2005 the compilation was reissued with new cover art as Aerosmith: Gold.

The last four tracks on Disc 3 are taken from A Little South of Sanity.

O, YEAH! ULTIMATE AEROSMITH HITS

Label: Columbia
Released: July 2002
Produced by: [see respective studio/compilation album for info]
Recorded: [see respective studio/compilation album for info]

Disc 1:
Mama Kin; Dream On; Same Old Song and Dance; Seasons of Wither; Walk This Way; Big Ten Inch Record; Sweet Emotion; Last Child; Back in the Saddle; Draw the Line; Dude (Looks Like a Lady); Angel; Rag Doll; Janie's Got a Gun; Love in an Elevator; What It Takes

Disc 2:
The Other Side; Livin' on the Edge; Cryin'; Amazing; Deuces Are Wild; Crazy; Falling in Love (Is Hard on the Knees); Pink (the South Beach Mix); I Don't Want to Miss a Thing; Jaded; Just Push Play (radio remix); Walk This Way (Run-DMC version); Girls of Summer (Tyler, Perry, Frederiksen); Lay It Down (Tyler, Perry, Donald DeGrate, Frederiksen)

Bonus tracks:
Come Together
Theme from Spider-Man (Paul Francis Webster, Robert Harris) (from the soundtrack to the 2002 film, *Spider-Man*)
Toys in the Attic

HONKIN' ON BOBO

Label: Columbia
Released: March 2004
Produced by: Steven Tyler, Joe Perry, Jack Douglas; except * by Tyler, Perry, Marti Frederiksen
Recorded: The Boneyard, South Shore, MA; the Bryer Patch, South Shore, MA; Pandora's Box

Road Runner (Ellas McDaniel); Shame, Shame, Shame (Ruby Fisher, Kenyon Hopkins); Eyesight to the Blind (Sonny Boy Williamson); Baby, Please Don't Go* (Joseph Lee Williams); Never Loved a Girl (Ronny Shannon); Back

Back Train (Fred McDowell); You Gotta Move (Rev. Gary Davis, McDowell); The Grind (Tyler, Perry, Frederiksen); I'm Ready (Willie Dixon); Temperature (Joel Michael Cohen, Walter Jacobs); Stop Messin' Around* (Clifford Adams, Peter Green); Jesus is on the Main Line (traditional)

Bonus track (Japanese version):
Jaded

Additional musicians:
Tracy Bonham—vocals on "Back Back Train" and "Jesus is on the Main Line"
The Memphis Horns—brass on "Never Loved A Girl"
Johnnie Johnson—piano on "Shame, Shame, Shame" and "Temperature"
Paul Santo—piano, electric piano, organ

ROCKIN' THE JOINT

Label: Columbia
Released: October 2005
Produced by: Marti Frederiksen
Recorded: The Joint at the Hard Rock Hotel and Casino, Las Vegas, NV, 2002

Beyond Beautiful; Same Old Song and Dance; No More No More; Seasons of Wither; Light Inside; Draw the Line; I Don't Want to Miss a Thing; Big Ten Inch Record; Rattlesnake Shake; Walk This Way; Train Kept a Rollin'

DEVIL'S GOT A NEW DISGUISE: THE VERY BEST OF AEROSMITH

Label: Columbia
Released: October 2006
Produced by: [see respective studio/compilation album for info]
Recorded: [see respective studio/compilation album for info]

Dream On; Mama Kin; Sweet Emotion; Back in the Saddle; Last Child; Walk This Way (Run-DMC version); Dude (Looks Like a Lady); Rag Doll; Love in an Elevator; Janie's Got a Gun; What It Takes; Crazy; Livin' on the Edge; Cryin'; I Don't Want to Miss a Thing; Jaded; Sedona Sunrise (Tyler, Perry, Vallance); Devil's Got a New Disguise (Tyler, Perry, Warren)

Notes: "Sedona Sunrise" and "Devil's Got a New Disguise" were culled from sessions for Pump. *Additional work was done to the latter during sessions for* Get a Grip.

VHS/DVD RELEASES

AEROSMITH VIDEO SCRAPBOOK

Label: CBS
Released: 1987

Collection of live performances, promotional videos, and band discussions. Performances culled from Pontiac Silverdome, Pontiac, MI, May 8, 1976; Ontario Speedway, Ontario, CA (California Jam II), March 18, 1978; and Capital Centre, Largo, MD, November 9, 1978.

Toys in the Attic; Same Old Song and Dance; Chip Away the Stone; Draw the Line; Sweet Emotion; Chiquita (promotional music video); Lightning Strikes (promotional music video); Walk This Way; Adam's Apple; Train Kept a Rollin'; S.O.S. (unlisted track)

PERMANENT VACATION 3X5

Label: Geffen
Released: 1988

Compilation of promotional videos from *Permanent Vacation*. Also includes behind-the-scenes footage.

Dude (Looks Like a Lady); Angel; Rag Doll

LIVE: TEXXAS JAM '78

Label: CBS
Released: 1989

Filmed July 4 weekend at the Cotton Bowl in Dallas, TX, at the Texxas World Music Festival.

Rats in the Cellar; Seasons of Wither; I Wanna Know Why; Walkin' the Dog; Lick and a Promise; Get the Lead Out; Draw the Line; Sweet Emotion; Same Old Song and Dance; Milk Cow Blues; Toys in the Attic

THINGS THAT GO PUMP IN THE NIGHT

Label: Geffen
Released: 1990

Compilation of promotional videos from *Pump*. Also includes band interviews and behind-the-scenes footage.

Love in an Elevator; Janie's Got a Gun; What It Takes; What It Takes (the recording of)

THE MAKING OF PUMP

Label: CBS
Released: 1990

Features rehearsal and recording segments, band interviews, and behind-the-scenes footage from the recording of *Pump*. Also includes uncensored video versions of "What It Takes" and "The Other Side."

BIG ONES YOU CAN LOOK AT

Label: Geffen
Released: 1994

Compilation of promotional videos from *Permanent Vacation, Pump,* and *Get a Grip*. Also includes band interviews and behind-the-scenes footage.

Deuces Are Wild; Livin' on the Edge; Eat the Rich; Cryin'; Amazing; Crazy; Love in an Elevator; Janie's Got a Gun; What It Takes (the recording of); The Other Side; Dude (Looks Like a Lady); Angel; Rag Doll

YOU GOTTA MOVE

Label: Columbia
Released: 2004

Filmed at the Office Depot Center, Sunrise, FL, April 3, 2004, on the *Honkin' on Bobo* tour. Also features band interviews, behind-the-scenes footage, and a photo gallery; bonus audio CD includes five additional tracks from the performance and a segment on the making of *Honkin' on Bobo*.

Toys in the Attic; Love in an Elevator; Road Runner; Baby, Please Don't Go; Cryin'; The Other Side; Back in the Saddle; Draw the Line; Dream On; Stop Messin' Around; Jaded; I Don't Want to Miss a Thing; Sweet Emotion; Never Loved a Girl; Walk This Way; Train Kept a Rollin'

Bonus DVD:
Fever; Rats in the Cellar; Livin' on the Edge; Last Child; Same Old Song and Dance

Audio CD:
Toys in the Attic; Love in an Elevator; Rats in the Cellar; Road Runner; The Other Side; Back in the Saddle; You Gotta Move (Umixit interactive track)

STEVEN TYLER

"WHEN I NEEDED YOU" B/W "THE SUN"

Band: Chain Reaction
Label: Date
Released: 1966
Produced by: Richard Gottehrer
Recorded: CBS Studios

When I Needed You (Barry Shapiro, Steven Tallarico, Don Solomon, Alan Strohmayer, Peter Stahl); The Sun (Barry Shapiro, Steven Tallarico, Don Solomon, Alan Strohmayer, Peter Stahl)

"YOU SHOULD HAVE BEEN HERE YESTERDAY" B/W "EVER LOVIN' MAN"

Band: Chain Reaction
Label: Verve
Released: 1968
Produced by: Artie Schroeck, Gene Radice
Recorded: CBS Studios

You Should Have Been Here Yesterday (Don Sloan [Don Solomon], Stahl); Ever Lovin' Man (Sloan, Stahl)

Personnel:
Steven Tallarico (a.k.a. Steven Tally)—vocals
Don Solomon (a.k.a. Don Sloan)—keyboards, vocals
Peter Stahl—guitar
Alan Strohmayer—bass
Barry Shapiro (a.k.a. Barry Shore)—drums

JOE PERRY

LET THE MUSIC DO THE TALKING

Band: The Joe Perry Project
Label: Columbia
Released: March 1980
Produced by: Jack Douglas, Joe Perry
Recorded: The Hit Factory, New York City

Let the Music Do the Talking (Perry); Conflict of Interest (Perry); Discount Dogs (Perry, Ralph Morman); Shooting Star (Perry); Break Song (Perry, David Hull, Ronnie Stewart); Rockin' Train (Perry, Morman); The Mist Is Rising (Perry); Ready on the Firing Line (Perry); Life at a Glance (Perry)

Personnel:
Joe Perry—guitar, vocals
Ralph Morman—vocals
David Hull—bass guitar, vocals
Ronnie Stewart—drums, percussion

I'VE GOT THE ROCK 'N' ROLLS AGAIN

Band: The Joe Perry Project
Label: Columbia
Released: June 1981
Produced by: Bruce Botnick
Recorded: The Boston Opera House, Boston, MA

East Coast, West Coast (Charlie Farren); No Substitute for Arrogance (Perry, Farren); I've Got the Rock 'n' Rolls Again (Perry, Farren); Buzz Buzz (Hull, Charlie Karp, Arthur Resnick); Soldier of Fortune (Perry); TV Police (Perry, Farren); Listen to the Rock (Farren); Dirty Little Things (Hull); Play the Game (Perry, Farren); South Station Blues (Perry)

Personnel:
Joe Perry—guitar, vocals
Charlie Farren—rhythm guitar, vocals
David Hull—bass, vocals
Ronnie Stewart—drums, percussion

Notes: Album was initially slated to be titled Soldier of Fortune.

"Buzz Buzz" was originally written and recorded by the Dirty Angels, David Hull's band prior to joining the Joe Perry Project, for their 1978 self-titled A&M album.

According to Charlie Farren, "East Coast, West Coast" and "Listen to the Rock" were originally written for, and recorded by, Balloon, the Boston-area band of which he was a member prior to joining the Joe Perry Project. In a 2008 interview with the website wickedlocal.com, Farren recalled, "[Balloon] had a couple of songs on area radio. The first was 'East Coast, West Coast' and the second was 'Listen to the Rock,' which was on the top ten at both WBCN and WCOZ for eleven weeks."

ONCE A ROCKER, ALWAYS A ROCKER

Band: The Joe Perry Project
Label: MCA
Released: September 1983
Produced by: Joe Perry
Recorded: Blue Jay Recording Studios, Carlisle, MA

Once a Rocker, Always a Rocker (Perry, Mark Bell); Black Velvet Pants (Perry); Women in Chains (Ronald Brooks, Harold Tipton, Tom Deluca); 4 Guns West (Perry, Bell); Crossfire (Perry, Bell); Adrianna (Perry, Bell); King of the Kings (Perry, Bell); Bang a Gong (Marc Bolan); Walk With Me Sally (Perry, Bell); Never Wanna Stop (Perry, Bell)

Personnel:
Joe Perry—guitars, six-string bass
Cowboy Mach Bell—vocals
Joe Pet—drums, background vocals
Danny Hargrove—bass, background vocals

JOE PERRY

Label: Sony BMG
Released: May 2005
Produced by: Joe Perry, Paul Caruso
Recorded: The Boneyard, South Shore, MA

Shakin' My Cage (Perry); Hold on Me (Perry); Pray for Me (Perry); Can't Compare (Perry); Lonely (Perry); Crystal Ship (Morrison, Krieger, Manzarek, Densmore); Talk Talkin' (Perry); Push Comes to Shove (Perry); Twilight (Perry); Ten Years (Perry); Vigilante Man (Woody Guthrie); Dying to Be Free (Perry); Mercy (Perry)

Personnel:
Joe Perry: guitars, bass, synth guitar, keyboards, lead and backing vocals
Paul Caruso: drums

HAVE GUITAR, WILL TRAVEL

Label: Roman
Released: October 2009
Produced by: Joe Perry
Recorded: The Boneyard, South Shore, MA

We've Got a Long Way to Go (Perry); Slingshot (Perry); Do You Wonder (Perry, Frederiksen, Billie Perry); Somebody's Gonna Get (Their Head Kicked in Tonite) (Jeremy Spencer); Heaven and Hell (Perry); No Surprise (Perry); Wooden Ships (Perry);Oh Lord (21 Grams) (Perry); Scare the Cat (Perry); Freedom (Perry)

Personnel:
Joe Perry—vocals, guitar, synth, percussion, programming, sound effects
Hagen Grohe—vocals
David Hull—bass
Ben Tileston—drums, percussion, glockenspiel
Marty Richards—drums
Scott Meeder—drums
Willie Alexander—piano
Paul Santo—Hammond organ, pipe organ, percussion
Glen McCarthy—sound effects

Notes: Though credited to "Joe Perry," the guitarist has often referred to the album as a Joe Perry Project release.

BRAD WHITFORD

WHITFORD/ST. HOLMES

Band: Whitford/St. Holmes
Label: Columbia
Released: August 1981
Produced by: Tom Allom
Recorded: Axis Studios, Atlanta, GA

I Need Love (Derek St. Holmes); Whiskey Woman (St. Holmes); Hold On (St. Holmes, Whitford); Sharpshooter (St. Holmes, Whitford); Every Morning (St. Holmes); Action (St. Holmes); Shy Away (St. Holmes); Does It Really Matter? (St. Holmes); Spanish Boy (St. Holmes, Whitford); Mystery Girl (St. Holmes, Whitford)

Personnel:
Brad Whitford—lead guitar
Derek St. Holmes—vocals, guitar
David Hewitt—bass
Steve Pace—drums

Acknowledgments

Thanks to Dennis Pernu for his stewardship, dedication, and always-discerning eye; all at Voyageur Press who labored to make this project read and look its very best; the many photographers whose striking images of a band at work and play grace these pages; the esteemed journalists who offered their time, words, and valued insights herein: Jaan Uhelszki in particular for additional assists and an amusing email or three; Robert "Nitebob" Czaykowski for always being game for a little guitar porn, as well as working to make NYC sound a little better each day; Neil Thompson for talking Biches and pups; Tom Beaujour at *Guitar Aficionado* for bullet truss rod wisdom and all-around guitar geekery; Brad Tolinski at *Guitar World* for the trips to Boston; Sian Llewellyn at *Classic Rock* for digging into the archives; Alexander Milas at *Metal Hammer* and Dave Ling for the quick and easy aid; Jacob Raddock for bringing the (box of) fire; and Steven, Joe, Brad, Tom, and Joey (and also Jimmy and Rick) for the music.

Last but actually first: Extreme gratitude to my wife, Carla Fredericks, for guidance, perspective, patience, and unyielding love and support, as well as for always getting the shots and asking for nothing more than a hoodie (and maybe a nice dinner) in return. Additional thanks to Hal Bienstock for a lifetime's worth of music appreciation (as well as that first Aerosmith cassette—even if it did house a poor radio edit of "Sweet Emotion"); Gary and Leslie Bienstock, because they deserve it; and, finally, Levi Bienstock for the daily reminder that a smile trumps all.

Sources

BOOKS

Aerosmith, with Stephen Davis. *Walk This Way: The Autobiography of Aerosmith*. New York: Avon, 1997.

Huxley, Martin. *Aerosmith: The Fall and the Rise of Rock's Greatest Band*. New York: St. Martin's Press, 1995.

Kramer, Joey, with William Patrick and Keith Garde. *Hit Hard: A Story of Hitting Rock Bottom at the Top*. New York: HarperOne, 2009.

TELEVISION

A&E *Biography*, 2009
A&E *Breakfast with the Arts*, 2005
VH1 *Behind the Music*, 2002

NEWSPAPERS AND WIRE SERVICES

Associated Press
Boston Globe
Boston Herald
Chicago Tribune
Globe and Mail (Canada)
Hartford Courant
New York Times
QMI Agency
Village Voice

MAGAZINES

Billboard
Blender
Circus
Circus Raves
Classic Rock
CREEM
Entertainment Weekly
Goldmine
Guitar for the Practicing Musician
Guitar Player
Guitar World
Hit Parader
Juke
Kerrang!
M Music and Musicians
Melody Maker
Metal Edge
Metal Hammer
Mojo
Musician
NME
Newsweek
Penthouse
Premier Guitar
Q
Rock Scene
Rolling Stone
RIP
Screamer
Sound on Sound
Sounds
Spin
Trouser Press
Uncut
Vintage Guitar

WEBSITES

aeroforceone.com
aerosmithtemple.com
filmposters.com
jimmycrespo.com
jimvallance.com
knac.com
mtv.com
rickdufay.com
rocksbackpages.com
rockthisway.de
roughedge.com
thegearpage.net
ultimate-guitar.com
wolfgangsvault.com

Currently (and unfortunately) offline:
Crossfire: The Joe Perry Project Homepage

Contributors

ROBERT ALFORD is a rock 'n' roll photographer of thirty-five-plus years who has photographed more than five hundred acts, from AC/DC to ZZ Top. His work has featured prominently in magazines (*CREEM*, *People*, *Rolling Stone*, and more), on album covers, in liner notes, on television, and in books and documentaries.

CHARLIE AURINGER enrolled in his first photography class after witnessing the Beatles and Bob Dylan in concert in 1964. In 1969, he helped create *CREEM* magazine and began shooting Detroit acts such as MC5 and Mitch Ryder. After *CREEM* went national in 1971, he photographed David Bowie, Led Zeppelin, the Who, the Rolling Stones, KISS, Alice Cooper, and others. In 1976, Charlie began devoting all his attention to design and photo editing at *CREEM*. Today he remains active in the music scene by designing *Big City Blues* magazine. He also publishes a community newspaper in his hometown.

DANIEL BUKSZPAN is the author of *The Encyclopedia of Heavy Metal*. He has been a freelance writer since 1994, and he has written for such publications as the *New York Post*, *Pop Smear*, *Guitar World*, the *Pit Report*, and *Hails and Horns*. He lives in Brooklyn with his wife, Asia, and his son, Roman.

NEIL DANIELS (neildaniels.com) is a freelance writer of rock and heavy metal. He has written books on Judas Priest, Journey, Robert Plant, Bon Jovi, and Linkin Park, among others. He has also contributed to numerous magazines, fanzines, and websites. He is a regular contributor to *Fireworks*, the revered British magazine on AOR and melodic rock.

CHUCK EDDY is the author of the books *Stairway to Hell*, *The Accidental Evolution of Rock 'n' Roll*, and the upcoming *Rock 'n' Roll Always Forgets: A Quarter Century of Music Criticism*. The Detroit native has served as music editor at the *Village Voice* and as a senior editor at *Billboard*, and has written thousands of pieces over the years for *CREEM*, *Rolling Stone*, *Spin*, *Blender*, *Entertainment Weekly*, rhapsody.com, and countless other publications and websites. He lives in Austin, Texas.

DANNY FIELDS began his career at *Datebook Magazine* in 1966, where he precipitated a great fuss by publishing, for the first time in the U.S., John Lennon's playful comments claiming that the Beatles were more popular than Jesus. He went on to work for the Doors, Iggy and the Stooges, Lou Reed, and the Ramones, and was an editor of *16 Magazine* and a producer of the syndicated radio program *Rock Today*. He is an avid amateur photographer whose work has been exhibited in New York, Paris, London, Tokyo, and Hong Kong. He is the author of a memoir about his close friend, Linda Eastman McCartney, and is most proud that the book *Please Kill Me: An Oral History of Punk Rock*, published in twenty languages, is dedicated to him.

KEVIN ESTRADA (kevinestrada.com) was a preteen when he began his photo career by smuggling his camera into some of the most legendary concerts in Los Angeles. For the last thirty-plus years he has photographed countless musicians in concert, backstage, on the road, and in the studio. He continues to make his living as a rock 'n' roll photographer and music video director in the L.A. area. He is blessed and supported by his wonderful wife and two beautiful daughters.

BILL HOLDSHIP is a longtime music journalist, critic, and historian. A former editor at *CREEM*, *BAM*, *New Times L.A.*, *Daily Variety*, *HITS*, *Radio & Records*, and, most recently, *Detroit Metro Times*, among others, he has written for numerous publications since the late 1970s, including *Mojo*, the *Los Angeles Times*, *SPIN*, *NME*, and *Us Weekly*, as well as websites and alternative weeklies. He is currently based back in his native Michigan.

GREG KOT (gregkot.com) has been the music critic at the *Chicago Tribune* since 1990, and the co-host, with Jim DeRogatis, of *Sound Opinions* since 1999. "The world's only rock 'n' roll talk show" originates at Chicago Public Radio and is distributed nationally. Kot also has written several books, including *Wilco: Learning How to Die* and, with DeRogatis, *The Beatles vs. The Rolling Stones: Sound Opinions on the Great Rock 'n' Roll Rivalry*. He lives on Chicago's Northwest Side with his wife, two daughters, and far too many records.

BOB LEAFE (bobleafe.com) has photographed over fifteen hundred music performers, ranging from Led Zeppelin to Liberace. He has been the house photographer for major concert venues, radio stations, TV shows, and for MTV, where he shot their first Christmas video, the first Video Music Awards, and the 1984 New Year's Eve Ball. He's been published in more than one hundred U.S. magazines and all over the world.

ROBERT MATHEU (robertmatheu.com) has been a music photographer since his teenage years in Detroit, where he attended that city's earliest shows by the MC5, the Stooges, Alice Cooper, Led Zeppelin, the Clash, Stevie Ray Vaughan, and the like. His work has appeared in *Playboy, Rolling Stone, CREEM, Time,* and *Mojo,* and on more than two hundred album covers. His books include *CREEM: America's Only Rock 'n' Roll Magazine* and *The Stooges: The Authorized and Illustrated Story.* As of this publication, he is at work on a book of his own photography entitled *Perfect View.*

MARTIN POPOFF (martinpopoff.com) is the author of twenty-eight books on hard rock and heavy metal. Additionally, he has written more record reviews than anyone living or dead. His band bios include works on Black Sabbath, Deep Purple, Judas Priest, UFO, Rainbow, Dio, Rush, and the mighty Blue Öyster Cult.

RON POWNALL started shooting rock 'n' roll as a staff photographer for the *Chicago Tribune* (his first three assignments were Jefferson Airplane, Janis Joplin, and Jimi Hendrix). Despite this auspicious beginning in Chicago, he moved to Boston and quickly linked up as the band photographer with Aerosmith, Boston, the Cars, J. Geils, and Ted Nugent. He has been a contributing photographer for *Rolling Stone, CREEM, Circus, Newsweek, People, Spin,* and others, and has over 250 LP, CD, and magazine cover credits. He licenses his image rights through RockRollPhoto.com and sells limited-edition, fine-art collector's prints through art galleries and FineArtRockRoll.com.

ROCK 'N' ROLL COMICS was launched in 1989 by Todd Loren to spin illustrated (and unlicensed) biographies of rock stars. Some were supportive, while others sued. Loren was convinced the First Amendment to the U.S. Constitution protected his "illustrated articles," and the California Supreme Court agreed. In June 1992, Loren was found murdered in his San Diego condo. The comics continued for two more years, with Jay Allen Sanford serving as managing editor. Loren's murder remains unsolved.

BUD SCOPPA is a music journalist and editor with a music business background, having worked primarily in A&R at Mercury Records, A&M, Arista, Zoo, and Sire. The author of *The Byrds* (republished as an e-book by rocksbackpages.com) and a Grammy nominee for the notes to Rhino's Little Feat box set, Scoppa is presently a senior editor at *Hits,* the L.A. correspondent for *Uncut,* and the co-author of iTunes' "School of Rock." He has written for *Rolling Stone, CREEM,* and other major music publications past and present.

London-based music journalist **PHIL SUTCLIFFE** has been writing about rock since 1974. His work has appeared in myriad publications, including *Mojo, Q,* the *Los Angeles Times, Sounds,* and more. He is also the author of Voyageur Press' *Queen: The Ultimate Illustrated History of the Crown Kings of Rock* and *AC/DC: High-Voltage Rock 'n' Roll: The Ultimate Illustrated History.* Phil's back catalog is mostly available on the world's best archive of music writing, rocksbackpages.com.

JAAN UHELSZKI was one of the founding editors at Detroit's legendary *CREEM* magazine. Since that time, her work has appeared in *USA Today, Uncut, Rolling Stone, Spin, NME, Classic Rock, Guitar World,* and the *Braille Musician's Guide.* Currently she is the editor-at-large at *Relix* and the only journalist to have ever performed in full makeup with KISS. Luckily she only had to put on eyeliner to write about Aerosmith.

FRANK WHITE began his photography career on February 12, 1975, shooting Led Zeppelin at Madison Square Garden after a few years of guidance from his mother, who had worked as a studio photographer in New York City during the 1950s. He began selling his images in 1982, first to *Relix* and then to several other music publications, including *Guitar World, Circus, CREEM, Kerrang!, Hit Parader, Rock Scene,* and others. His images have also been licensed to record companies, MTV, and VH1. In 1986, he began the Frank White Photo Agency. He continues to photograph music and other subjects today.

Index

Album, DVD, and song titles are found under the heading "Aerosmith releases" (bold numbers indicate reviews written for this book).

Rockin' the Joint tour, Staples Center, Los Angeles, February 22, 2006. KEVIN MAZUR/WIREIMAGE/GETTY IMAGES

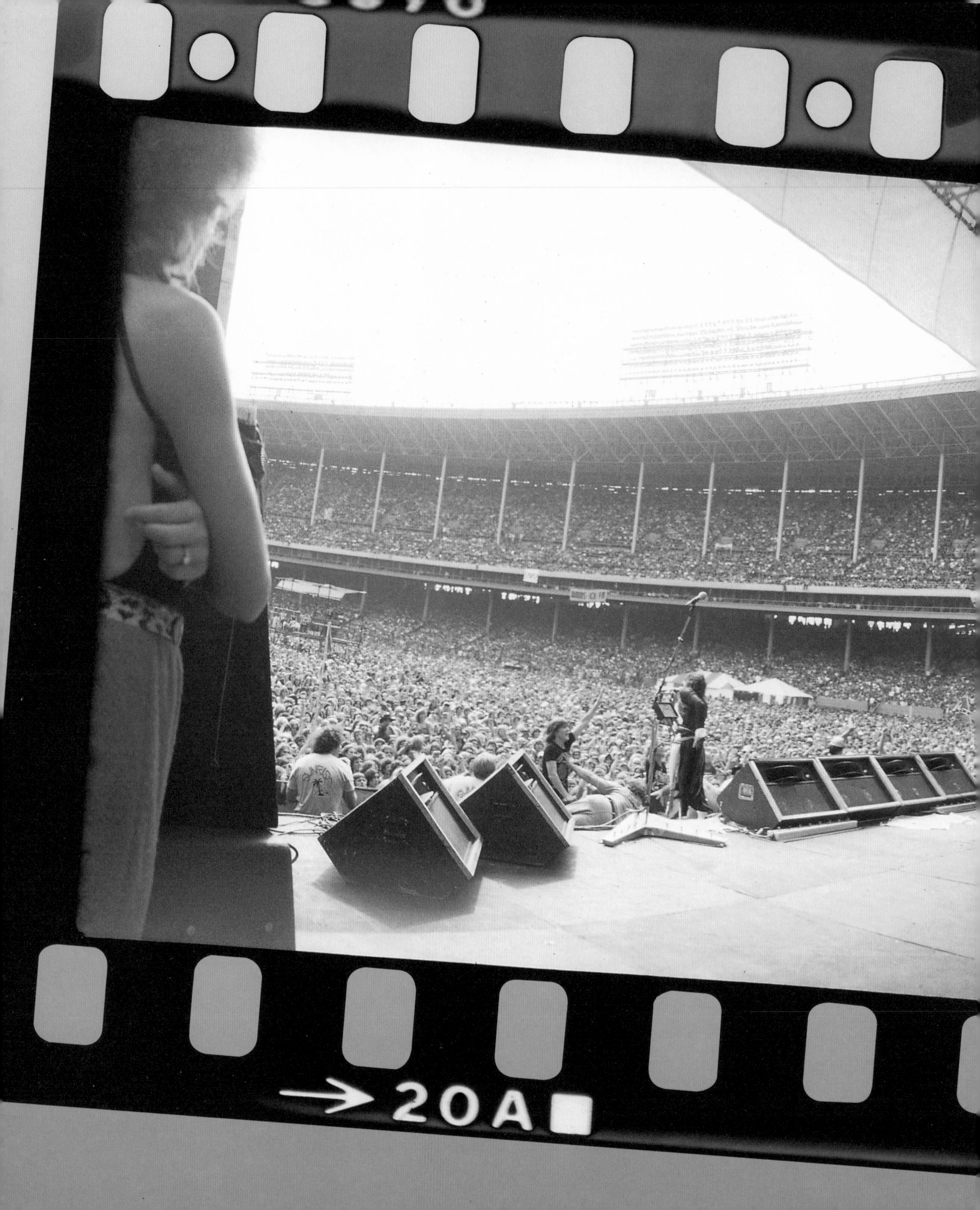
20A